# THE
# CAPITALIST
# REVOLUTION

## FIFTY PROPOSITIONS ABOUT PROSPERITY, EQUALITY, AND LIBERTY

## PETER L. BERGER

BasicBooks
*A Division of* HarperCollins*Publishers*

Library of Congress Cataloging-in-Publication Data

Berger, Peter L.
  The capitalist revolution.

  Includes bibliographical references and index.
  1. Capitalism.   2. Liberty.   3. Economic development.
I. Title.
HB501.B4518   1986        330.12′2        85–73882
ISBN   0–465–00867–4 (cloth)
ISBN   0–465–00868–2 (paper)

# CONTENTS

# A NEW
# INTRODUCTION
# —FIVE YEARS LATER

Thε word *revolution* in the title of this book was, of course, intended to denote the fundamental changes, the radical transformation, that capitalism brings about in a society. It did not imply an overthrow of existing regimes and, alas, did not constitute a prediction of the cataclysmic events that have shaken the socialist world since the spring of 1989 (I can console myself with the thought that hardly anyone predicted these events). All the same, much of the international scene today is dominated by what can only be described as a "capitalist revolution" of massive dimensions. It seems plausible, in view of this, to ask whether these developments support or weaken any of the propositions around which the book was constructed. But first I would like to make a few observations about the current capitalist upsurge and the triumphalist mood it has engendered among advocates of capitalism.

The most spectacular manifestations of this turn toward capitalism have, of course, occurred in the socialist societies of Eastern Europe and, to an extent, within the Soviet Union itself. The speed with which the new democratic or democratizing regimes in Eastern Europe have begun to dismantle the structures of socialism and to move toward a market economy has been astonishing, as has been the pro-market-economy rhetoric that has accompanied this revolution. At the time of this writing, Poland, under its Solidarity-dominated government, has opted for the most radical form of the transition to capitalism, rejecting a gradualistic process in favor of a cold-turkey treatment, the success or failure of which remains to be revealed. Within the Soviet Union there has been more talk than action about marketization of the economy, but there seems to be a growing consensus within the Soviet elite that something along these lines is a condition of survival (though clearly this consensus does not extend to the political implications of such a change).

The attention of world media has rightly been focused on the upheaval within what used to be the Soviet empire. The outcome of this upheaval will have far-reaching and long-lasting consequences, not only for those countries themselves, but for the world as a whole. Yet the current capitalist revolution, if it is to be called that, is not limited to this one region. There has been turmoil in that other socialist giant, China, at least temporarily coming to a brutal halt with the repression of the summer of 1989. It is not at all clear, though, that the gerontocracy now in charge will manage to put the revolutionary genie back in its bottle; it is not even clear whether the present regime really wants to reverse the economic liberalization that has occurred, or whether it rather wants to put a stop only to the democratizing movement the former has engendered. In many other parts of the world, however, market-oriented policies and pro-market rhetoric is flourishing. This is notably the case in Latin America, where a number of democratically elected governments have embarked on vigorously capitalist economic policies. The same has been true, though to a lesser extent, in a number of African countries. It has been true for quite a long time in most of East and Southeast Asia. Since *capitalism* continues to be a negatively charged word in many places, especially among intellectuals, it is often avoided in favor of the less upsetting synonym *market economy*. Conversely, where *socialism* is still a word that uplifts some hearts, it will also be avoided as the term to describe a *non*market economy; instead, reference may be made to *command, communist,* or even *Stalinist* economies. These are semantic games. What is being described is, very clearly, a broad shift from socialist to capitalist models of economic organization.

Understandably, this turn has created a rather euphoric mood among those who have been in favor of capitalism all along. There is great satisfaction to be had for anyone who is in a position to say, I told you so!—especially anyone who used to be in a minority often treated with derision. It is also very satisfying to feel that one is ideologically attuned to the wave of the future or even (heaven forfend) the "end of history." The Left used to bask in just these satisfactions. Fair enough. Needless to say, I'm a member of this pro-capitalist party within the West's intelligentsia. This membership has not been altogether comfortable over the last twenty years, and it is nice for a change to be able to indulge in a bit of *Schadenfreude.* All the same, I think that the triumphalist mood prevailing at the moment in right-of-center circles is somewhat premature.

One hears the statement that socialism is "finished" or "discredited." Both adjectives are ambiguous. To say that socialism is finished implies that there can be no successful attempts to restore it, in the same way that one might declare, for example, the Holy Roman Empire or the Albigensian heresy to be finished. That, however, is by no means clear. Not only may socialism survive for a long time in enclaves ranging in size from gargantuan China to minuscule Albania—even if most of the world goes capitalist—but there is also the very real possibility of restorations in countries that have already moved some distance in another direction. No sensible person would predict today what the Soviet Union will look like some ten years from now. A neo-Stalinist scenario can by no means be ruled out, and such a scenario would inevitably have powerful repercussions beyond the Soviet borders. In a different part of the world, the pro-capitalist governments in Latin America do not have many years to demonstrate that their policies can indeed help to solve the intractable economic and social miseries of that continent, and there is every reason to expect that, in the wake of failure, socialist solutions would gain credibility once more. I'm convinced, of course, that such a return to socialism would be disastrously misguided, but I've learned not to confuse my own intellectual convictions with the logic of history.

If one then says that socialism has been discredited, one would have to answer the question, Discredited with *whom*? With those who used to believe in it? With objective, informed analysts? With historians in the future? In some sense, I tend to think, no *idea* is ever finally discredited, once and for all finished. Even the Albigensian heresy has resurfaced in some versions of contemporary feminism, and while the resuscitation of the Holy Roman Empire would not appear to be a promising political project, some of the notions now in vogue in Central Europe are surprisingly consonant with at least the later manifestations of that empire's ideology. Historians in the future, looking back to our time, will presumably be as confused, as divided, and as opinionated as our own historians: There is no such thing as a "verdict of history," only the stumbling and often silly interpretations of those who make it their business to judge the past. I regard myself as both informed and objective, and socialism is certainly discredited with me; there is probably a growing number of reasonably informed and analytic people who agree with me. Again, this is gratifying, but one should not make too much of it: Most of mankind is neither objective nor informed. As to those for whom socialism has been a sustaining faith, they will find ways of reinterpreting current events in such a way as to leave their faith intact. This process of reinterpretation can already be observed daily in various commentaries on the transformations in Eastern Europe: What is being swept away is "communism" (or "state capitalism," or "Stalinism"), but *not* "socialism"—which will live to see a better incarnation. Or: These countries are being delivered from one bad system ("state capitalism" and the like) only to be plunged into one just as bad or worse—greedy, exploitative, oppressive capitalism. Or: The present situation is temporary; once these societies settle down and come to their senses, they will appreciate the advantages they still have over the West—precisely the fruits of socialism, however distorted this socialism may have been in other ways. And so on. To be sure, there will be some, perhaps even many, who will avow that their god has failed; there will be others who will confront the contradictions between their beliefs and reality *not* by changing their beliefs but by making the necessary corrections in their definitions of reality.

Groups as much as individuals are ingenious in denying inconvenient or disagreeable facts. This is what psychoanalysts call rationalization. But, to stay within the Freudian universe of discourse one instant longer, there is also something called the "reality principle." Facts have a way of *being there,* stubbornly resisting efforts to wish them away and haunting those who deny them. They even haunt those (such as, understandably, many on the Left) who theorize that there *are* no facts outside our interpretations of them (an immensely convenient theory, by the way, for those with an interest in denying reality). It follows that, while one must not exaggerate the historical efficacy of rational argument and empirical evidence, one must not fall into the opposite exaggeration of regarding the latter as having no effects at all. Actually, Freud put it very well when he observed that the voice of reason is quiet but persistent. This very modest optimism may serve as grounds for expecting that the scientific study of human affairs (including the social sciences) may be something more than the pastime of an esoteric underground—that is, it may have some public relevance. Be that as it may, let me now turn to the issue of what, if anything, may have to be revised in this book in the light of recent events.

As is to be expected, many propositions in the book are unaffected, either way, by recent events: These propositions are as plausible or as implausible as they were five years ago. There are four important areas, though, to which recent events are indeed relevant: the relation of capitalism and prosperity, the relation of capitalism and democracy, the nature of socialism, and perhaps also the mythic power of the socialist idea.

When I say that recent events are relevant, I mean relevance in the business of theory construction to which the book was intended to contribute. In that strict sense one might say that recent events have added nothing that we didn't know before or, more accurately, should have known as social scientists or otherwise as people attentive to empirical evidence. The crucial fact here, of course, is the vast superiority of capitalism in improving the material standards of living of large numbers of people, and *ipso facto* the capacity of a society to deal with those human problems amenable to public policy, notably those of poverty. But, if this fact had been clear for a long time, recent events have brought it quite dramatically to the forefront of public attention in much of the world, and by no means only in Europe. It is now more clear than ever that the inclusion of a national economy in the international capitalist system (*pace* all varieties of "dependency theory") favors rather than hinders development, that capitalism remains the best bet if one wishes to improve the lot of the poor, and that policies fostering economic growth are more likely to equalize income differentials than are policies that deliberately foster redistribution.

Whereas these propositions have long appeared credible in economics departments in Western countries, they are now being propounded by governments from Budapest to Buenos Aires, by communist *apparatchiks* and Péronist politicians, even here and there by revisionist Marxist intellectuals. This widened resonance is, strictly speaking, scientifically irrelevant, but it certainly improves the cultural context within which social scientists must operate. Put simply, social scientists uttering these propositions about capitalism sound less and less like the proponents of flat-earth theory that, to many, they still appeared a few years ago. To be sure, there are holdouts, and not only among so-called conservatives in the communist parties of China and the crumbling Soviet empire—for example, in the political and intellectual establishments in India, in the English-speaking universities of South Africa, or in the social-action bureaucracies of mainline Protestantism in the United States. But it is these holdouts, rather than their intellectual adversaries, who now appear as people who argue that the earth is flat.

In this connection the propositions in this book about the relation of capitalist prosperity and equality should also be reemphasized. We continue to hear that, yes indeed, capitalism increases prosperity, but at the price of gross inequalities. Since I wrote the book, nothing has changed my mind about the strong probability that the notion of a trade-off between growth and equality is false. The weight of the evidence indicates that the Kuznets effect does indeed hold (increased inequality as a modern economy takes off, with a leveling-off occurring within a reasonable time thereafter), but that it holds *regardless* of whether economic growth takes place under a capitalist or a socialist system. In other words, the basic choice between capitalism and socialism is irrelevant to the issue of equality, *except* that capitalism greatly accelerates the growth process, thus accelerating both the inegalitarian and the egalitarian phases of the Kuznets curve. It follows that to opt for capitalism is *not* to opt for inequality at the price of growth; rather, it is to opt for an accelerating transformation of society. This undoubtedly produces tensions and exacts costs, but one must ask whether these are likely to be greater than the tensions and costs engendered by socialist stagnation. Moreover, the clearer view of the European socialist societies that has now become public radically debunks the notion that, whatever else may have ailed these societies, they were more egalitarian than those in the West: They were nothing of the sort. One must also remember that, comparatively speaking, these European societies were the most advanced in the socialist camp. The claims to greater equality are even hollower in the much poorer socialist societies in the Third World (China emphatically included).

We also hear a good deal today about social democracy as the putative "third way" between Soviet-style socialism and the allegedly brutal capitalism of the West. This talk is based on both a conceptual confusion and a lot of empirical uncertainty. Conceptually, it continues to be important to insist (as Marxists have always done, correctly) that capitalism and socialism are systems of *production;* under either one, there can be very different systems of *distribution.* Social democracy is precisely an approach to distribution. Thus Sweden, the utopia of those who consider themselves social democrats, has an overwhelmingly capitalist production system; what distinguishes it (though not as much as some would think) from other capitalist societies is the size and the scope of its welfare state. This is *not* a third way; it is a variant of the first way. It is thoroughly confusing to refer to it as a variant of socialism (as, incidentally, its critics often do as much as its advocates).

There continues to be a lot of empirical uncertainty about the amount of welfare-state expenditures a modern capitalist society can afford without undermining its productivity. And, by the way, the present condition of Sweden does not exactly enhance the utopian perspective on it. The same uncertainty prevails about the economic and social costs of non-welfare-state interventions of government in the economy. These are and will continue to be important issues between right-of-center and left-of-center parties in capitalist democracies; they are issues that have nothing to do with socialism. Very few people in the respectable spectrum of Western politics favor the abolition of the welfare state or the withdrawal of government from all economic interventions other than the printing of money and the enforcement of contracts. In other words, die-hard libertarians are a possibly endearing but politically irrelevant sect. In terms of the capacity of capitalist societies to safeguard the welfare of their weaker members, the difficulties of integrating the former German Democratic Republic into Federal Germany throw sharp light on this matter: The problem was *not* how to integrate the superior welfare system of the DDR into the ruthless social policies of the Federal Republic; it was precisely the opposite. In this context it is worth recalling that from 1948 on (the beginning of the West German economic miracle), the phrase used by all, especially conservatives, to describe the system prevailing in the Federal Republic has been *social* market economy *(soziale Marktwirtschaft)*. In that important sense, we are all social democrats.

By far the most dramatic relevance of recent events to the propositions in this book is in the relation of capitalism and democracy. And here I would say, at the risk of sounding self-congratulatory, that the plausibility of two key propositions has been enhanced—to wit, that capitalism is the necessary but not sufficient condition of democracy, and that market forces in a socialist or heavily statist society have a democratizing effect.

The former proposition is now being shouted from the rooftops in the formerly communist societies in Europe. The urgency with which these governments now seek to install market economies is, of course, motivated by the desire to get out of the economic disaster created by forty years of socialist mismanagement; but it is also due to the insight that, without an effective market economy, the prospects for democracy are very poor indeed. The theoretical issue here is the relation between economic and political liberalization; in Soviet terms, one might substitute *perestroika* and *glasnost*. It seems likely that the underlying relation between these two processes was not clear at all to the Soviet elite that launched the reform process; it may not be quite clear even now in those circles (though there are indications that it is becoming more so). Put simply, to open up a socialist society politically while leaving in place most of the structures of the command economy is asking for trouble: The economic gains will be sparse, slow, and very unequally distributed, and those who are thereby hurt will have increasing opportunity to complain, to organize politically, and to destabilize the process. Put simply, the Soviet regime would have been better advised to keep *glasnost* limping a few steps behind *perestroika;* in the event, it did precisely the opposite and by now it is probably too late to reverse the effects of the sequence.

By contrast, the Chinese regime did have something like the "correct" sequence in mind, and it pursued this course with a good deal of success for several years. It seems that what the reformist elite in Beijing had in mind was not too different from what happened in Taiwan after the Kuomintang regime was installed there following its retreat from the mainland—a broad economic liberalization presided over by an authoritarian government (indeed, in mainland debates the phrase "the new authoritarianism" was used to describe the political management of the marketization process). I, for one, am not competent to judge why the regime abruptly changed course in 1989, not only repressing the political liberalization with great brutality but also putting brakes on the economic liberalization. It requires no great Sinological competence to predict that, unless there is a reversion to the earlier course, a very high price will have to be paid in terms of China's economic development.

It is also important to reiterate that, while capitalism appears to be a precondition for democracy, the converse is *not* the case: Much as one might deplore this, it is quite possible for capitalism to develop under nondemocratic regimes (although these will be of the authoritarian rather than totalitarian variety). The entire history of capitalism both in the West and in East Asia testifies to this, but recent history provides additional examples. The astounding economic takeoff of Spain in recent years began with the pro-capitalist policies during the final years of the Franco regime; a similar economic drama has been unfolding in Pinochet's Chile. Needless to say, this in no way justifies the atrocities committed by these two governments, both distinguished by odious records in the area of human rights. But it is important to understand that the relation between capitalism and democracy is *asymmetrical*—the latter presupposes the former, but not vice versa. It might be observed that economic success is not necessarily hindered by tyrannical and inhumane governance. Thus the Kuomintang regime brutally suppressed an independence movement in Taiwan in the early years of its establishment there, with bloodshed that, in that smaller territory, can probably vie with the massacres on the mainland in 1989. The further observation is equally important, though: As the Taiwanese economic miracle took off, the regime progressively liberalized itself and is now decisively on the road toward democracy; the Beijing rulers appear headed in the opposite direction, with socialism still intact.

To reiterate, while there can be capitalism without democracy, successful capitalism releases democratizing forces; similar democratizing effects can be observed if a socialist or heavily statist society makes successful moves toward the market. Both Spain and Chile can be cited by way of evidence. It may well be that this relationship was understood only too well in Beijing in 1989. I see no reason to change the way I formulated this relationship earlier: Peasants who are no longer hungry become uppity—a very inconvenient situation for those who used to lord it over them, no matter whether the lords are feudal oligarchs or socialist *nomenklatura*. The differences between these two types of elites are not as great as their respective rhetorics would make one think—which is why socialist regimes are so easily superimposed on traditionally feudal or oligarchical societies. One might even say that the only genuine revolution under modern conditions is that of democratic capitalism.

So recent events have not instilled doubts in my mind about my earlier characterization of socialism, neither about its economic inefficiency nor its propensity toward dictatorial governance. The events of 1989 and 1990, however, do necessitate an important theoretical adjustment and raise an important question. The theoretical adjustment concerns the understanding of totalitarianism. Ever since Hannah Arendt, Zbigniew Brzezinski, and Carl Friedrich gave the concept of totalitarianism wide currency in political science, a common view (initiated by them, especially by Arendt) has been to the effect that a totalitarian system, once established, is very difficult if not impossible to remove from within—only outside force can do so (as was the case with Nazi Germany). The collapse of communist regimes in Europe and the unfolding political drama in the Soviet Union itself, no matter the eventual outcome of these developments, can already be said to have falsified this proposition of totalitarianism theory. On the contrary, it became clear that only outside force (the might of the Soviet military) had kept these regimes going; remove that outside force, and these governments collapsed like card houses. The steps by which this collapse then took place, from the first stirrings of popular discontent to the defection of security forces to the side of the revolution, closely resemble similar stages in nontotalitarian dictatorships, indeed closely follow the prescriptions of Leninist revolutionary theory. This falsification of at least Arendt's notion of the invulnerability of totalitarianism does not invalidate other features of her theory, nor does it detract from the usefulness of the concept (including the distinction it makes between the two types of dictatorial regimes). But I certainly regard as good news our new insight into the fragility of the totalitarian project and into the dogged persistence of elements of "civil society" even after decades of relentless assault.

The important question about the transition from socialism raised by recent events is that of the optimal way to manage it. The basic alternative is between incremental and "big-push" approaches, and there are good theoretical arguments to be made for both. General knowledge of history and, more specifically, of the rapid revolutions of modern times make one lean toward gradualism, toward incremental rather than cataclysmic change. Both capitalism and democracy require special institutions through which to operate, and institutions take time to be constructed and to become taken-for-granted presences in people's lives. On the other hand, even a general bias toward incremental change cannot foreclose the possibility that there may be particular situations in which something else is called for; the transition from socialism to capitalism may well be such a special case.

The long experience with gradualism in Yugoslavia and Hungary does not encourage the incremental approach; it appears that the half-measures toward the market are economically unsatisfactory and that they create new problems, notably that of widespread corruption. Almost inevitably, in a partially marketized economy there must be collusion between the new entrepreneurs and the bureaucrats who still control the "commanding heights" of the economy. This type of corruption evidently reached heroic dimensions in China and was the most immediate grievance of the students' protest movement (an unfortunate fixation on a symptom instead of the disease, one might say). These considerations in turn would favor a single, radical push—the cold-turkey treatment currently being tried in Poland and being at least considered in other socialist societies in Europe. In a nonsocialist but statist context, similar big-push strategies are now being implemented in several Latin American countries. At the time of writing, the question must remain unresolved. Fortunately or unfortunately, some answers are likely to be forthcoming fairly soon.

Just as there is no third way, there is no such thing as market socialism. Not that recent events were needed to demonstrate this (I tried to make the case in this book), but it appears that this conclusion has now been reached by quite a few people who previously held out this expectation. Among these has been no less than the current pope, who in his recent encyclical *Sollicitudo Rei Socialis* explicitly repudiated the idea, widely popular on the Roman Catholic Left, that it should look for a third way between what it considered two morally equivalent evils. (I will not comment here on the peculiar morality that makes such a perspective possible.)

My earlier proposition about the superior mythogenic power of socialism has not been falsified, either. It may yet be. But even if the glittering vision of socialism should seriously pale, it is still very doubtful whether capitalism as such would generate a myth of its own (for more people, that is, than can be counted as followers of Ayn Rand). I doubt it. Democracy is a more likely candidate. There are less attractive possibilities. Nationalism continues to be an ideology (or, more accurately, a collection of ideologies) of unbroken appeal, and the homicidal tribalisms breaking out throughout the decomposing Soviet empire suggest even more chilling scenarios for the age that was to be the end of ideology (*a k a* the end of history).

The questions about totalitarianism and nationalism adumbrate the topic that has preoccupied me most intensely since completing the book, namely, economic culture. Not quite by accident, the completion of the book coincided with the start of the research center I have been directing since then, the Institute for the Study of Economic Culture at Boston University. This is hardly the place for a commercial in behalf of this undertaking, but I must mention it here because the research of the people associated with it has been instrumental in pushing my own thinking further in this direction.

The startling aspect of the collapse of communist regimes in Europe has been its rapidity and relative ease, once the restraining force of Soviet bayonets was removed. It is this aspect that has, I think, falsified that portion of the theory of totalitarianism that asserted the invulnerability of such regimes against internal challenges, and this would be so even if the democratic and pluralistic tendencies in the region were to be reversed in the near or distant future. The monolith, it is now evident, had many more holes in it than Arendt and others envisaged. But equally startling has been the survival, beneath the glacial structures of the totalitarian states, of a variety of social and cultural traits that faithfully replicate the pretotalitarian situation. Institutionally, these are especially rooted in the family and in religion. But there are also cultural configurations (or, if one prefers, structures of consciousness—beliefs, values, moral and ideological propensities) that have reemerged, seemingly unscathed, with the demise of communist power (or even, as in the Soviet Union at the time of writing, with a diminishment of that power). Nationalism, an emphatically modern ideology, is only one of these. There are other beliefs and values, some of them reaching far back into the premodern past. They range from ancient ethnic antagonisms to ways of looking at work. Some of them may turn out to be decisive obstacles to the establishment of democratic and pluralistic societies. They are also likely to influence in an important way the success or failure of efforts to establish market economies in these countries. The cultural differences between, for example, Czechs and Rumanians, or Slovenians and Serbs, simply cannot be ignored in the considerations of economic reformers, not to mention the even more glaring differences among the nationalities that make up the Soviet Union.

As I noted earlier, it is very doubtful whether any body of ideas can ever be declared to be "finished" in human history, particularly socialism, with its mythopoetic power. I would say, however, that this particular idea should be finished as a serious topic of inquiry for social science, except for its continued relevance in the analysis of specific groups (be they African dictators or Western intellectuals) with a vested interest in its survival. Not only the economic dynamics but also the political and social consequences of the two basic modes of production of the modern era should by now be quite clear. Put differently, as far as social science is concerned, the question of socialism may now be safely put to rest.

What may *not* be put to rest, however, is the question of why capitalism (or the transition from socialism to capitalism) succeeds brilliantly in some places and fails miserably in others. Not for a moment would I suggest that an explanation of this discrepancy can always be found in culture. Such a notion would be utterly simplistic, indeed *as* simplistic as the pseudo-explanations of historical materialism. Every important phenomenon in history has many causes. All the same, I would ever more strongly contend that economic culture must be seriously considered as social science tries to unravel the causal constellations that shape the course of human events. This, of course, was the grand intention of the work of Max Weber (though he never used the phrase *economic culture*), and to that extent what I'm recommending here is a neo-Weberian enterprise. This does not imply some sort of sectarian allegiance to his heritage—it can easily be seen now that Weber was very wrong in many of his specific propositions (for example, about the modernizing potential of Confucian cultures). It is not Weber's answers but his questions that are most useful to us today. And they continue to have a remarkable timeliness.

The phrase *economic culture* itself, as explained in the book, does not refer to some mysterious, empirically inaccessible element. Quite simply, it denotes the sociocultural context within which economic activities and economic institutions exist. It points to a certain set of relations; it does *not* imply a theory about those relations. Thus, to speak of economic culture by no means implies that culture always determines economics, or even that cultural factors must be taken into account in all phenomena that an economist studies. Whether culture does or does not enter into the explanation of any economic situation must always be a matter of empirical inquiry. In the absence of the concept, though, such empirical inquiry is foreclosed from the beginning—precisely the foreclosure that characterizes the work of most (not all) economists. My own reading of the empirical evidence leads me to think that economic culture is a very important aspect of many economically relevant phenomena.

One of the questions discussed at some length in the book is the relation between capitalism and what I called the culture of individual autonomy. I refer to Alan Macfarlane's *The Origins of English Individualism,* which strongly suggests what might be described as an inversion of modernization theory: Whereas modernization theorists have seen individualism, and the social and cultural configurations that go with it, as *consequences* of modernity, Macfarlane's findings about the individualistic characteristics of medieval England suggest that, on the contrary, individualism should be seen as a *precondition* of modernity. Brigitte Berger, in *The War over the Family,* has made the same suggestion with regard to the so-called nuclear, conjugal family, allegedly the result of modernization but quite possibly one of its necessary antecedents, at least in Europe. More recently, Macfarlane, in *The Culture of Capitalism,* has dealt with the storm of critical controversy that his earlier work aroused. The nonhistorian can only tread cautiously on such ground.

All the same, I find myself inclining to the revisionist views held by Macfarlane and an apparently growing number of historians of Europe. If they are correct, some of Weber's ideas about the relationship of capitalism and the Protestant ethic will also have to be revised. One could then continue to accept the linkage made by Weber between these two phenomena, more or less in the manner in which he did so, but one would also have to ask why Protestantism triumphed in some parts of Europe and hardly got off the ground in other parts. It could well be that the answer lies in very ancient patterns of society and culture (as, notably, in the structure of the family and the household) that differ, as between different areas of Europe. Thus one need not disparage the role of Protestantism in legitimating the capitalist development of England and the Netherlands, for example. But one would also have to look at social and cultural patterns that divided Northern and Western from Southern and Eastern Europe. It is very unlikely that a colleague of Macfarlane will find medieval roots of individualism in, say, Spain or Russia. In other words, what emerges here is an intriguing new picture of the economic culture of early capitalism in its continent of origin.

Even more intriguing, at least to the nonhistorian, is the question of whether similar differences in premodern patterns are relevant to the understanding of contemporary economic developments. Berger's current work focuses on this question, especially as it relates to family and household patterns. Take the case of the Overseas Chinese, arguably one of the economically most successful groups of people in the contemporary world. One persistent puzzle has been why the Chinese have had such phenomenal success in other countries but not in China itself. There are a number of plausible answers to this question in terms of the political constraints on economic activity in China both before and (obviously) after the communist takeover. Thus certain values conducive to economic success (the much-vaunted Confucian ethic, for instance) would lie dormant or latent in the unfavorable circumstances of traditional or communist China, but erupt into intense economic relevance in places where these unfavorable constraints are absent, as in many countries of the Chinese diaspora. But Berger suggests another possibility: Emigration removes people from the constraining network of the traditional extended family and forces them into patterns strangely similar to the nuclear, conjugal family characteristic of Northern and Western Europe. The same consideration may apply to other economically successful migrants—for instance, Indians and Arabs in many African countries. Thus, in a surprising way, Macfarlane's inversion (if I may call it such) may be important to our understanding of what is happening today in places far removed from the village commons of England.

I continue to think that, as argued in this book, East Asia constitutes a theoretically important second case of advanced industrial capitalism. And I continue to be fascinated by the question of the role of cultural factors in the economic success stories of the region. It is perfectly valid to approach this question by way of broad historical considerations (as Michio Morishima did in *Why Has Japan Succeeded?*). But it also seems to me that what is called for is detailed ethnographic work providing what American anthropologists have aptly called "thick description." One of the first projects of our Institute has now yielded such a work, with Gordon Redding's study of the business ethos of Overseas Chinese managers *(The Spirit of Chinese Capitalism).* What Redding shows, with much detail, is how the Confucian ethic actually operates in the workaday life of Chinese business people. Here is a plausible account of how a premodern cultural ensemble is adapted to modern conditions and transformed into an ethos for modern business activity. The Chinese family firm, as it operates in all the Pacific Rim societies and beyond, here provides an ethnographic laboratory in which to explore this cultural transformation. The essential formula in this instance is an old cultural pattern taking on radically new functions in a changed environment. In some ways, nothing has changed; the ancestors, if you will, are greatly pleased. But in other ways, everything has changed, as the Confucian ethic is transformed from an ideology of conservative bureaucrats (the people Weber described in his marvelous essay "The Chinese Literati") into a value system upholding a dynamic modern capitalism.

It is instructive to compare the Chinese family ethos, as described by Redding, with other family values that some superficial observers would regard as similar, such as those common in Latin America. One might compare Redding's work with Lawrence Harrison's rather pejorative description of Latin American culture in his *Underdevelopment Is a State of Mind.* Both Hong Kong Chinese and, say, Mexicans have a value system that can accurately be described as "familistic," in the sense that in both cases the family is a key focus for the individual's aspirations and efforts. But the economic consequences of Chinese and Mexican "familism" are very different indeed. The Chinese family (among the Overseas Chinese) functions as an institution geared to productivity—source of capital and credit, trusted network of business contacts, employment agency, and social security system—an economic mini-culture that, under auspicious circumstances, can generate truly impressive results. By contrast, the Mexican family is an institution geared to redistribution—a system of obligations by which every gain of individual social mobility is quickly redistributed to a large number of relatives, *compadres,* and other free riders, with the consequence that no capital accumulation occurs and nobody gets very far from the place from which he started. The key differential here, in all likelihood, is in the realm of values, perhaps finally in the realm of religion (Confucianism versus a distinctive Iberian Catholic ethic). It is a culture of emulation ("One of our boys made it!") as against a culture of envy ("Who does he think he is?"). In other words, two variants of the genus "familism" exhibit dramatically different forms of economic culture.

The same point can be made succinctly in the form of a joke that compares (admittedly in a less than scientifically rigorous manner) three economic cultures on the continent of North America. An American, a Canadian, and a Mexican farmer are asked to describe their best wish for the future. The American says, "I want my barn to be bigger than my neighbor's." The Canadian says, "I don't want my neighbor's barn to be bigger than mine." The Mexican says, "I wish my neighbor's barn to burn down."

There are two equally serious mistakes that one can make in these matters: One is to neglect culture as a factor in social change, the other to look upon culture as an inert, unchanging factor, always acting in the same way on the course of events. As also discussed in the book, there is good evidence to the fact that there is cultural change in East Asia. There are great differences in the interpretations given to these changes. The data on changing values among young people in Japan were mentioned in the book as a case in point, with some analysts citing these data as evidence of a cultural sea change, while others (especially Japanese social scientists with an attachment to the unique qualities of "Japaneseness") interpret the evidence as offering yet another illustration of the ingenious way in which Japanese culture absorbs foreign influences, accommodating them and simultaneously domesticating them within the perduring matrix of Japaneseness.

Since then there has been an ongoing, often acrimonious debate in Japan on these value changes, especially as they affect education (arguably the only area in which policy can have much of an impact upon culture). The debate is directly related to the question of whether Japan will retain its competitive edge (its "comparative cultural advantage," in my own terminology) in the international economy. There are some interesting variations in this debate. Variation 1: Japanese values are changing, more or less in the direction of the West (individualism and all that), and this will damage the nation's competitiveness ("Soon we'll be in the same mess that they are in already"). Variation 2: Japanese values are changing, and this will be good for the economy, because the old values, while helpful in an earlier period of modern economic development, have become a hindrance now ("What is good for steel manufacturing is not good for high technology"). Variation 3: Japanese values are *not* changing, and therefore the nation will retain its competitive edge (here belong the, from a Japanese point of view, optimistic interpreters of the data on youth). Variation 4: Japanese values are indeed not changing; the nation is failing to adapt to a changing world, and therefore its economic future looks dim. Needless to say, these different interpretations lead to very different educational policies.

In discussing Redding's work on the practical consequences of the Confucian ethic, I suggested a formula whereby culture remains intact but has different results in a new situation (the same formula would apply to variation 4 in the argument over Japanese values). Quite a different formula applies in situations where the culture loses its intactness (variations 1 and 2). There are some cases in which such cultural change occurs rapidly and massively, to the point where one can legitimately speak of a cultural revolution. One such case, also studied in one of the first projects of our Institute, is the enormous growth of Evangelical Protestantism, especially in its Pentecostal form, in vast areas of the Third World—specifically, in much of East Asia (with the exception of Japan) and the South Pacific, in sub-Saharan Africa, and (most dramatically) in Latin America. The results of our study are reported in the recent book by its principal researcher, David Martin, *Tongues of Fire: The Explosion of Protestantism in Latin America*. Martin focuses on Latin America, but also compares it both with other areas in the contemporary Third World and with the earlier history of Protestantism in the Anglo-American orbit.

The evidence indicates that these masses of Latin Americans converting to Protestantism are also converting to a radically new lifestyle. It is in many ways the very opposite of traditional *latino* culture— uptight rather than relaxed, puritanical and hard-working rather than sensual and leisurely, sensitive to the concerns of women rather than *macho*. What is in the making here is an economic culture given to disciplined effort, restrained consumption, saving, and prudent planning for the future. The most important consequences of the Protestant repudiation of *machismo* are for children: Not only do the economic prospects for the family look much brighter with a father who no longer drinks or runs around with women, works hard and saves, and puts his obligations to the church ahead of those to his *compadres* (strictly speaking, as a Protestant, he has no more *compadres*), but there is now a strong emphasis on the education of the children—an emphasis classic in Protestantism but quite new among poor people in Latin America. Martin describes a sort of "feminization" of Latin American culture here: A large number of Protestant evangelizers are women. They are, as it were, the shock troops of the Protestant movement; but in the process they also "domesticate" their menfolk, or perhaps recruit those men who, for whatever reasons, are ready to be so domesticated. *Feminization* and *domestication* are apt terms to describe what Martin found. Another, slightly more frivolous formulation suggests itself: "Max Weber is alive and well, and living in Guatemala City!" (Guatemala, incidentally, is one of the epicenters of this Protestant earthquake, somewhere between one-fourth and one-third of the nation's population having joined the new faith.)

All of this would be interesting and theoretically significant if it occurred on some margin of society. This is not the case here, though. The phenomenon is of staggering dimensions, growing at breathtaking speed, and worldwide in scope. In terms of dynamism and disregard of national boundaries, its only serious competitor is conservative Islam, but it can be argued, I think, that Protestantism wins out in its rate of growth as well as in its cross-national expanse (the two faiths, by the way, clash directly, frontally, in sub-Saharan Africa). In any case, the cultural revolution of Evangelical Protestantism is anything but a marginal, sectarian phenomenon. On the contrary, I would argue that it is one of the most important cultural developments in the world today. This is not the place to discuss the implications of this for the future of Latin America as well as some of the other regions affected by this explosion; the point here is that we don't have to go far afield in history to find cases where rapid and massive cultural change occurred, with far-reaching and often lasting consequences for the economy: an enormously significant case is to be found today, right on our doorsteps.

Nascent capitalism has different requirements than mature capitalism. If Max Weber is living in Guatemala City, what about Manchester and Milwaukee? It would appear that quite a different cultural dynamic is in evidence there.

The question of what is happening in the meantime, on the farm (the old farm, in Europe and North America, where capitalism was first grown), was raised in the book in the discussion of the knowledge class. Here I followed the idea of Joseph Schumpeter and, more recently, the American authors who spoke of the New Class, to the effect that capitalism has produced its own adversary, not as Marx thought in the industrial proletariat but rather in a class of educated knowledge workers who are needed in increasing numbers in an age of high technology and greatly diminished labor-intensive production. The hypothesis that this class of professionals is politically and socially to the Left was analyzed by John McAdams in an Institute study of American survey data; his findings, not yet published at the time of writing, support the hypothesis. At the present time we are bringing to an end a five-country study of the culture of the newer professions in Western Europe and the United States, under the direction of Hansfried Kellner. This study, while not contradicting the New Class hypothesis, raises new and as yet unresolved questions.

First the intelligentsia (when they were few) and then the new knowledge class (of which there are many, indeed millions) created what Lionel Trilling aptly called an adversary culture—adversary, that is, to the old bourgeois culture that accompanied (perhaps caused, perhaps was caused by) capitalism in its formative period. Whatever the Protestant ethic was, the antagonistic culture was *not*. As this antibourgeois culture burst into public view in the 1960s throughout the Western world, it saw itself and was seen by others as standing in sharp counterpoint to the earlier middle-class culture, which was still identified with the business community and capitalism. It was a *counter*culture indeed. Its advocates besmirched all the old ideals of the middle class, the entire catechism of the Protestant ethic. If the cultural revolution of Latin American Protestantism is the triumph of uptight respectability, *this* cultural revolution prided itself on its defiance of respectable middle-class virtues in all areas of life, from patriotism to sexual morality. Emphatically included in this repudiation of bourgeois culture was anything conducive to the maintenance of an effective capitalist economy, now pejoratively characterized as "the system" or, from the vantage point of the individual caught in it, "the rat race."

I continue to think (and McAdams's findings have strengthened my view) that one can speak of class conflict here. That is, the new knowledge class has both vested interests and a culture (if you will, a class consciousness) that put it in conflict with the old middle class, which still has the business community at its core. The class conflict is clearest if one looks at directly political behavior and attitudes: The new professionals diverge in statistically significant ways from business people when it comes to voting and political opinions. But what is also emerging is a certain symbiosis between the two cultures to the point where *conflict* doesn't quite seem an appropriate word to use. The popular term *yuppie,* though sociologically imprecise, intended the same phenomenon: Here are individuals whose general worldview and whose lifestyle have been greatly influenced by the counterculture, but who accept "the system," who wish to succeed in it in conventional capitalist terms, and who are prepared to give up (indeed, have given up) the wilder political stances of the original counterculture. This intriguing symbiosis can be observed quite sharply in new management philosophies and practices in such "soft" areas as human resources, corporate identity, and (needless to say) public affairs. The language of the campus protests now emerges from the glossy pages of corporate propaganda, and erstwhile revolutionaries are drawing excellent salaries peddling countercultural themes and practices in the boardrooms of the capitalist establishment.

What is one to make of this? There are two sets of questions here. If there really is such a confluence of previously antagonistic cultural trends, who is the winner, who the loser, in this deal? And is this symbiosis good or bad for the international competitiveness of Western economies?

The first question is more ideological than analytic. To be sure, from the viewpoint of the would-be revolutionaries of the 1960s, their later selves have sold out. But, from the viewpoint of an earlier middle-class ideology, it is business that is selling out to its enemies. Analytically, it is not at all clear who is co-opting whom here. The system survives, by incorporating its adversaries, and in this sense wins. But, on the other hand, "the long march through the institutions" succeeds beyond the wildest dreams of those who coined this phrase, by invading the very centers of capitalist power with at least some of its cherished values. Thus Western capitalism, of course, does not become socialist or go back to some primitive communalism, but is becoming heavily influenced by the countercultural ideas embodied in feminism, environmentalism, and (perhaps most important) by a style of human relations best described as "sensitive." Put differently, capitalism survives, but it has become softer, more gentle. Whether one welcomes or deplores this depends on philosophical choices that need not concern us here.

The second question—Will such a softer capitalism be more or less competitive?—is of great importance indeed. I must confess that, at this time, I'm very uncertain about it. Intuitively and also on the basis of historical experience, one would tend to think that this "sensitivization" of Western capitalism will erode its competitive edge: When the going gets rough, soft people lose. On the other hand, it is quite possible that what holds in an earlier phase of capitalism (in England two hundred years ago, or in Guatemala today) may *not* hold in a later phase. Also, if people really believe that becoming more sensitive will make them more productive, it may actually do so (no matter what an outside observer may feel about the claims of the sensitivity advocates). And, if the West is going soft, so may its principal competitors (see the earlier discussion of Japanese value change); in other words, if we all soften together, no one will have an edge. Of course, in the background somewhere, in a country that no one is paying attention to now, may be lurking the hard-nosed, *macho,* insensitive son-of-a-bitch who in the end will do us all in!

As I tried to express emphatically in the opening pages of this book, science deals in probabilities, not certainties; in hypotheses, not dogma. Social reality is ever in flux, and recently it has been in flux with a vengeance. It is gratifying to see some of one's hypotheses confirmed, annoying to have to admit that one was wrong or not prescient enough. Unanswered questions can gnaw and irritate, especially if they *remain* unanswered for many years. But what draws one back to the social-scientific enterprise, ever again, is what drew one in the first place: the rich diversity and often stunning surprises of human actions. Capitalism is a phenomenon of rich diversity indeed, and again and again its vitality and its inventiveness surprise us. It is unlikely to lose its fascination in the lifetime of even the youngest reader of this book.

*1991*

# INTRODUCTION

CAPITALISM is widely viewed as a conservative force in the contemporary world. Consequently, the phrase "capitalist revolution" in the title of this book may appear odd to some. Like many widely held views, the notion of capitalism as conservative is misleading. On the contrary, from its inception capitalism has been a force of cataclysmic transformation in one country after another. Capitalism has radically changed every material, social, political, and cultural facet of the societies it has touched, and it continues to do so. Understanding this revolutionary impact of capitalism on modern society is a formidable and important intellectual task.

The purpose of this book is to draw the outline of a theory concerning the relation between capitalism and society in the modern world. Each chapter (with the exception of the first and the last, which deal, respectively, with matters of definition and with summary reflections) contains various propositions which I put forth on the basis of the empirical evidence cited. These propositions are hypotheses, in the strict sense in which this term has been used within the social sciences. That is, these propositions are not of a philosophical, ethical, or any other a priori sort. As hypotheses within a social-science framework, they are subject to empirical testing and thus to falsification. I expect that they will be challenged, in part or as a whole; I hope that such challenges, like the propositions themselves, will be grounded in empirical evidence.

As is spelled out in more detail in the first chapter, an empirically oriented theory of capitalism and society does not exist at present, unless one wants to accord this status to Marxism. Clearly, I do not. Marxism, of course, comes in many versions, some of them sharply contradictory of each other. All share that peculiar mixture of science and prophecy that is both the major intellectual flaw of Marxism and the source of its immense mythopoetic appeal. It remains the case, however, that only Marxists have consistently sought to integrate in a single theoretical construction the economic, social, political, and cultural dimensions of the capitalist phenomenon. Thus it will be necessary in various portions of this book to deal with the Marxist interpretations of this or that aspect of the phenomenon, usually in a critical vein. A few observations should be made right in the beginning as to why Marxism in any of its versions will not meet the requirement of a comprehensive theoretical framework for an understanding of the relation between capitalism and society in the modern world. It is further appropriate to indicate why various non-Marxist theorists, such as Max Weber, Joseph Schumpeter and F.A. Hayek, do not meet this requirement either. In other words, it is important to establish that a great lacuna exists on the contemporary intellectual landscape. Not for a moment is it intended to suggest that the present book, by itself, can fill this lacuna. Such a suggestion would not only be an exercise in insufferable hubris (of which, if only because of a pervasive sense of the comic, I find myself incapable), but it would also lift the book out of the context of the social sciences, which can never do more than provide partial, provisional, and in principle refutable interpretations of human reality. In the present state of our knowledge, no individual is in a position to supply the full-blown theory that must be a final if ever-elusive goal. What an individual can do is to produce a blue-print for the task at hand and to suggest some building blocks. This is what I have tried to do here—no more, but also no less.

Karl Marx was one of the intellectual giants of the modern age, and especially social scientists remain indebted to his work at many points. One may only mention here, by way of an important example, the concept of class, which Marx first put squarely into the center of the analysis of modern society. However, from its inception, Marxism has been plagued by its methodological starting point, which supposedly grounded its scientific investigations in philosophy and which did this in a manner that undermined its status as an empirical discipline. To this day Marxists criticize "bourgeois" (that is, non-Marxist) social scientists for their putatively illusionary ideals of objectivity and value-neutrality; by contrast, Marxists claim to base their own science on a correct understanding of underlying historical forces. Unfortunately, these superior insights into the historical process are not susceptible to empirical testing; rather, they are a priori assumptions, which are nonfalsifiable, but which determine both the approach and the results of particular historical or social-scientific investigations. Not to put too fine a point to it, Marxist social scientists typically ask questions about matters on which they already believe to have the answers, at least in broad outline. This is a very useful methodology for prophets; it decisively flaws the work of social scientists.

Those who are not convinced by the philosophical outlook foundational to Marxism have no alternative to bracketing this outlook (a difficult feat, in view of the way in which philosophy and science are intertwined in Marxist works) and then to exploring those Marxist propositions that are, one by one, susceptible to being tested empirically. (Marxists, of course, repudiate such treatment as illegitimate, indeed as a trick of "bourgeois ideology," but non-Marxist social scientists have learned to live with this.) Thus, for instance, Marx's own labor theory of value (the notion that the true value of a commodity is the labor expended in producing it) is based on an a priori notion that cannot be empirically tested or falsified; but Marx's prediction of falling wage rates can be empirically tested outside the context of his philosophy of labor; and, indeed, this prediction has been consistently falsified in the economic history of the advanced capitalist societies. The list of other falsified Marxian propositions is long and embarrassing—to mention but a few of the more important ones, the deepening "immiseration" *(Verelendung)* of the working class and the consequent ever-sharper polarization of society, the inability of "bourgeois" democracy to cope with modern class conflicts and the consequent ascendancy of dictatorial regimes in the heartlands of capitalism, or the progressive exclusion of the working class from the culture of the capitalist classes. Post-Marxian Marxism, in all its various forms, has not done much better in withstanding empirical testing. The inability of Marxist theory to explain the realities of socialist regimes in the contemporary world is a particularly serious weakness, as is the failure of the Marxist prediction that only socialism can generate successful development in the Third World.

It is of the nature of prophecy that it manages to survive despite repeated empirical falsifications (a psychologist of religion may even argue that such falsifications actually strengthen the devotion of true believers). Thus Marxism continues to have strong appeal in various places and, because of this, it must be taken seriously by the social scientist (later on in this book, there will be some discussion of the nature of this appeal). But the social scientist who, for whatever reasons, cannot be counted among the believers, must look elsewhere for a satisfactory theoretical framework. There is, alas, no embarrassment of riches.

If one is to look for such a non-Marxist framework, the three authors mentioned above—Weber, Schumpeter, and Hayek—are probably those who would suggest themselves first. It is by no means a derogatory statement about them if one says that none of them supplies this framework. Each of the three made enormously important contributions to our understanding of the modern world, and some of these contributions will have to be taken up in the pages to follow. But it must be stressed that none of the three set out to construct the kind of theory that is being called for here. Weber's intellectual enterprise was essentially one of comparative history, designed to uncover the roots of the unique Western development of what he called "modern rationality." Capitalism was one important phenomenon explored by Weber in this connection, but he never intended to come up with a comprehensive theory of capitalism as such. Schumpeter remained essentially an economist and his most durable contributions have remained in economics (for example, his theory of the economic role of entrepreneurship). His profoundly astute analysis of the relations between capitalism, socialism, and democracy constituted a sort of intellectual excursion, never intended to result in something to be called a theory of capitalism in sociopolitical or sociocultural terms. Hayek, finally, also made some highly astute observations about the relation of capitalism to various other phenomena in modern society, such as democracy and the rule of law, but, once again, he never set out to construct a comprehensive theory embracing all these relationships. Indeed, his later works are primarily concerned with what he considered to be the preconditions of a "free society," among which capitalism is but one of several. There are many aspects of capitalism—social, political, and cultural—that interested none of these authors. Finally, it should be emphasized that Weber and Schumpeter did not live to see the luxuriant flowering of both capitalist and socialist experiments in the era following World War II, while Hayek apparently has had little interest in those that have taken place outside the orbit of Western civilization. Yet the development of a vast socialist world in recent decades, both within and outside the parameters of the Soviet empire, and the great variety of Third World economic and sociopolitical "paths to development," constitute exceedingly important materials for any adequate theory of modern capitalism.

This having been said, though, it should be added that the present book is not primarily intended to be either a refutation of Marxism or a development (let alone an exegesis) of the non-Marxist authors just mentioned. There is no shortage of refutations of Marxism, be it in toto or in parts (suffice it to mention the magisterial work of Leszek Kolakowski in this connection). But what I have set out to do here is positive rather than negative—to begin to put in place a viable theoretical framework rather than to demolish other people's frameworks. I have learned very much from Schumpeter, somewhat less from Hayek, but I have had to turn elsewhere for most of my theoretical building blocks. I'm indebted to Max Weber more than to any other author in the social sciences, and this debt will be clear on many pages of this book. But I have never been very much taken with the endless enterprise of interpreting and reinterpreting the Weberian opus. I'm convinced that Weber asked many of the crucial questions; I tend to think that many of his answers are no longer tenable and that today we must ask many questions that he could not possibly have asked. At least in science, one shows the greatest respect for an author by leaving him behind.

What, then, is the theoretical approach I want to propose here? It is expressed in a key concept recurring in various parts of the book —the concept of "economic culture." The phrase is a deliberate neologism. It is inspired by the concept of "political culture," as it has become common in political science due to the work of Gabriel Almond, Lucian Pye, Sidney Verba and others. Mutatis mutandis, the theoretical intent is the same here. An "economic culture" theory of capitalism (or, for that matter, of any other economic phenomenon) will explore the social, political, and cultural matrix or context within which these particular economic processes operate. No unidirectional causality is assumed by the term. That is, it is not assumed that culture determines economics or, conversely, that economic factors are always determinative of culture. The specific causal relations are left open to empirical inquiry, case by case. The concept of "economic culture" simply draws attention to the relationships that such inquiry must explore.

Thus, for example, it will be necessary to explore in what way a capitalist economy is linked to the particular type of stratification that ever since Marx has been designated by the category of "class." It so happens that here I find myself in agreement with an important Marxian view, namely, that capitalism does indeed demolish other types of stratification (such as feudalism) in favor of a class system, though I cannot agree with many of Marx's particular characterizations of such a system. Thus I devote considerable space to an exploration of the relation between capitalism and democracy and, farther on, to the relation between capitalism and the amalgam of values commonly called "individualism." My propositions about these two sets of relationships are stated as succinctly as I can make them in the appropriate places of the following argument. Further exploration may or may not sustain the empirical validity of these propositions. My point here is simply this: The theory of capitalism that must be constructed will have to deal with these relationships—capitalism and stratification, capitalism and forms of polity, capitalism and various value systems —be it in the way I have attempted here or in some quite different ways. Only as systematic inquiry into these relationships proceeds, with different social scientists both building on the work of their predecessors and demolishing the latter, will a comprehensive theory of the economic culture of capitalism emerge.

As the argument of the book develops, a number of propositions (fifty in all) will be formulated. I want to stress, as emphatically as I can, that *each one of these propositions is to be understood as a hypothesis within an ongoing empirical inquiry.* The book constitutes a prima facie argument for these propositions. It follows, though, that *each proposition is, in principle, falsifiable.* My own view of the likelihood of this happening varies from case to case. Some of the propositions impress me as very well founded, and I would be much surprised if falsifying evidence could be brought up. In other cases I find myself quite uncertain as to the ultimate validity of a particular proposition and would be much more comfortable if additional data clarified the issue one way or the other. There are also some propositions that I don't like at all, so that I would dearly welcome it if someone came along and falsified them for me. In any case, it should be clear beyond the shadow of a doubt that what is being proposed here is hypothetical, open-ended, and nondogmatic. To use a juridical analogy, I have prepared an "indictment," based on the evidence presented; the "verdict" remains to be pronounced—by the ongoing "jury" which is constituted by the community of scholars committed to the discipline of empirical inquiry.

It should be clear, then, that the theory I wish to adumbrate in this book is one that belongs squarely within the ongoing enterprise of the empirical social sciences. This statement implies what the book is *not*. It is not a book of philosophy or ethics. I have no a priori principles to proclaim (and I have been unpersuaded by the principles of this sort that have commonly been adduced by both protagonists and critics of capitalism). Nor do I claim to know anything about the inner logic or direction of history. I hold no philosophical (or, for that matter, theological) positions that would lead me either to embrace or to reject capitalism. Thus this book also does not intend to constitute a moral argument in favor of capitalism. As will become clear, I do indeed think that such an argument can be made, and in the final chapter I spell out the values on the basis of which one may so argue. But I do not argue for these values here (I have on occasion done so elsewhere), and it follows that anyone not holding these values may reach quite different moral and political conclusions on the basis of the same empirical evidence. Thus, for example, I submit that both the values of an ongoing improvement in the material standards of life and of the institutionalization of individual liberties will favor an option for capitalism over the empirically available alternatives. But anyone who repudiates these values—say, a traditionalist who believes in the superior virtue of austerity and of collective solidarity—may agree with me on the empirical evidence regarding the effects of capitalism but will then draw very different practical conclusions from this evidence.

All the same, since the values spelled out are not idiosyncratic but are shared by many if not most people who have addressed themselves to these matters, I cannot gainsay the conclusion that this book has clearly procapitalist implications. I'm too much of a sociologist not to anticipate the criticism that a procapitalist bias inspired the argument from the beginning and determined its outcomes; the same sociological tristesse makes me resigned to the improbability that critics making this assertion will be convinced by my protesting the contrary. For my own sake if not for theirs, I will protest all the same. As a description of my own intellectual odyssey, this criticism would put the cart before the horse. I did not start out with a procapitalist bias. When I began to occupy myself with these questions more than fifteen years ago, I was very open to the possibility that socialism may be a more humane form of economic and social organization. It was the sheer pressure of empirical evidence, registered in my mind over years of work, that compelled me to arrive at the position I now hold. Perhaps it is one of the ironies of my professional career that, very largely because of my perception of capitalism, I moved to the "right" while a sizable segment of my colleagues in the social sciences moved to the "left." But this is hardly the place to ruminate about this accident of biography.

While the subject under discussion is vast and immensely complex, the structure of the book is simple. Chapter 1 does the necessary job of definition and delineation of capitalism as a phenomenon; it also amplifies the foregoing observations about the kind of theory that is called for. Chapter 2 deals with the impact of capitalism on the material life of people and with the distribution of material benefits. Chapter 3 discusses class, chapter 4 the relation of capitalism and democracy, and chapter 5 the relation between capitalism and what is commonly (and quite accurately) called "bourgeois culture." The major focus in all these chapters is on the advanced industrial societies of the West, where modern capitalism began and where it has reached its most "mature" forms. Historical developments are, of necessity, touched upon, but obviously these chapters do not purport to present a history of Western capitalism. Likewise, economic data and theories have to be taken into account (a particularly nervous-making thing for the noneconomist), but there is no attempt here to develop an understanding of the strictly economic mechanisms at work. A theory of economic culture is not a theory within the science of economics; rather, it is an intellectual exercise on the borderline of economics and the other social sciences. Put differently, the emerging theory of capitalism proposed here deals primarily with the *non*economic ramifications of the capitalist phenomenon.

The realities of the contemporary world forbid the construction of a theory of capitalism limited to its Western manifestations. As is suggested in the book, a useful way of looking at the contemporary world is to do so through the image of three gigantic test tubes, in each of which the process called "modernization" has reached a degree of high intensity, and the image can be augmented by adding a number of test tubes in the background where this process is still in an earlier or less-developed phase. In other words, the image is that of a global laboratory in which the "chemical reaction" of modernization may be observed in a series of more or less complete experiments. The three crucial test tubes represent Western industrial capitalism, East Asian industrial capitalism, and industrial socialism; the additional test tubes represent various Third World societies. I contend that the economic culture of our time can only be understood in such a cross-national, indeed global, perspective.

Chapter 6 deals with the expansion of capitalism into the Third World and its effects on development. Chapter 7 deals with the successful capitalist societies of East Asia, which, I believe, can no longer be seen as a mere extension of Western capitalism but rather must be analyzed as a theoretically most significant "second case." Comparison between Western and East Asian capitalism allows the empirical testing of a number of hypotheses concerning economic culture. While the boundaries of "success" in East Asia are shifting, the focus here is on Japan and the so-called Four Little Dragons (South Korea, Taiwan, Hong Kong, and Singapore). Industrial socialism—specifically, the Soviet Union and its more advanced European allies—constitutes an equally important "control case" (chapter 8). The systematic comparison between industrial capitalism and industrial socialism allows one to discriminate between the effects of modernization as such and effects that may be ascribed to the particular forms of socioeconomic organization. This comparison also begins to make clear that any adequate theory of capitalism will necessarily imply a theory of socialism. These two forms of organizing the economy are, willy-nilly, twin manifestations of modernity, and to understand one requires of necessity an understanding of the other.

Chapter 9 deals with the question of how capitalism is legitimated in the minds of people (the sociology-of-knowledge question par excellence in the present context). Finally, chapter 10 tries to sketch the shape of the theory as it has come into view, mainly by pulling together the propositions scattered throughout the preceding text, and to discuss how capitalism can be morally assessed in the light of a number of commonly held values.

This book has been many years in the making. It began subcutaneously in the late 1960s, when I became interested in Third World development and when the nefarious role of capitalism regarding the latter was widely proclaimed by the then-ascendant New Left. I was never persuaded by the arguments of the latter, but I took them seriously (in retrospect, more seriously than they deserved). In 1974 I published a book on the ethical dilemmas of development, *Pyramids of Sacrifice* (Basic Books), largely shaped by my experience in and my reflections about Latin America (at that time, except for a short foray into Africa, the only part of the Third World with which I had some familiarity). In this book I tried very hard to be evenhanded as between capitalist and socialist models of development, arguing that both should be assessed in terms of a number of moral criteria I proposed (notably a "calculus of pain," referring to the avoidance of human suffering, and a "calculus of meaning," by which I meant respect for the values of Third World people). I have had no reason to change these moral criteria since then, but precisely their application to the empirical evidence led me step by step to my present position, which is that capitalism is the morally safer bet. The turning point for me came in the mid-1970s, when I first experienced Asia and especially the societies of what one may call the "prosperity crescent" stretching from Japan down to the Malay peninsula. The experience of East Asia makes it difficult to remain evenhanded as between capitalist and socialist development models.

It would be impossible to name all the individuals who over the years have helped me in my understanding of these matters. I will limit myself here to thanking those who have been immediately helpful as I was writing this book.

As with all my previous books, this one could not have been written without the support and the critical interest of Brigitte Berger. To say that I am indebted to her would be a monumental understatement. The problems discussed in this book were greatly clarified in my mind through many conversations with Richard Neuhaus over the years. From 1981 to 1984 I served as chairman of the Seminar on Modern

Capitalism, conducted under the auspices of the Institute for Educational Affairs with a grant from the Smith Kline Corporation. At the time of writing, the papers of the seminar are as yet unpublished, though publication of the papers of the first two years is projected for 1986 in two volumes entitled, respectively, *The Arithmetic of Justice: Capitalism and Equality in America* and *The Calculus of Hope: Capitalism and Equality in the Third World* (both edited by me and Philip Marcus, both to be published by University Press of America). While the focus of the seminar was much narrower than that of the present book, being solely on the issue of equality, the discussions of those sessions have been invaluable to me. Without wanting to imply invidious distinctions, I have particularly profited from the counsel of Walter Connor, Nick Eberstadt, Grace Goodell, Alan Kantrow, Hansfried Kellner, Laura Nash, Gustav Papanek, Myron Weiner, and Jeffrey Williamson, all of whom were members of the seminar at different stages.

In fall 1984 I gave two visiting seminars at Georgetown University, one for faculty and one for graduate students, on the theory of capitalism. I found these occasions very helpful during a crucial stage of writing the book, providing as they did both positive feedback and astute criticisms. I am particularly grateful to Karl Cerny and Bruce Douglass for making this experience possible.

My understanding of the East Asian "second case" was greatly helped by a study trip in 1982 under the auspices of the Council on Religion and International Affairs, and I want to thank Robert Myers, the president of that organization, for his continuing interest in my work. The Asia and World Institute sponsored two seminars on the relation of culture and economic performance in East Asia that I have found very instructive, in Taipei in 1984 and in New York in 1985. I have profited from my intermittent collaboration with Michael Hsiao. Thomas Berger helped me with bibliographical suggestions on the economic and social history of Japan.

I want to thank the Earhart Foundation for awarding me a grant during the final writing stage of the book.

In a book dealing with capitalism it may be appropriate to include what could well be construed as a commercial message. In the fall of 1985 the Institute for the Study of Economic Culture at Boston University was inaugurated under my direction. It is my hope that the work of this institute will carry forward the agenda suggested by this book, opening up new areas, compelling me to revise (and, who knows, perhaps to recant) some of the propositions made in the following pages. In this connection I also want to thank John Silber and Jon Westling, respectively president and provost of Boston University, for their sympathetic encouragement of a venture that administrators at other academic institutions might well regard as outlandish.

Last not least, I want to thank Judith Greissman and Martin Kessler, of Basic Books, for their unstinting support and editorial criticisms.

*1986*

# I

# CAPITALISM AS A PHENOMENON

I<small>T IS</small> of the essence of the human mind to take apart what experience presents as a whole. This essentially dissective quality is, of course, accentuated when the mind subjects itself to the discipline of scientific reasoning. Individuals experience their own society (or, for that matter, other societies they may encounter) in terms of aggregates. Similarly, as one looks back in history, aggregates present themselves for one's inspection. This is what makes it possible, even in ordinary language, to speak of particular "worlds"—say, "the middle-class world," "the world of American Evangelicals," "the world of seventeenth-century France," and so on. Each such "world," contemporary or in the past, is made up of a seemingly infinite or near-infinite number of elements. Any attempt at understanding or explaining a human "world" necessarily entails an intellectual task of disaggregation. The purpose of this is not to deny the richness or the wholeness of human experience but rather to grasp the latter within an intellectually meaningful framework. The enterprise known as "theorizing" in any science is, of necessity, an operation whereby empirical aggregates are disaggregated in the mind and whereby the resulting elements are then ordered in terms of some sort of causal or functional or hermeneutic hierarchy. Poets will decry the loss of wholeness brought on by such an activity, and they are quite right (that is why poets are needed); theorists will have to live with the loss as an inevitable price of their calling.

The term "capitalism" refers to a set of economic arrangements both in ordinary language and in scientific terminology. These economic arrangements, however, rarely if ever manifest themselves in experience as isolated from other elements of experience that have nothing to do with economics. The ordinary citizen of a "capitalist" society encounters the economic arrangements so labeled as part and parcel of much larger social "worlds." Thus, in America, "capitalism" appears inextricably linked with the material cornucopia of an advanced industrial civilization, with a highly dynamic class system, with political democracy, and with an array of cultural patterns (for example, "individualism"); yet each of these can be seen as being distinct from the economic arrangements as such. The outside observer of American "capitalism" (no matter whether he is friendly, hostile, or neutral) similarly perceives the economic arrangements as embedded in a much larger picture, as does the historian of American society looking back in time. To say the least, it is not easy to excise the capitalist phenomenon from this wider context and look at it, as if holding it with pincers under a lens, in any kind of "pure" form.

But "capitalism" is not only an element of experience; it is also a concept. For historical reasons that are not difficult to reconstruct, it is also a concept that is typically charged with valuations, both negative and positive ones. Thus capitalism is habitually defined in a manner that already includes a valuation—say, as an economic system in which some exploit the labor of others or, alternatively, as an economic system that respects the natural rights of property. Such definitions may have their place in political propaganda; they emphatically do not belong in the framework of science. Any attempt at a theory of this phenomenon is, therefore, under an unusually strict mandate to devise a definition that will not automatically condemn or praise what is being defined. The purpose of definition must be to delineate the boundaries of the phenomenon—no more, and no less. It is strictly in this sense that it is necessary to ask the far from simple question: What is capitalism?

Capitalism is a *historical* phenomenon.[1] To say this is more than a truism. It implies that capitalism grew over a long period of time; consequently, historians will differ as to the point in time where the phenomenon may be reasonably said to exist. In this, of course, capitalism is just like any other historical phenomenon; by comparison, one may recall all the controversies concerning the decline of Rome: Just when did Rome reach its apex and when did it begin its decline? When can the phenomenon of the Roman Empire be said to have disappeared? Or has it perhaps not disappeared at all but only been transmuted? Yet, despite the many difficulties of periodization and causal explanation, there is a remarkable agreement among major historians of capitalism, ever since the great work of Werner Sombart on the subject was published in 1902, about certain features of this history (the agreement is all the more remarkable in view of the violent ideological differences among the historians concerned). Among these agreed-upon features are the following: The expanding market economies of medieval Europe, with various peculiar institutional accompaniments (such as the development of European cities, merchant houses, and guilds), were the foundation on which later capitalism developed. Sometime in the late Middle Ages the economic center of Europe shifted from the Mediterranean littoral to Northern Europe, a shift that became further stabilized in the early modern period, with its first focus in Holland and a second (decisive) focus in England. Modern capitalism became firmly established between the sixteenth and eighteenth centuries. But a decisive leap forward came with the eighteenth century, first in England, with the merging of a capitalist economy with the immense technological power released by the Industrial Revolution. The modern capitalist world system became established in the nineteenth century and has been further solidified in the twentieth.

Obviously, there are important differences between historians as to the causes and many of the details of these stages of development. But the most important implication that enjoys widespread consensus is that capitalism, however defined, was at first only a small part of Western economies and then gradually became the basic organizing principle of these economies as a whole. None of this, though, frees one from the necessity of defining the phenomenon.

The etymology of the term is mildly helpful for this.[2] The term "capital" (*capitale,* from Latin *caput* for "head") first emerged in the twelfth and thirteenth centuries, denoting funds, stocks of merchandise, sums of money, and money carrying interest. Fernand Braudel quotes a sermon of St. Bernardino of Siena (1380–1444), who refers to *"quamdam seminalem rationem lucrosi quam communiter capitale vocamus"* (that prolific cause of wealth we commonly call capital).[3] The term came to denote, more narrowly, the *money* wealth of a firm or a merchant. In the eighteenth century it gained common usage in this narrower sense, especially referring to *productive* capital. And, of course, it was Karl Marx who made this term into a central concept, denoting what he called a "mode of production." The noun "capitalist" probably dates from the mid-seventeenth century, to refer to owners of "capital." Curiously, the term "capitalism" is the most recent. Adam Smith, commonly regarded as the classical theorist of capitalism, did not use the term at all; he described what he regarded as the natural system of liberty. Marx rarely used the word "capitalism" as a noun. It became common only after the publication of Sombart's magnum opus, and by then was generally seen as the opposite of "socialism." Yet this etymology does point to some key elements of the phenomenon: It is rooted in money, and it is a particular way of organizing production.

Max Weber defined capitalist enterprise as an economic activity that is oriented toward a market and that is geared to making a profit out of market exchanges.[4] Clearly, such activity can be (and originally was) only a small part of a total economy. Thus, in the Middle Ages, there were enclaves of capitalist enterprise within the overall feudal economy, which was organized in a very different way. Gradually, these enclaves expanded. Weber suggests that the term "capitalism" applies to a situation in which the economic requirements of a society or a group are predominantly met by means of capitalist enterprise as defined above. In all likelihood it makes little sense, then, to speak of fully capitalist economies prior to the nineteenth century, when capitalism combined with industrialism to create what is now the modern world. Braudel made it his major life work to trace the steps by which capitalist enterprise was progressively superimposed on the entire economies of Europe. And, as Braudel points out, the Marxian term "mode of production" adequately catches this increasingly all-embracing character of the capitalist phenomenon.

The historical characteristics of this modern industrial capitalism can be further specified.[5] It presupposes rational calculation by means of double-entry bookkeeping, which is much more than a clerical technique; rather it constitutes a new mind set for economic activity—the rationally calculating pursuit of profit. Further characteristics are the appropriation of all the material means of production (land, tools, machines, and so on) as private property; freedom of the market (as against various precapitalist, typically feudal restrictions); rational technology geared to economic activity; a rational (and thus predictable) legal system; free labor (as against various forms of slavery or serfdom); and, last not least, the commercialization of the economy, which means above all the growing importance of freely traded shares and securities.

Needless to say, this list of characteristics is arguable; it is not axiomatic or doctrinaire but rather an attempt to reasonably delineate the phenomenon.[6] Still, the most useful definition of capitalism is one that concentrates on what most people have long had in mind in using the term—*production for a market by enterprising individuals or combines with the purpose of making a profit.* Whatever may be the defects in his theory of capitalism, it was the historic achievement of Marx to show how such a system (as he thought, through the autonomous "movements" of *das Kapital*) generates vast and unprecedented productive power. This power has dramatically transformed the material conditions of human life, first in the capitalist "core countries," then increasingly throughout the world.

Through most of human history, economic processes (those processes that deal with the production and distribution of scarce resources and services) were firmly embedded in the overall institutional order of society. Put differently, it would have been difficult until very recently to even conceive of "economic man" acting on the basis of autonomously functioning economic processes.[7] This also meant that economic processes (what was produced and how it was produced and to whom it was distributed) were largely determined by tradition. This was very probably even so in the early capitalist period in Europe, when capitalist enterprise was still "contained" in relatively small enclaves within economies operating on very different principles. As these enclaves expanded, and especially as the vast accumulation of productive resources made possible by capitalism merged with the quantum jump in technological power made possible by the Industrial Revolution, all this changed. It now became possible to think of the economic apparatus of society working away according to its own laws; not so incidentally, a science to study these laws, that of economics, became possible.

Historically, the capitalist phenomenon in its full-blown form coincided with the phenomenon of industrialism. Together, the new economic institutions and the new technology (in Marxian terms, the relations and the means of production) transformed the world. One way of describing the socialist vision, at least since Marx, is as an act of the imagination that would take these two forces apart again. Socialism intends to replace production for profit by production for human use, which means that the same power of modern technology would now be operating under different economic institutions—specifically, institutions that would *not* be enterprising individuals or combines operating for profit in a market system. In order to produce for human use rather than profit, private ownership is to be replaced by public ownership and market mechanisms by (putatively more equitable) mechanisms of political allocation. But tradition as an economic criterion has as little place in this vision (or in the socialist realities brought about by this vision in the twentieth century) as under capitalism. Socialism, like capitalism, is a thoroughly rational vision of the world; put differently, both socialism and capitalism are thoroughly modern phenomena (and, incidentally, are typically perceived as such by traditional people). This has many implications, some of which will be addressed later in this book. But it has one very interesting implication, which is a narrowing of institutional options. In premodern societies, where tradition generally rules, there is a great variety of economic arrangements, all studied with loving care by anthropologists, many of whom rather prefer their favorite tribe to modern societies. Under modern conditions (that is, under the conditions brought about by industrial technology—conditions that of course include the astronomically large populations made possible by the technological transformation), the options are sharply reduced. Specifically, the basic option is whether economic processes are to be governed by market mechanisms or by mechanisms of political allocation. In social-scientific parlance, this is the option between market economies and command economies. Without too much terminological quibbling, this is what most people have in mind when they contrast capitalism and socialism. And that is not a bad way of roughly conceptualizing existing societies in the contemporary world.

However, the adverb "roughly" in the preceding sentence indicates a fundamental empirical problem, namely, that neither market nor command economies exist in the real world in anything like a "pure" form. Market mechanisms in societies classified as capitalist are severely modified by monopolistically inclined corporations and labor unions, and the advent of what Joseph Schumpeter called the "tax state" has massively introduced political allocation as a very important factor in the economies of these societies.[8] This, of course, has led procapitalist critics (for example, F. A. Hayek) to complain that these societies are already well on the way toward socialism. There can be no doubt that no society commonly classified as capitalist (including all of North America and Western Europe) remotely resembles what Adam Smith would have recognized as a "free" society. In other words, in these societies mechanisms of political allocation are constantly intervening to modify (the critics would say to distort) the working-away of the market. Meanwhile, on the other side of the fence, market mechanisms continue to interfere with the carefully laid plans of socialist command economies (from the viewpoint of orthodox ideologists in those places, to subvert socialism). Thus even the Soviet Union, not to mention other, less stringently controlled, socialist societies, gives ample leeway for enterprise oriented toward market profits. Some of this is legal (as the private plots on collective farms), much of it illegal (the flourishing black market in "socialist property," ingenuously diverted from the official economy by countless little underground entrepreneurs). In some socialist countries (very strongly in Yugoslavia, more mutedly in Hungary, beginning recently in China), there has been a deliberate effort to introduce market mechanisms into the official command economy. But even in countries where, at least for a while, no such concessions are made, market mechanisms have an apparently invincible way of creeping in. Indeed, given the intrinsic problems of socialism as an economic system (of which more later), the question may be raised whether socialist economies could survive at all without these modifications by "creeping capitalism." Conversely, given the political pressures engendered by those who get the short end of the bargain on the market, it is questionable whether those capitalist societies that are also democracies (which, let it be noted, includes all the technologically advanced ones) could survive without the interventions of political allocation policies.

Given this inconvenience imposed by empirical reality on the purity of concepts, it is plausible to think of existing economies as located on a continuum between two extreme poles, which as such do not empirically exist at all.[9] One pole (presumably to be placed on the right end of the continuum) represents a pure market economy, in which all decisions of production and distribution are determined by market forces. Here one may luxuriate in an imagined paradise of laissez-faire economics, a libertarian utopia presided over by the approving specter of Adam Smith. The other pole (it should certainly be placed on the left extremity) represents an economy in which all decisions are determined by political allocation. By all means let this alternative utopia be purged of all unpleasant associations of existing socialist regimes; let the political characteristics remain blank; all that is said about this imagined economy is that it is utterly purged of the vicissitudes of the market. Thus anyone with a philosophical commitment to socialism remains free to project into it any and all principles of democracy, equality, and human rights (which, by the way, means that, if such an economy ever appeared in the empirical world, the presence of these principles could be proposed as hypotheses).

Neither of these poles exists today (or, for that matter, has existed for any length of time or in any large-scale society in the past). They are theoretical constructs. As such, though, they are quite useful. For what does exist is a set of economies, each one of which can be located on an imagined scale as being closer to the one or the other imagined pole. In this sense it makes good sense to say that some societies are more capitalist or more socialist than others—the United States more capitalist than the Soviet Union, North Korea more socialist than South Korea, Switzerland more capitalist than Sweden. And, as long as one keeps in mind the constructed character of the entire continuum, it is quite permissible to say, flatly, that Belgium is a capitalist society and Bulgaria a socialist one. Obviously, especially if one wants to use such flat terms, there is an element of arbitrariness as to just where on the continuum one will place specific societies. Is Yugoslavia still to be called a socialist society? Would Sweden still be capitalist if some of the reform plans of its socialist party were realized? There can be no axiomatic answers to such questions (how many hairs does a man have to have on his head before one stops calling him bald?). At the same time, however, the choice of designation is not all that difficult in most cases. Only the most dedicated methodological purists are likely to lose sleep over the designations of Belgium and Bulgaria or of the two Koreas.

This attempt at definition, using the two differentiating criteria of market mechanisms and mechanisms of political allocation, has the advantage of permitting the delineation of empirical phenomena without prejudging any other characteristics these may have *other than* the characteristics that serve to define them. By analogy, a Martian zoologist studying humans may decide after some research that this species may be divided into two groups, males and females, on the basis of specific physical organs. Having achieved this conceptualization, the zoologist may now explore what other characteristics may be differentially distributed in the two groups. But if the zoologist defined males as humans with physical organs X who have superior nurturing ability and females as humans with physical organs Y conducive to higher aggression, one would be justified in saying that these definitions prejudge matters that should be left to empirical investigation. In other words, empirical issues should not be decided by definitional tricks.[10]

Back to the phenomenon of capitalism as it developed in history: One perceives this highly distinctive mode of economic activity, entrepreneurs (individually and then increasingly in combines) producing for profit in market exchanges, spreading out of a few early enclaves, penetrating more and more sectors of European societies, and finally establishing a global system of immense capital wealth and productive power. It is tempting to perceive all this in the image of an economic machine pumping away all by itself, an autonomous force with respect to all other social institutions. It is not unfair to say that this sort of perception represents the fondest dreams of many economists (at least the non-Marxist ones). In this view of things, the economist can analyze (and perhaps even tinker with) the capitalist machinery as the cardiologist diagnoses (and occasionally treats) the cardiovascular system. Let this approach not be dismissed too quickly. For heuristic and pragmatic reasons it may be useful to look upon the capitalist economy as a gigantic machine pumping away in accordance with its own rules, just as a cardiologist may apply his diagnostic tools while bracketing such little details about his patient as the fact that the latter has just gone into bankruptcy or been sentenced to a long prison term. But it is clear that, in either case, there are important factors at work that are not, respectively, economic or cardiovascular.

Empirically, both today and in the past, the capitalist phenomenon appears in aggregation with a multitude of other phenomena. This already is clear if one looks at the rather sparse list of characteristics used above to elucidate the definition of modern industrial capitalism. For example, an item in this list is already implied in the phrase "modern industrial," then elaborated as meaning rational technology geared to economic activity. For another example, a rational legal system was listed as a presupposition. But these are *historical* characteristics. That is, as capitalism developed in history up to its present shape, it has evinced these characteristics. Put differently, capitalism presents itself empirically in these particular aggregations. But could they not be disaggregated? Could one have a modern capitalist system that is purely agrarian in character? (One might think of an accentuated Denmark or New Zealand.) And then, surely, the advanced socialist societies of Europe employ rational technology for economic purposes. One might also ask whether, under some conditions, capitalism might not dispense with a rational legal system administered by an outside agency such as the modern state. (Perhaps Hong Kong gives one at least an idea of what such a society might look like.) In other words, an important question is whether specific historical, empirical aggregations are essential to the phenomenon at issue. This, of course, is a question one can ask about *any* historical phenomenon. Could one have feudalism without an aristocracy? Can one conceive of Roman Catholicism without the papacy? Is atheism a necessary element of Marxist regimes? And so on. Such questions are not frivolous games of the imagination; rather, they are useful in getting a firmer theoretical grasp on an empirical reality.

It is precisely to address this type of theoretical question that the concept of "economic culture" is useful, when the question is applied to economic institutions and their relations to other components of society. Economic institutions do not exist in a vacuum but rather in a context (or, if one prefers, a matrix) of social and political structures, cultural patterns, and, indeed, structures of consciousness (values, ideas, belief systems). An economic culture (be it of capitalism or of socialism or of classical Hindu society or of any other historical constellation) then contains a number of elements linked together in an empirical totality. The question concerns the manner of the linkage.[11] Say, there are elements A and B. Are these necessarily linked, or is their linkage an accident of history? Is A the causal presupposition of B, or the other way around? And similar questions pertain to elements C and D and so on.

For example, contemporary South Africa represents a very distinctive economic culture in which capitalism is linked to a system of racial dominance by whites over nonwhites, the system that has become known (and notorious) as that of "apartheid." In the empirical reality of South Africa these two elements—the capitalist economy and the sociopolitical system of apartheid—are intertwined; that is, they present themselves as a single comprehensive totality, so that virtually every time that one encounters one, one also encounters the other. Yet there are sharp differences of opinion as to the underlying character of their linkage. Opponents of apartheid have coined the phrase "racial capitalism" to describe the South African reality. Many of these opponents, especially among intellectuals, are socialists of this or that variety, and the intent of the phrase is to suggest that a capitalist economy is part and parcel of the system of racial domination and that, conversely, the abolition of the latter requires the abolition of the former. Thus a postapartheid South Africa will have to be a socialist South Africa. This view finds support in the historical record, which shows how South African capitalism developed on the basis of cheap and docile labor, the supply of which was certainly facilitated by the system of racial dominance. All the same, a quite different interpretation of contemporary South Africa is possible. Thus businessmen who are increasingly hostile to apartheid and politically active in opposing it have been arguing that the racial system is an *obstacle* to capitalist development today (even if it might have facilitated such development in the past). Indeed, this view would hold that contemporary South Africa is not capitalist at all but is a superimposition of capitalist forms on a society that is essentially feudal, so that the term "racial feudalism" would describe the society much more aptly. Salient characteristics of feudalism have always been domination by a hereditary elite, unfree labor or serfdom, and the coincidence of economic and political power (especially on the local level) with appropriate values and belief systems legitimating these arrangements.[12] South Africa, especially as it has been reconstructed under the apartheid legislation since 1948 (when the National Party came into power), exhibits very similar characteristics: Whites constitute a hereditary elite; the laws on "influx control" and "group areas" impose a type of serfdom on nonwhites; at least as far as nonwhites are concerned, economic and political power coincides in the controls imposed on them; and the mythology of Afrikanerdom powerfully legitimates this social order. To bring about a postapartheid

South Africa, then, it will be necessary to *liberate* the dynamics of capitalist development from these feudal handicaps.

Placing the South African case in a larger theoretical framework, there are two elements here, linked in this particular economic culture —a capitalist economy and a system of racial dominance. Are these two elements always linked, or are they (as it were) accidental products of the peculiar history of South Africa? A single case is never enough to argue the necessity of linkage; rather, one must look at as many cases as possible, to see whether the same linkage appears under different historical circumstances.[13]

To put this more concisely, the question is this: Which elements within the given matrix are intrinsically linked and which are merely linked extrinsically? An intrinsic linkage is one without which the phenomenon could not be imagined; conversely, an extrinsic linkage can be ascribed to this or that historical contingency and can, therefore, be "thought away" from the phenomenon. For example, the linkage between modern technology and a rational engineering mentality appears to be intrinsic; one cannot imagine the first without the second. On the other hand, the linkage of the engineering ethos with individualism may well be an accident of Western history; it may easily be hypothesized that it is an extrinsic linkage; it can be "thought away" in this or that highly collectivist society employing modern technology.

Employing the concept of economic culture in this way makes no a priori assumptions on causality. Thus to say that certain economic processes are intrinsically linked to certain contents of consciousness does not assume that consciousness is necessarily determined by the economic substructure (in the manner of "vulgar Marxism"), but neither does it assume that the reverse is so (as in certain "idealist" theories of history). Causality can never be assumed; it must be established empirically. In the case of extrinsic linkages, of course, there is not even the temptation to assume necessary causation; accidents are always caused, but there are no theoretical shortcuts to finding out by empirical methods who hit whom and why. Furthermore, it is wise to have an overall bias against unicausal explanations; it is very unlikely that any significant event in history was caused by a single factor.

It is in this sense, then, that the concept of economic culture is employed here. Capitalism, defined as a particular economic system (or, if one prefers, a particular mode of production), presents itself empirically in aggregation with other social phenomena. In its modern or "mature" form, capitalism is linked to technology and thus to the vast transformations brought about by the latter in the material conditions of human life. Capitalism is also linked with a new stratification system based on class (as against the old status groups of earlier Western history), a new political system (the modern nation-state and the institutions of democracy) and a new culture (historically linked to the bourgeoisie as a class and characterized, among other traits, by a new emphasis on the individual). All of these elements are intertwined within the economic culture of capitalism, experienced by ordinary people as a totality or unity, and often conceptualized as such both by advocates and by critics of capitalism. It should be clear from the preceding discussion how the principal theoretical task is envisaged here, namely, as a procedure whereby these linkages come to be understood as either intrinsic or extrinsic. Put more loosely, a theory of capitalism will have to explain how these different elements are related to each other.

As discussed in the introduction to this book, Marxism has been the most ambitious effort to achieve such a theoretical integration.[14] Perhaps the closest to an alternative paradigm is what, very broadly, has been called modernization theory. In a narrower sense, this term is applied to a set of theoretical efforts, since World War II, to explain the rapid changes undergone by the developing societies of Asia, Africa, and Latin America.[15] Modernization theory in this sense has been self-consciously competitive with various Marxist theories of Third World underdevelopment and change. But one may also use the term in a broader sense to refer to a general view of modernity emerging mostly from a central tradition of classical sociology, including not only the works of Weber and Simmel but also the contributions of such authors as Ferdinand Toennies, Emile Durkheim, and Talcott Parsons. If one adds up all these contributions, one does indeed arrive at a synthetic paradigm in which the category of modernity is central and which differs in important respects from the Marxist paradigm.

This book clearly stands within this sociological tradition, broadly speaking, and more specifically its argument is heavily influenced by the Weberian approach to the modern world. What does this mean?

A case can be made that the central question of sociology, from its inception in the rather fanciful philosophy of August Comte, has been the question about the nature of modernity.[16] In the Jewish ritual of Passover, the question is asked: "How is this night different from all other nights?" Sociologists for at least the last hundred years have been asking: "How is modernity different from all other periods of human history?" Needless to say, their answers have differed, as have their presuppositions and methodologies. All the same, a sort of paradigm has emerged from their cumulative efforts.

Max Weber, as is well known, paid very direct attention to capitalism, especially to its origins. But his treatment of capitalism was in a much broader context of intellectual endeavors to understand the driving forces of the modern world. For Weber, the most important driving force was what he called "rationalization"—the progressive imposition of rational thinking and rational techniques on every sector of society. He believed that specific features of Judaism and Christianity laid the ideational groundwork of this rational transformation of the world (the first "rationalizing" step, taken long ago in ancient Israel, was to replace magic by faith in a God with very high moral demands) and that these features came powerfully to the fore as a result of the Protestant Reformation (especially its Calvinist wing). Having satisfied himself that this explanation made sense in explaining the origins of modernity in Europe, he then embarked on a gigantic enterprise of comparing Europe with various non-Western cultures, notably those of India and China. He took the position that the religious and ethical traditions of these cultures did *not* foster the sort of "rationalization" that occurred in the West. Weber's views on these matters, of course, have not been unchallenged. The controversy over the modernizing (and capitalism-prone) character of Protestantism goes on to this day. Later in this book, in the chapter on capitalism in East Asia, it will be argued that, very probably, Weber was quite wrong in his view of the modernity-inhibiting character of Confucianism and other East Asian traditions. But even if some of Weber's answers are doubtful, there can be no doubt that his questions continue to be highly relevant today. Weber's opus remains a very important building block for any theory of modernity and ipso facto any theory of capitalism.

But other sociologists, even if they looked at different materials and employed different methods, circled around the problem of modernity in their own way. Georg Simmel, another classical German sociologist, discussed under the heading of "abstraction" the same question that Weber addressed as "rationalization": The modern world (partly because of capitalism and the money economy it brought about) has become ever more abstract, as against the highly concrete relations of premodern societies. Ferdinand Toennies, a contemporary of both Weber and Simmel, coined the terms *"Gemeinschaft"* and *"Gesellschaft,"* which continue to be used in English-speaking sociology. A *Gemeinschaft* (German for "community") is characterized by a sense of all-embracing, undifferentiated belongingness in a particular group of people; by contrast, in a *Gesellschaft* ("society") people relate to each other only in particular roles, partially, typically in the form of contractual arrangements ("my obligations to you, and yours to me, are exactly as laid down in our agreement—no more, no less"). And Toennies argued that modern society is characterized by a massive shift from *Gemeinschaft* to *Gesellschaft;* as a conservative thinker, he thought that this was a very unfortunate change. Emile Durkheim, the father of modern French sociology, had very much the same transformation in mind when he spoke of the shift from "mechanical solidarity" to "organic solidarity." This shift produced a high vulnerability of modern people to what he called *"anomie"*—a condition of having no roots, no sense of belonging, and no firm norms. The description of the change is very similar to Toennies's; but Durkheim, as a progressive thinker very much in the Enlightenment tradition, believed that, despite the costs (such as the cost of *anomie*), the change was for the better, especially because it enhanced individual liberty. Finally, more recent American sociologists have continued to be fascinated by the question of how modernity differs. Thus Talcott Parsons, the most ambitious theorist of this group, capped his work with a set of writings about modernity. The key category here is what Parsons called "differentiation": modern society segments, dividing up into distinct institutions what in earlier periods of history was integrated within the same institution (for example, the "functions" of kinship are divided among separate social, economic, and political institutions). Once again, the themes of older sociological thinkers are reiterated and carried further in new formulations.

During the formative period of sociology (roughly, the fifty years from 1880 to 1930), there also occurred the development of Marxism into a number of distinctive theoretical schools. Both paradigms were refined in interaction with each other. Indeed, several of the classical sociologists (notably Weber) thought of their own work as an alternative to Marxism. Needless to say, there was a good deal of polemics, often vitriolic, between the two camps of social theorists, and of course this is still true today. But it is also possible to compare the two paradigms in a dispassionate manner.

The Marxist paradigm perceives capitalism as the central causal force in the contemporary world, with all other elements within its matrix being more or less in the role of dependent variables (whether more or less will depend on the degree of economic determinism of any given Marxist school). The modernization paradigm, on the other hand, perceives capitalism as one of several causally central elements; in its more recent versions (particularly as applied to Third World societies) technology tends to move to center stage, in some instances suggesting a technological determinism replacing the economism of the Marxists.[17] These different emphases naturally color the perceptions of the other paradigm. Marxists will look upon any interpretation of the contemporary world that fails to put capitalism in the center of attention as an obfuscation. Thus the technological focus obfuscates the real economic and political relationships between different societies (for instance, in understanding Brazil it is misleading to concentrate on its degree of technological development rather than on its degree of "dependency" on the international capitalist system). Conversely, from the viewpoint of modernization theory it appears that Marxism is above all prone to what logicians call the fallacy of *pars pro toto,* taking a part for the whole. Thus Marxists will ascribe to capitalism a large set of processes that are actually the result of modernization, no matter whether under capitalist or socialist auspices (for instance, the miseries of the northeast of Brazil are due to differential technological and economic modernization and would take a similar form even if Brazil were a socialist society). Given this emphasis on technology and its consequences (such as urbanization, the breakdown of traditional patterns, rapid population growth, and unstable political systems), modernization theorists have often tended to downplay the differences between capitalist and socialist societies, in some cases suggesting that a "convergence" between the two is very likely.

The position taken here certainly shares the perception of the Marxist paradigm as being distortively one-sided, indeed as a large-scale fallacy of *pars pro toto*. At the same time, the position taken will seek to avoid an overemphasis of the technological element and will especially seek to avoid the distortions of so-called convergence theory, which trivializes very important economic, social, and political differences. There is no a priori assumption that capitalism as such is either the single most important element in the modern world or nothing more than a dependent variable of other forces, such as those of modern technology. And there is certainly no doctrinaire reluctance to accede to such particular Marxist interpretations as may, from case to case, be empirically supportable, even if the Marxist paradigm as a whole must be rejected.

The nature of the theoretical challenge should by now be clear. It is to begin constructing a theoretical framework within which the linkages between economic, technological, social, political, and cultural elements of the capitalist phenomenon can be more adequately understood. This is a slow, painstaking, never fully completed enterprise. No individual, working alone, can hope to accomplish it. What is more, because of the very nature of science, this enterprise can never yield prophetic certainties, only probabilities, tentative conclusions that further evidence may overthrow. Such an enterprise is particularly difficult in an area literally throbbing with prophetic pathos, both on the "left" and on the "right." (It depends on one's zip code which set of prophets one is mainly afflicted with: In Boston the prophets of the "left" are a greater affliction than they would be in, say, Dallas.) These difficulties have always been endemic to the scientific vocation. Those who require certitude should not turn to science. They should worship at the ideological shrine of their choice and settle the choice with their conscience. But the scientific vocation has its own rewards, intellectual as well as moral. The intellectual rewards are obvious to anyone with the gift of curiosity. The principal moral reward is a sense of the ambiguity of all human projects, of the inevitable trade-offs in all social change, and this in turn leads to a reluctance to risk the highest human costs for projects of change the outcome of which is unknown. People kill each other for prophetic certainties, hardly for falsifiable hypotheses. The social scientist's insistence that he has no certainties to offer and that his hypotheses are falsifiable thus has a moral as well as an intellectual warrant.

# 2

# MATERIAL LIFE:
# THE HORN OF PLENTY

I T IS POSSIBLE today to travel in the less-developed countries in such a way that at no point does one leave the amenities taken for granted in North America or Western Europe. But if one strays even a little from the narrow swath of modern hotels, tourist shops, and airport lounges, and especially if one ventures into the villages that still contain the majority of mankind, one readily senses that one is entering a totally different world of human experience. All the major categories of experience are transformed. Space shrinks: Where the modern traveler traverses continents, the life of the villager is confined to a radius of a few miles from his home. Time slows down: Modern life is decisively marked by speed and acceleration; life in a village moves slowly, every day as light and shadow shift during the long hours, every year as the seasons alternate in their eternal cycles. Other human beings appear in different forms: Modernity means life with large numbers of strangers; in the village one lives with a small group of people, most of them known intimately from childhood to old age. Last not least, there are vast differences in power and possessions. The modern traveler, even if he comes from a relatively modest background, carries with him tokens of power far beyond the experience, and in many cases even the imagination, of the villager—passport, credit cards, airline tickets, address book (probably containing telephone numbers to call in every conceivable emergency). And even the sparse luggage of the seasoned traveler contains goods beyond the means of most villagers, including marvels of minituarized technology like pocket calculators or automatic cameras. These comparisons, of course, serve to highlight the reality of underdevelopment in the contemporary world. They may also serve, though, as a window on the past for a very simple reason: The world of the villager is still very close to the way most people lived through most of human history.

History first of all impresses one by its variety—all those kings and their empires, rising and falling—a kaleidoscope of languages, costumes, idiosyncratic gestures. At the same time, though, there is a remarkable continuity of forms of life, especially on the lower levels of society and in the area of material life.[1] No matter what king was ruling (usually far away) or what empire supposedly held sway (most of the subjects probably had never heard of it), the great mass of human beings eked out their existence in a very similar manner. This substratum of material life was characterized by very high rates of infant mortality, low life expectancy (both at birth, where of course it was determined by the infant mortality rates, and at later points in the individual life cycle), inadequate nutrition and frequent starvation, very high vulnerability to disease and pain, very high vulnerability to the ravages of nature, with all of this sustained by a simple and relatively unchanging (more precisely, very slow-changing) technology and by a zero-growth subsistence economy. In this form of existence both the life of individuals and of societies were determined to a large degree by the pressures of the physical environment and of the sheer demographic facts upon the feeble structures of human technology and economic arrangements. Fernand Braudel has coined the apt phrase "the biological ancien régime" to denote this millennia-old shape of human existence. It forms the stable underside of all the glittering events that are conventionally evoked by the word "history." Most of it is a reality of pain beyond the experience of virtually all people, even the poorest, in an advanced industrial society.

Needless to say, this does not imply that this ancien régime was without human values, some of them perhaps superior to those of twentieth-century peoples. However, it is important to keep in mind the long-lasting realities of material life so as to avoid the recurring romanticisms about premodern times. As a mental exercise, for example, one might focus on the fact that almost all of human history took place without the benefits of modern dentistry. This means, quite simply, that most individuals either suffered from toothaches or had rotten teeth; it probably means that their mouths both looked and smelled accordingly. Focus further then on some favorite glittering event or personage, with this fact in mind: Demosthenes addressing the citizens of Athens . . . Caesar crossing the Rubicon . . . even Louis XIV amid the splendors of Versailles.

The coming of modern technology, first gradually and then with a cataclysmic acceleration, radically changed this situation. It brought about an unprecedented and vast transformation of the realities of material life. Thus the conventional phrase "industrial *revolution*" is thoroughly and precisely correct. Each of the aforementioned characteristics of life was fundamentally revolutionized: Infant mortality descended sharply, life expectancy shot up. Diets improved dramatically in nutritional value, and starvation became progressively infrequent if it did not disappear altogether. One disease after another was brought under control, as was physical pain. The destructive forces of the physical environment were likewise tamed. And these achievements, of course, were part and parcel of a near-total transformation in the technological apparatus of society (not a once-and-for-all transformation, as the invention of the wheel must have been long ago, but a *continuing* transformation) and of an economy moving from zero-growth subsistence into sustained and self-generating growth. It should be emphasized how *very recent* these events are. Even in England, the country in which the Industrial Revolution first took place, the full effects of this transformation can only be observed in the second half of the nineteenth century.

One says "Industrial Revolution" or "modernization," and the associations tend to be with rather dry technological and economic processes. It is all the more important to remain aware of the human realities affected by these processes. Take what is arguably the most fundamental reality here: Through most of human history, most children (even the children of the very rich) died before reaching adulthood. Today, in advanced industrial societies (and increasingly in the less-modernized societies), most children (even the children of the very poor) live to become adults. This one fact, all by itself, provides a measure of the revolution in human life that has taken place. Now, of course, to say this in no way implies that the fact is unproblematic.

Thus the population explosion, largely caused by the decline in infant mortality, poses unprecedented human problems. Thus the overall decline of infant mortality, even though it has affected all strata of the population, has not affected them equally; consequently, there is a much sharper sense of moral offensiveness about the unequal life chances of rich and poor children. Once more, though, those who romanticize about the allegedly superior qualities of premodern societies should be compelled to compare a situation in which most children died with a situation in which most children remain alive.

This technological transformation of material life is at the core—indeed, *is* the core—of what is commonly meant by modernization. Marion Levy has described modernization as "the ratio of inanimate to animate sources of power."[2] This is, of course, a simplification (Levy intended it as such), but a useful one. For it points to the essential fact that there has been an astronomical increase in the amount of sheer physical power available to human societies. The essential effect of the Industrial Revolution has, in consequence, been a vast increase in productivity. The dimensions of this would have been unimaginable to people until the very recent past.

It is not the present purpose to describe in detail or to trace the stages of this technological transformation.[3] All that is necessary in the present context is to keep before the mind this Promethean vista of unleashed power, beginning with steam and coal, then passing on to other sources of energy. It is also, to repeat, necessary to hold on to the fact that this transformation did not happen once and then stop. Rather, it is not only continuing but is continuing at an accelerating pace, and at least to date there is no indication that the acceleration is diminishing. The works of the modern Prometheus, for better or for worse, did not stop with the gift of fire.

Now, it is a historical fact denied by no one (Marx stressed it emphatically) that this technological revolution took place within the context of a developing capitalism; or, if one prefers to put it this way, the Industrial Revolution was a historical achievement of capitalism. At the same time, the two processes of capitalist development and technological modernization are analytically distinct. *Historically,* though, the two processes are very difficult to disentangle. They constitute what has earlier been called an empirical aggregate (Fernand Braudel uses the term *"ensemble"* for this). One can ask, looking at the present realities of socialist industrial societies, what modernization looks like in the absence of capitalism. One may also ask such questions with regard to the future, as one tries to imagine possible future reassemblies of technological and socioeconomic elements. But there can be little disagreement (and, indeed, there *is* little disagreement) about the past.

Thus it is possible to formulate the first two propositions for the theoretical enterprise at issue here:

*Industrial capitalism has generated the greatest productive power in human history.*

*To date, no other socioeconomic system has been able to generate comparable productive power.*

Even those highly critical of Western societies are likely to agree with these propositions. They will then go on, of course, to criticize the alleged costs of this socioeconomic system and to predict that this or that future version of a noncapitalist society will have equal or even greater productive power *without* these costs. The question of costs is, to a large extent, open to empirical inquiry, and this is a very important issue to which attention must be paid within the present theoretical undertaking. The future, of course, is by definition empirically inaccessible; it is a matter of faith (as Antonio Gramsci put it nicely, it is "fideistic"); to some extent (as will also be done later in this book) the social and psychological context of these acts of faith can also be explored empirically.

Caveat: This second proposition does *not* mean that the productive power of modern technology cannot unfold at all except under the socioeconomic arrangements of industrial capitalism. One need only look at existing socialist societies and also at various still largely traditional or semifeudal societies. Modern technology clearly has an autonomous power that creates its effect in just about *any* socioeconomic context. Thus it is difficult, indeed is quite an achievement, to introduce modern technology into a society and *not* generate at least some of the changes in material life listed above. Similarly, most societies into which modern technology is introduced, even modestly, do experience a measure of economic growth. It follows that the demonstration of improving standards of living in a socialist society, or of economic growth in a semifeudal society, will *not* in itself falsify the above proposition. The proposition refers to the *degree* of productive power, not to its simple presence.

Different analysts of the capitalist phenomenon are much less likely to agree on the *reasons* for the historical conjunction of developing capitalism and the Industrial Revolution. A further step in theory building, however, must address this conjunction. It is plausible to find an explanation in the coming together of two kinds of human ingenuity—that of the entrepreneur and that of the engineer. In principle, to be sure, these two constitute very different human types, despite some common characteristics. But an economy based on production for market exchange on a large and expanding scale gives unprecedented opportunity for the unfolding of *both* forms of human inventiveness. This, of course, is what the advocates of capitalism have always maintained.[4] The position here is that market forces provide the best, indeed a unique, incentive for ever-improving productivity. As someone once observed, the market, with its price signals, is the first computer ever invented by man; to date, it has found no rival in providing both information and incentives for ingenious individuals intent on improving their economic lot. These individuals, of course, are those who in the "right" circumstances will become entrepreneurs. The engineer may have very different motives; he may have no economic aspirations at all; he simply wants to improve his gadgets and see how they can be made to work. But a market economy provides the most promising socioeconomic context within which this other type of human ingenuity, that of the engineer, can unfold.[5] And that is why the conjunction of capitalism and modern technology has been such a productive one. It follows that this explosion of productivity is more than a historical accident; rather it is rooted in intrinsic economic and social characteristics of capitalism.

Proposition: *An economy oriented toward production for market exchange provides the optimal conditions for long-lasting and ever-expanding productive capacity based on modern technology.*

Or, more simply put, capitalism provides the optimal context for the productive power of modern technology. To date, there are no empirically available countercases.

Even on the level of material life, and leaving aside for the moment all more "refined" questions of individual or collective value, the expansion of productive power per se need not necessarily mean a general amelioration of the human condition. Even a vast augmentation in productive capacity may generate material benefits that are available only to very few people, leaving most others as badly or even worse off. Allowing that capitalism is a gigantic cornucopia, just who benefits from this new plenty? Industrial capitalism can accurately be described as an enormously powerful machine for the generation of wealth. But who has access to these riches?

Any discussion of these questions takes place against the background of the Marxian notion of "immiseration" which has had a very great influence not only on Marxists but on others trying to understand the socioeconomic dynamics of capitalism. Marx predicted that, because of intrinsic features of the capitalist mode of production, there would be an increasing polarization of society. The bourgeoisie, the capitalist class, would become ever more wealthy and ever fewer in numbers. The proletariat, or working class, would become progressively poorer and more numerous. Intermediate strata, and indeed portions of the bourgeoisie itself, would become "proletarianized" and sink into this ever-growing mass of impoverished, propertyless, and desperate humanity. This prediction, of course, had great political import, since it made it appear that a revolutionary change of this situation was inevitable: Eventually, the growing proletariat would become sufficiently conscious of its condition and sufficiently organized to overthrow the class that had been exploiting it. Since this increasing inequality of capitalist society was a built-in feature, the historical process could be interpreted as capitalism digging its own grave.

If one statement can be made with considerable assurance, it is that the history of Western capitalism has thoroughly falsified this Marxian theory. If Marxism were nothing but a social-scientific theory, and in view of the central place occupied by the immiseration thesis within it, this falsification might well have spelled the end of Marxism as a plausible interpretation of modern history. Marxism, of course, is much more than a social-scientific theory; it is also a powerful myth (in Georges Sorel's sense of the term) and a political program (or, more accurately, a set of political programs). The falsification of the Marxian theory of immiseration has, in consequence, led not to the demise of Marxism but to a series of reinterpretations, all designed to show that, contrary to what may seem to be the empirical evidence, capitalism *does* breed misery, and therefore, its eventual overthrow *is* inevitable (and, of course, is morally just). This long effort of ideological reinterpretation is a fascinating topic, especially if viewed within the frameworks of the sociology of knowledge and of social psychology.[6] The different forms of reinterpretation, however, cannot be pursued here.[7]

None of this, however, negates the importance of the question of who benefits from the productive gains of industrial capitalism. For purposes of analysis, this question can be subdivided. First, there is the question of absolute material standards of life: What was, or is, material life like at different levels of society? It has become customary, in dealing with this question, to concentrate on the poorest levels; this is not only morally plausible but also analytically appropriate. But then there is the second question: What was, or is, the degree of material inequality between different levels of society? The two questions, of course, are quite distinct. Thus it is possible to have a general rise in living standards, even including the very poor, while relative inequality remains the same (or perhaps even increases). Conversely, it is possible to have increasing equality while living standards plummet. It is a matter of moral judgment which condition, misery or inequality, one finds more offensive—or, put positively, whether one puts a higher value on general material well-being or on material equality. But the moral judgments are invariably made on the basis of empirical assumptions; these assumptions are susceptible to social-scientific exploration. What is more, such exploration must be a part of any credible theory of capitalism.

The continuing debate over the effects of the Industrial Revolution on living standards in England, the mother country of industrial capitalism, is very relevant to the first of the just-mentioned questions (the absolute rather than relative question about material benefits). The question is not simply a historical one, because it is raised again and again in terms of the human costs of capitalism and thus of its moral status.

A deeply ingrained view, both among historians and laymen, has been the one that the Industrial Revolution in England (and presumably elsewhere) was characterized by great and indeed worsening material misery. This view has not only been held retrospectively but was widely propagated at the time. Then as now, both those who maintained this view and those who criticized it or maintained the opposite had high ideological stakes in their respective positions.[8] Literature played an important part in the codification of the view of industrial misery, as in the novels of Charles Dickens and the poetry of William Blake. Interestingly, the negative view of the Industrial

Revolution was propagated not only from the left, by various strands of socialist critics, but also from the conservative right (as in "Tory radicalism" in the vein of Benjamin Disraeli) with its disdain for the money-grubbing bourgeoisie and its (probably paternalistic) identification with the common people. On the left, of course, Friedrich Engels's book, *The Condition of the Working Class in England* (first published in German in 1845), attained virtually canonical status. There can be little doubt that Engels's depiction of the situation was highly partisan and hardly concerned with a dispassionate weighing of the evidence.[9]

The passions have remained, on both sides of the debate, and it is not easy for an outsider to arrive at a sensible assessment. Recent economic historians, broadly speaking, have been divided into two camps—the "pessimists," maintaining that the Industrial Revolution created vast and unprecedented misery, as compared with pre-industrial conditions; and the "optimists," taking the contrary and more benign position.[10] Both positions, needless to say, are characterized by strong ideological undertones, with "pessimists" and "optimists" generally dividing along left/right lines politically (at least in the sense of "left" as tending toward socialist views and "right" as not so tending). As one delves into this literature, one occasionally thinks that "critique of ideology" *(Ideologiekritik)* is about all one can do with this. Fortunately, though, there is a growing body of literature that appears to transcend this barrage of propaganda. The outsider can orient himself by this literature; he can also take some steps forward by zoning in on those areas where some measure of consensus seems to be emerging on both sides.[11]

The data under debate are complex and often ambiguous. For example, how is one to assess late eighteenth-century reports on the health or the housing conditions of the poor? Still, it appears that the "pessimist" position is more tenable for the earlier period of the English Industrial Revolution (roughly 1750 to 1820) but less tenable for the later period (after 1820), at least as far as absolute measures of material well-being are concerned. The "pessimists" can draw some comfort (if that is the word) from the fact that, while material life improved after 1820, there was also rising inequality and a good deal of social disorder, so that *subjective* well-being may not have much improved for the poor. Where there is general agreement, however, is that there was a definite shift by the middle of the nineteenth century, with material life improving remarkably on all levels of English society. This development, while now agreed to by most "pessimists," does not detract from their insistence that early industrial capitalism exacted a high price in human suffering.

The following proposition has to be put forward very tentatively, then: *The early period of industrial capitalism in England, and probably in other Western countries, exacted considerable human costs, if not in an actual decline in material living standards then in social and cultural dislocation.*

The controversy among historians goes on, and the above proposition may have to be revised drastically, be it in a "pessimist" or "optimist" direction, as more data emerge. For the moment, the proposition is so formulated as to lean toward the "pessimists" as far as the early period is concerned and also to lean toward them to the extent of acknowledging that social and cultural tensions should also be subsumed under the category of "human costs," even if the "optimists" should turn out to be right on material standards as such. But the following caveat is important: However one may eventually come out on the human costs of the Industrial Revolution in England (and, for that matter, elsewhere in Europe or in the United States), there is no a priori warrant for proposing that the *same* costs will have to be borne by other societies undergoing industrialization today. Present-day conditions are very different—technologically, economically, politically, and socially—and the costs of industrial capitalism may be correspondingly different (whether more *or* less exacting than in the earlier cases). Put differently, there is no law of history by which all societies have to replicate the English experience. This caveat, of course, applies both to those who would draw a "pessimistic" lesson from the English case and to those who look on it as conducive to "optimistic" predictions.

Controversy among historians diminishes greatly as one turns to the period since the middle of the nineteenth century. Here, there is little doubt: There occurred an immense increase in the material well-being of virtually all strata in Western societies, proceeding steadily despite some severe disruptions (notably the two world wars and the Great Depression), and then spurting forward dramatically in the period following World War II.[12]

During this period, standards of longevity and health rose to levels that would have been looked upon as wildly utopian only two or three generations earlier. Thus, the average life expectancy at birth in the United States reached seventy-four years in 1984; what is more, these benefits reached deep down into the lower strata.[13] Similar developments occurred with regard to nutrition, clothing, and housing. To be sure, Western societies continue to have slums that contrast starkly with the housing of upper-income groups, but the hovels of pre-industrial times have disappeared even from most of the countryside. As Samuel McCracken has put it, "The poor live in what would have been thought of in the pre-capitalist period as ill-maintained castles."[14] The increase in purchasing power, even of most of the poor, is comparably dramatic (as measured by the number of hours that any category of worker must work in order to acquire the purchasing price of any commodity). This point was made eloquently in a well-known passage by Joseph Schumpeter: "Queen Elizabeth owned silk stockings. The capitalist achievement does not typically consist in providing silk stockings for queens but in bringing them within the reach of factory girls in return for steadily decreasing amounts of effort."[15]

Of course, those who are accustomed to the standards of material life in North America or Western Europe today will be shocked when encountering even modestly inferior situations. McCracken points to this when suggesting that a contemporary slum be looked at through the eyes of, say, an English peasant of the sixteenth century. Such shifts of vision are still possible today in comparison with Third World countries. A concrete image may help to make this point. A few years ago an American, who had been traveling in Southeast Asia, decided to stop over in Hawaii on his return trip to the East Coast. He checked into a hotel in Waikiki and, still groggy with jet lag, walked the streets there. His mind still full of images of the slums of Jakarta and of the huts inhabited by the poor in Philippine villages, he felt that he had been parachuted into the wealthiest and most exclusive preserves of American capitalism. Then his familiarity with his own society reasserted itself. He recognized, in a sort of reverse culture shock, what he had for a moment overlooked: *These people were not the rich of America.* They were secretaries, skilled factory workers, dental technicians, insurance salesmen—in other words, he was in the midst of masses of lower-middle-class and working-class people, spending their vacations, more or less as a matter of course (and, no doubt, on all sorts of bargain tours), in the tropical splendor of one of the most beautiful spots on earth. To be sure, there were no welfare recipients in this crowd. But neither, it seemed, were there any millionaires (*they* would stay in private clubs or homes or in luxury hotels a bit farther up the coast—places distinguished not so much by greater physical luxury, though there would be some of that, but by much greater social exclusiveness). A pedagogical exercise may thus be suggested: To understand the transformation of material life under industrial capitalism in the second half of the twentieth century, go for a walk on Kalakaua Avenue![16]

Proposition: *Advanced industrial capitalism has generated, and continues to generate, the highest material standard of living for large masses of people in human history.*

The future, of course, may force a revision of the proposition, in one of two ways: The standards of living in the advanced capitalist societies of North America, Western Europe, and Japan may collapse. Or, these standards of living may be surpassed by societies operating under different socioeconomic systems. In terms of explaining the proposition, of course, one will have to link it to the preceding proposition about the productive power of industrial capitalism. Two caveats here: The proposition, by itself, has no implications for the question of whether all this affluence has occurred at the expense of others (notably those others in the Third World mentioned before); *that* question will have to be taken up separately. Also, the proposition should not be taken as implying that there is no poverty in the advanced capitalist societies: Of course there is; but poverty is, almost by definition, a relative concept; one *can* say that poverty in the United States is, both quantitatively and qualitatively, a different phenomenon from poverty in Southeast Asia.

As has been pointed out above, a massive improvement in the standards of material life, even of the poor, does not ipso facto settle the question of the relative distribution of wealth and income. It is quite possible that the poor get richer while the rich also get richer, so that the relative gap between them remains the same or even widens. A theory of capitalism must also address this second question on the egalitarian agenda.

Here too one is immediately plunged into a complex—and in parts forbiddingly technical—debate among economists and economic historians. At the center of the debate is the so-called Kuznets curve, proposed as a hypothesis by Simon Kuznets in 1955 in a presidential address to the American Economic Association.[17] Shorn of some of its more controversial problems (such as the issue whether income should be figured per capita or by households—most economists now seem to favor the latter method), the hypothesis is not difficult to grasp: It proposes that income and wealth distribution follow a pattern that, when pictured in a diagram, looks like an inverted U. That is, as modern economic growth continues over time, there occurs first a sharp rise in inequality and then, later, a leveling effect.

There is widespread agreement today that, to date, the hypothesis has been confirmed, both historically and cross-nationally.[18] That is, not only do the capitalist societies of Europe and North America seem to follow the Kuznets curve, but so do the socialist industrial societies and Third World societies of either socioeconomic persuasion. (There may be some disconfirming cases in the capitalist societies of Eastern Asia, a matter that will have to be looked at later in this book.)

In all Western capitalist societies, the Industrial Revolution was accompanied by a sharp and long-lasting rise in inequality. (Note again: This statement does *not* prejudge the question of absolute standards of living.) There were differences in degree and timing between different countries, but the same general trend can be observed everywhere. By the late nineteenth century, there was very high inequality in all industrial or industrializing countries, highest of all in Britain (where, indeed, it was higher than in most Third World countries today). The peak of inequality, in most of these countries, was reached just before World War I. Between the 1920s and 1950s, again with differences in degree and timing, there took place a pronounced leveling trend in all these countries. Since the 1950s there has been a generally steady situation; that is, inequality has not greatly changed in either direction.

It is theoretically important that the Kuznets curve appears to hold for both capitalist and socialist countries. Thus, the Soviet Union appears to have been characterized by great income inequality from the early 1930s through World War II, with a sharp leveling occurring after that. In 1966, for example, income inequality in the Soviet Union was higher than in Sweden and Britain, though lower than in the United States. There are serious technical problems in the comparison of data from capitalist and socialist countries, but, despite these, the overall trends seem quite clear.[19]

The cross-national support for the Kuznets hypothesis has frequently been cited by "hard-nosed," procapitalist development experts to argue that inequality is a precondition for growth and thus for the eventual rise in everyone's income (including the poor's) because inequality favors the rich, who are the ones who save; that is, inequality favors capital accumulation, which in turn leads to economic growth. The argument is logical; it *may* be empirically valid; but its conclusions do *not* necessarily follow from existing data on the Kuznets effect. For example, in the American case (not exactly a marginal one), it is difficult to establish direct correlations between different points on the Kuznets curve and rates of capital accumulation. Thus, in the United States, income per capita was growing at comparable rates during both the period of high inequality and the succeeding period of greater equality.[20] The "anti-Kuznets" data from Eastern Asia (countries combining high growth rates with decreasing inequality) have already been mentioned. Also, it is plausible that growth rates per se are not the cause of the Kuznets effect but rather the *extended duration* of growth, with the technological and demographic consequences of the latter.

This is related to another important point: The Kuznets curve primarily refers to what economists call "pre-fisc" income, that is, to income before taxes and without taking into account miscellaneous government-sponsored distribution measures (such as all those that constitute the modern welfare state). Can the leveling phase of the curve be explained by government redistribution policies? Is the leveling effect the result of liberal government policies and would it not have taken place if capitalism had been left alone politically? There seems to be broad agreement on some important aspects of the question among economists with quite different political views.[21] This position is that government interventions do indeed have a sizable effect on income distribution, but that this is *on top of* various pre-fisc forces that tend toward leveling. Put differently, governmental redistribution measures do indeed strengthen and perhaps accelerate the leveling phase of the Kuznets curve, but considerable leveling would take place in any case, even in the absence of these political interventions. This view is supported by evidence that leveling set in *before* any large-scale redistributional policies and also by calculations pertaining to income distribution that take fisc effects into account.

Caveat: This view obviously appeals to liberals, who welcome government action to improve income and wealth equality. However, strong redistributional policies, operating by way of tax and transfer mechanisms, may well serve as a disincentive to productivity. If so, there would be a trade-off between equality and economic efficiency; in the long run, greater equality may lead to a lowering of the standard of living.[22] There may also be noneconomic costs: The strongly redistributional state must become ever more intrusive, and the final trade-off may be between equality and liberty.[23]

There is also the question of the role of labor unions in the leveling process. It seems likely that there is such a role—in terms of the income of unionized workers. However, these workers tend not to be in the lowest income groups to begin with. The overall effect of labor unions on inequality is doubtful.

It is most plausible that the Kuznets curve is basically caused by intrinsic technological and demographic features of the industrialization process as it continues over time. Labor requirements change in the course of this process. So does the supply of labor (particularly as a result of changes in fertility and of migration). Jan Tinbergen has insisted that the most important cause of inequality is the differential in wages between different categories of skilled and unskilled labor.[24] If so, then it is indeed plausible that the demand for and supply of unskilled labor may be a crucial factor, with leveling occurring as the economy changes from "labor-saving" to "labor-using" technology. This change is in turn made possible by the development of what economists (somewhat antiseptically) call "human capital"—that is, the quality of the available labor force. The most important factor in thus improving the quality of the labor force appears to be education. (It might follow from this that the most effective "redistribution" policy is to provide education, and possibly other "quality of life" services, to the poor rather than seek a redistribution of income or wealth.) Statistical evidence for this view is that cross-nationally in advanced industrial societies, there has occurred a decline in the pay differential between skilled and unskilled labor. Again, the important fact that these developments can also be observed in the socialist societies strongly suggests that the whole complex of Kuznets effects is due to forces intrinsic to modernization rather than to capitalism.[25]

With all due caution, the following propositions may then be formulated: *As technological modernization and economic growth perdure over time, inequalities in income and wealth first increase sharply, then decline sharply, and then remain at a relatively stable plateau.*

*These changes are caused by the interplay of technological and demographic forces and are relatively independent of the forms of socioeconomic organization.*

*The leveling phase of this process can be strengthened and accelerated by political interventions, but if these interventions exceed a certain degree (which at this time cannot be precisely specified), there will be negative consequences for economic growth and eventually for the standard of living.*

The first proposition, of course, is a simplified version of the Kuznets hypothesis. The second proposition, if sustained, would cut the ground from under many contemporary criticisms of capitalism (or, for that matter, criticisms of the *economic* inequalities in existing socialist societies); as far as Marxism is concerned, it would support the view that it commits the fallacy of *pars pro toto,* that is, the view that Marxism ascribes to capitalism many traits that appertain to *any* modern society. As to the third proposition, it cannot be automatically used to argue against liberal redistribution policies, as long as the tilting point (that is, the point at which redistributional policies begin to undermine the productive capacity of the economy) cannot be clearly located; the question of the noneconomic consequences of political redistribution cannot be pursued at this point of the argument; it should be stressed, though, that this important contestation between right-of-center and left-of-center parties in Western democracies does not deal so much with the issue of capitalism per se but rather with the scope and character of the democratic welfare state, a related but distinct matter.

In summary, the record of industrial capitalism in its countries of origin differs depending on its being scrutinized in terms of material well-being or in terms of material equality. In terms of the former, with the possible exception of the early period, capitalism does indeed appear as a gigantic horn of plenty, benefiting virtually all strata and having far from exhausted itself. In terms of the latter, capitalism is subject to certain intrinsic forces of modernization that affect the distribution of income and wealth; in consequence, capitalism is neither more nor less egalitarian than other technologically advanced societies. Whether material well-being or material equality is the higher value or whether either should be subordinated to values of a noneconomic sort (such as personal and political liberty) are questions that are, of course, beyond the scope of empirical inquiry. The social sciences cannot provide moral judgments. They can, however, clarify the likely empirical consequences of this or that morally induced option, in the form of "if . . . then" propositions. In the present context, those are fairly clear: If one wants to improve the material condition of people, especially of the poor, one will do well to opt for capitalism. If one wants to modernize, under *any* form of socioeconomic organization (capitalist *or* socialist), one will probably have to settle for a considerable measure of material inequality. If one wants to intervene politically to bring about greater material equality, one may eventually disrupt the economic engine of plenty and endanger the material living standards of the society. The "if" portions of these propositions are, in the strictest sense, meta-scientific and thus empirically nonfalsifiable. The "then" portions, as is in the nature of all empirical statements, are hypothetical and probabilistic. Those who seek to act in society are, inevitably, faced with the less than happy necessity to reconcile moral preferences with highly uncertain predictions. In other words, they must guess and they must gamble. Still, some guesses are better than others, and some bets are safer.

# 3

# CLASS: THE LADDER OF SUCCESS

A FEW YEARS AGO a sociologically pregnant conversation between two women could be overheard in a small park in a fashionable neighborhood in New York City. The women were sitting on a bench, keeping an eye on their children toddling around in a large sandbox thoughtfully provided by the park management. One woman, looking pensively at her little boy (aged about two, an onlooker would estimate), turned to the other and asked, "Do you really think he is Princeton material?" The question may be filed away as indicating the pathological success orientation of upper-middle-class parents. But other classes in America also expect their children to be successful beyond the station of birth and indeed tend to believe that a chance at such success is an inalienable birthright (canonized as the right to the "pursuit of happiness" in the founding document of the American republic). The specifically American cult of success has found many expressions, one of them being the image of the diligent newspaper-delivery boy, who, with proper application and maybe a little luck, ends up as head of a big corporation. In this generalized expectation of success, however, America is only a specially virulent case of modernity as such. The process of modernization has been aptly described as a "revolution of rising expectations." This does not necessarily imply egalitarianism in the sense that at the end of the day it is expected that all individuals will have attained an identical measure of success. It does imply that they all should have a roughly equal crack at it or, put the other way around, that no one should be sentenced to stay in the place to which he was born. In this, modernity is at odds with what people expected through most of history. Louis Dumont, the great French Indologist, has argued that the refusal to accept immutable hierarchies is what sets modern man off most sharply from his traditional ancestors. Dumont has coined the phrase *"homo hierarchicus"* to describe the latter, while modern man can be described as *"homo aequalis."* Modernization everywhere has meant that age-old hierarchical orders have become shaky and that a new dynamism has appeared in the relations of men with each other.

It is possible that, say, five individuals living together on an island could do so in a state of equality. Larger numbers might do so, provided that the time spent together is short. Forms of inequality will appear if a human community consists of more than a handful of individuals and if it continues over time. The questions of why this is, whether it is just, and whether it is possible to change, have occupied some of the best human minds for a very long time. These questions cannot occupy us here. All that we can do here is to explore the empirical forms of inequality with which capitalism has been associated, to compare these with inequality in other empirically available socioeconomic arrangements, and perhaps to begin exploring the reasons for these differences. *That* agenda is formidable enough.

Needless to say, the terms "inequality" or "equality" are quite vague. Probably the discussion of the relevant issues would be greatly helped if the terms were always used in the plural rather than the singular. Thus it is difficult to know what it means empirically to say that "society X has great equality," but it is quite clear what one means by saying that "society X has a more equal income distribution but less equal political participation than society Y." The statement about "equality" is vague and probably ideologically charged, while the latter statement refers to specific equalities or inequalities that are open to empirical inquiry. Be this as it may, all societies that we know of to date have been ranked—or, as many sociologists like to say, have been stratified (a term that suggests geological strata and thus some sort of hierarchy, which is helpful but which also suggests that the strata have a rocklike quality, which is not helpful at all). But the ranking can be based on very different criteria and bestow very different benefits.

Broadly speaking, the benefits of ranking are of three kinds—privilege (in the sense of access to material goods and services), power (that is, in Max Weber's understanding, the likelihood that one will get one's way even against resistance by others), and prestige (in the usual sense of the word). Those three benefits *may* go together, but not necessarily so. Thus, for example, the traditional Hindu system of stratification divided the three benefits among the three top *varnas,* or castes, in such a way that, at least theoretically, the benefits were sharply divided. Also, very different criteria may be used in locating an individual in this or that rank—physical prowess, age, sex, descent, economic achievement, the favor of the king, or the verdict of an oracle. It is no wonder, then, that the mysteries of ranking have agitated philosophers, historians, and, lately, social scientists.

In terms of modern social thought, there is a vast literature on the subject and a great variety of theoretical conceptualizations, many of them going back to the class theories of Marx and Weber.[1] It is necessary to state the assumptions and to define the concepts employed here, even if the methodological reasoning behind these choices cannot be explicated in the present context.

It is assumed that all stratification categories are theoretical constructs rather than photographlike renditions of social reality; this implies that these categories cannot be falsified or supported by data—they can only be shown to be more or less useful in the interpretation of data.[2] It is further assumed that the complex and dynamic character of stratification makes it very unlikely that any monolithic or monocausal conceptualizations will be useful in grasping the relevant phenomena; this implies that different forms of ranking are likely to overlap or crisscross in most societies; thus two societies may differ greatly in the way ranking by privilege relates to ranking by power. The category of "class," which at least since Marx has been central to most stratification theories, is thus understood here as one category of stratification but by no means the only one; therefore, to speak of a "class system" is to refer to a specific pattern of stratification that can be differentiated from other patterns.

Definition: *A class is a group deriving its privilege from its role in the production process and is characterized by common interests and by common cultural traits; a class society is one in which class is the dominant form of stratification.*

This definition (emphatically a theoretical construct, to be deemed more or less useful but not as such to be falsified) is frankly eclectic.[3] It refers to privilege, as described above in terms of access to material goods and services, and leaves open the question of how this relates to power and prestige.[4] It insists that class must have a political aspect, in that classes have vested interests in common, interests that must always be pursued *against* other interests.[5] It further insists that classes, to be called that, must form recognizable human groups and thus must have certain common cultural traits.[6] Thus a particular income category is not, in itself, a class (if it were, incidentally, this chapter would be an unnecessary sequel to the preceding one). There are two implications to this way of conceptualizing class that should also be put on the table. Defining class by reference to the production process implies that occupation will be of crucial importance in determining class position. This has the advantage that data on occupation are, at least in modern societies, relatively easy to obtain. The definition also seems to suggest that a class system of stratification will be relatively open as compared to other systems (say, the Hindu caste system just mentioned)—openness referring to the chances of an individual to move up from one stratum to another. But this should *not* be construed to imply that the empirical degree of such openness is prejudged by way of definition, *nor* is it denied that nonclass forces may be at work even in a class society. Thus the question of social mobility (movement of individuals up or down within a stratification system) is one that cannot be answered by definition but must be explored empirically. And another empirical agenda is the degree to which factors other than class affect an individual's or a group's privilege (factors such as race or gender or political rectitude). It should also be clear that an investigation of social mobility will not only have to look into the *amount* of movement across class lines but also into the *methods* employed for purposes of movement (for instance, educational credentials as against size of investment portfolio or, for that matter, membership in the ruling party).

But this is more than enough of general sociologizing; it is high time to narrow in on the phenomenon of class in modern Western capitalism.

Proposition: *Under industrial capitalism there has been the progressive displacement of all other forms of stratification by class.*

What this means can best be seen by comparing class under modern capitalism with the stratification system that preceded it in Europe. This system of the *ancien régime,* itself a development out of feudalism, was one of "estates" (*états* in French, *Staende* in German). An estate was a stratum in which all the three major benefits—privilege, power, and prestige—were largely determined at birth and, also, were fixed as *legal* inequalities.[7] The aristocracy, of course, constituted the dominant estate (stratified within itself). The church constituted a separate stratum (this one, of course, *not* determined by birth). But even in the "Third Estate," the stratum of urban tradesmen and artisans, the guild system carefully regulated the distribution of benefits. The modern bourgeoisie, the class that "carried" capitalism, grew out of this Third Estate (as the developments preceding the French Revolution make very clear). It is very significant that one of the first demands of this new class (at first not visible as a new class at all, seeming to be just a more militant expression of the old third estate) was *legal* equality of all—or at least of those above a minimal economic line. In other words, the relation of an individual to the order of privilege should no longer be determined by birth or by royal favor but rather by his role and success in the production process.

The social character of this demand, and of the class that made it, is better seen by looking at it through the spectacles of those who opposed it.[8] From the viewpoint of the aristocracy, the bourgeoisie appeared above all as "vulgar." What did this mean? It meant above all that these people insisted that economic success—more simply, the sheer possession of money—should count as much as noble birth, family virtue, personal honor, and proximity to the throne. This "vulgarity" was morally shocking as much as it was politically threatening. Imagine: Any tradesman who by sweaty effort or by cheating or perhaps by plain luck had managed to accumulate a fortune now claimed the same legal standing as a peer of France who could trace his lineage to the age of Charlemagne! The bourgeoisie was vulgar and so was the capitalist society that was coming to replace the ancien régime. Similar sentiments were held by the aristocrats of England and of other European countries, and they were also voiced by whatever quasi-aristocracies developed in America (as in the Old South). It is significant that the charge of vulgarity against bourgeois capitalism continues to be made by its critics, be it from the right or the left: There is an intriguing continuity here from the Duc de Saint-Simon, via John C. Calhoun and Tory radicalism, to Herbert Marcuse. But that is another story.

The point to be made here is this: Leaving aside the pejorative content of this description, those who have called capitalism and its class system vulgar are perfectly correct. The word itself, of course, derives from the Latin *vulgus,* denoting common, ordinary people, as against the patricians. But more than etymology is involved here. A class system creates a situation in which, at least in principle, economic achievement in and of itself determines the material privilege accessible to an individual. Such a situation, again correctly enough, may mean that other benefits as well—specifically, prestige and power—may be acquired in the same way. Put differently, class means that "money speaks loudest"—a thoroughly vulgar proposition if there ever was one. What, then, would no longer "speak"? Well, it would be precisely those attributes that mattered most to an aristocracy—lineage, family tradition, personal honor—all of which, under the ancien régime, not only conferred prestige and power but also guaranteed a high degree of privilege. The position in society that an individual previously received at birth as the end result of centuries of careful cultivation could now be purchased, cash-on-the-barrel, by just anyone coming from nowhere. And these upstarts not only practiced this approach to society, but they had the effrontery to demand that it be legitimated and legalized as a human right.

It is heuristically useful to imagine what a "pure" class system would look like. *All* privilege—that is, *all* access to material goods and services—would be the result of individual achievement within the processes of economic production. Now, a moment's reflection will make clear that such a situation has never existed. To begin with, the individual's participation in the economy, no matter how much he may have equal rights to such participation, will be greatly helped or hindered by the accident of birth. Put more sociologically, family origin is a very important variable in the individual's career within the class system. This is why egalitarians of different descriptions have always been bothered by the family.[9] That, in itself, would still be incorporable within the notion of a "pure" class system, as long as one acknowledges that the individual players within the system do not necessarily start out with an equal number of chips.[10] In addition, however, every empirical class system is modified by other criteria that help or hinder an individual's access to privilege, such as sex, race, ethnicity, political allegiance. Every existing class system is "impure," in the sense that non-class factors interfere with the operation of the class system. An important example of this, extensively studied by sociologists, is the way in which class and race have interacted in American society; in this case it can be plausibly argued that two distinct stratification systems have been superimposed on each other, one the general American class system, the other a "caste" system based on racial criteria.[11] It follows that one should never think of a class system in monolithic terms; one must always see such a system in relative terms, with class being the dominant but not the only form of stratification.

Given this conceptualization, it is clear that class is not a phenomenon limited to modern industrial capitalism. It is quite possible to speak of class in analyzing, say, the society of ancient Rome (though one will obviously want to be careful and not assume that this Roman class system followed the same patterns found in a modern society). Later in this book it will be necessary to ask whether contemporary socialist societies, contrary to their official ideologies, are also analyzable in terms of class. At the same time, though, it is plausible to say that industrial capitalism has a natural affinity to class. One way of putting this is, once more, to refer to market mechanisms as the core of a capitalist economy. Just as the market determines the course of the production process, so there is also a market on which privilege is obtained. In a "pure" capitalist class system the two markets would coincide perfectly: *All* privilege would be purchased, and in principle purchasable, by the income and wealth generated within the market economy. Empirically, as we have indicated, this is not so. But the empirical reality of capitalist societies, when compared with other societies either in the past or in the present, does correspond to the "pure" notion of a class system sufficiently to allow one to make the above proposition on capitalism and class.

It is not possible within this context to present the very great changes undergone by the class systems of Western societies since the advent of industrial capitalism. But a few of these changes must at least be mentioned if the above proposition is to remain plausible.

One very significant change has been the enormous expansion of the middle strata, in a way that could not possibly have been predicted by anyone (Marx included) writing in the nineteenth century.[12] The basic cause of this development was undoubtedly technological: An ever smaller portion of the labor force was required for the actual chores of material production, allowing the diversion of ever larger numbers of workers into administrative and other white-collar activities. But there were also social changes not directly based on technology. Thus, as business enterprises grew, their administration became increasingly bureaucratized and required growing numbers of bureaucratic personnel. Also, there occurred a vast expansion of government bureaucracy, largely necessitated by the development of the welfare state, and here too a large new labor market for white-collar personnel opened up. In consequence, to say the least, the class system became much more complicated—a fact that also had important political consequences.[13] This change has meant that both the social and (inevitably) the social-psychological character of the capitalist class have been transformed: Bureaucratic types have come to supersede entrepreneurial ones.[14] Now, this is not to be understood as a complete supersession. Entrepreneurs have by no means disappeared; they still play a leading role, very much in the classical mold, in important sectors of the economy (for instance, in the high-technology industry in America); also, even the bureaucratic types, or at least some of them, must have entrepreneurial traits as long as their organizations operate in a market economy. All the same, different skills and behavior traits are at a premium today, given these changes, than was the case in an earlier phase of industrial capitalism.

Closely linked to the above change has been the rise of the corporation as a new and immensely important form of economic organization.[15] This, of course, has greatly encouraged the growth of bureaucracy, with all its social and social-psychological consequences, at the very center of industrial capitalism. But it has also meant a separation of property, in the legal sense, from effective economic control. Corporate managers, of course, may or may not be personally wealthy, but their control over economic decision making is based on their office in the corporation and not on their possession or lack of personal property. Since Marxists have always placed great stress on property (necessarily so, since their entire view of capitalist society and its alleged evils is based on a theory of property and expropriation), this change has produced endless problems for them.[16] Many non-Marxists have maintained that this change has brought about a fundamental transformation of the class system.[17] This, in all likelihood, is an exaggeration. But one result of the controversy over this matter has been to suggest that effective control over economic resources rather than legal ownership of them is to be the defining criterion for the top capitalist class—probably a useful theoretical result. In any case, in the conceptualization of class employed here the question of ownership (or property in the legal sense) has been left aside.[18]

Finally, there has been a more recent change of great significance. This has been the development of the service sector of the economy, leading to a massive shift in the labor force to service occupations that is at least as significant as the earlier "white-collar revolution." One part of this change has been the emergence of yet another stratum, that of the new knowledge class. This change, however, will have to be taken up by itself toward the end of the present chapter.

The subject of social mobility has been a very central one in recent sociology.[19] Once again, as is to be expected, there has been a good deal of disagreement and controversy, and again much of that ideologically colored (obviously, sociologists leaning to the left have tended to say that social mobility in Western society is unimpressive, while sociologists of a more conservative bent have taken a more benign view of the matter). Social mobility, as that term is commonly used in sociology, simply means the movement of individuals, either up or down, within any system of stratification. That is a very broad concept. Much of the empirical work, luckily, has had a more precise focus, dealing with occupational mobility of males from one generation to the next—that is, with the occupational position of adult males as compared with that of their fathers. The large-scale entry of women into the paid labor force is sufficiently recent to make intergenerational comparisons more difficult; there is now a lot of work concentrating on female mobility. The occupational emphasis, of course, is very congenial to the conceptualization of class employed here: If one understands class in the manner of the above definition, then occupational mobility will give one a good picture of mobility in the class system *tout court.*

Despite the disagreements, there is a measure of consensus on some aspects of the phenomenon. No one disputes that the Industrial Revolution inaugurated massive changes in the occupational structure. Increasingly large numbers of people shifted from rural to urban employment; indeed, the progressive shrinkage of the proportion of the labor force employed in agriculture is one of the basic indicators of industrialization to this day. This shift, in the early days of industrialism as today, included massive migrations both within and between national societies; the gigantic immigration into the United States in the nineteenth and twentieth centuries is the most dramatic case of this. Also (as Marx saw more clearly than anyone else in his time), the Industrial Revolution gave birth to an altogether new stratum, namely, the industrial working class. Needless to say, as the Industrial Revolution progressed there were ongoing changes in the occupational stratification of the middle class as well, and the old aristocratic upper class was replaced by the new capitalist bourgeoisie in one country after another. There is wide (though not general) agreement to the effect that all these changes meant a great increase in social mobility as compared with the pre-industrial period. Put more directly, *industrialization brings about an increase in social mobility.* There is less agreement on the history of social mobility in societies already industrialized, in Europe and the United States in the nineteenth century. As to the twentieth century in the advanced industrial societies, there is general agreement that no decline in mobility has occurred, and also that there had been no sharp increase at least until World War II.[20] For the first half of this century, some take the position that there has been a moderate rise in mobility, others that the mobility rate has remained fairly constant.

Looking at the industrial countries since World War II, a number of empirically plausible generalizations can be made.[21] The line between manual and nonmanual labor continues to be the hardest to cross, going *either* way. There is a good deal of downward mobility (even from the top strata), but it is greatly exceeded by upward mobility. At a very rough estimate, intergenerationally (that is, between fathers and sons), about 25 percent of individuals move from manual to nonmanual occupations, while about 10 percent move in the reverse direction. Downward mobility, it goes without saying, is a personal misfortune in most cases, but it is as important as upward mobility in gauging the "openness" of a stratification system: As upward mobility shows that there is real opportunity for the "outs," downward mobility shows that there are no guarantees for the "ins," despite the fact that, in a modern class system as in any other type of society, a prudent choice of parents helps a lot.

Not only is it more difficult for an individual to move up from manual to nonmanual labor (and, conversely, less likely for an individual to move down in the opposite direction), but generally most mobility takes place between adjacent occupational categories. For example, it is more likely for the son of an unskilled worker to become a skilled worker than to become a professional and for the son of a clerk to become a professional than to become a top executive. While the family "point of origin" continues to be important in predicting the mobility of an individual, the educational level attained by the latter is by now more important (though, of course, family background is in turn important for the amount of education an individual is likely to obtain). Thus the son of a blue-collar worker with a college degree has better chances than the son of a white-collar worker without such a degree. The importance of education as a mobility vehicle, as against "raw" economic achievement, is very clearly related to the previously mentioned bureaucratization of the economy.

Contrary to many popular assumptions, the overall mobility rates, at least in this century, have been similar in all Western industrial countries.[22] There continue to be considerable differences in the subjective perception of mobility chances, with Americans tending to be more optimistic than Europeans. This is an interesting phenomenon, relevant to an understanding of class consciousness and its political consequences, but it probably has limited bearing for a theory of capitalism.[23] Another set of data, however, has very great bearing for the latter—namely, data indicating that there is also overall similarity between the mobility rates in Western countries and in the socialist industrial societies (the Soviet Union and its European allies). Now, there are considerable difficulties in making comparisons between these two sets of countries, and the similarity in gross mobility rates should not be allowed to obscure the very real differences in the workings of the two systems. Still, it is very important to recognize that most of the above generalizations on mobility hold as much for, say, East Germany as for West Germany: There is more upward than downward mobility, the manual/nonmanual line is more difficult to cross, education is the most important predictor of mobility, and so on. This similarity between capitalist and socialist industrialism gives added weight to another broad generalization: *Social mobility is basically driven by the industrialization process as such.* That is, the amount of social mobility in a particular society basically depends on the degree of its industrialization rather than on other characteristics. This in no way denies that this basic "engine" of mobility is modified by social, political, and (very important) demographic forces, such as prejudice against minority groups, government policies (notably in education), and the differential fertility rate between classes (it seems to be cross-nationally true that the higher strata have fewer children, so that demography ensures that there will be "room at the top"). None of these modifications, however, change the underlying fact that social mobility is basically the result of changes in the occupational structure of the economy, which in turn are determined by technological changes in the production process.

The reader, we trust, will register a sensation of déjà vu. The finding just stated, of course, is very similar to one conclusion of the discussion of income distribution in the preceding chapter. This wondrous convergence between economic and sociological data should not surprise us. It also has important theoretical consequences.

Proposition: *Ongoing industrialization, regardless of its sociopolitical organization, is the basic determinant of social mobility.*

Social mobility is determined by essentially the same forces that determine the Kuznets effect. As far as the theory of capitalism is concerned, the implication of this proposition is quite clear: It is modernization, not capitalism, that accounts for the basic shape of social mobility in Western societies. Thus, depending on whether one regards mobility in these societies as quite high or unacceptably low (to a large extent, this is a subjective decision), capitalism as such should not be either praised or blamed for this state of affairs. As far as Marxist analyses of the matter are concerned, they would seem to repeat the fallacy of *pars pro toto* that has been touched upon before in the present argument—that is, they ascribe to capitalism, which is but one version of modernity, characteristics that properly should be ascribed to all of modernity. Obviously, the way to falsify the above proposition would be to produce data indicating that social mobility varies significantly with forms of sociopolitical organization after all (notably with the difference between capitalist and socialist forms of organization); in that case, capitalism *could* be either blamed or praised for the existing mobility rates in Western societies.

Proposition: *In all advanced industrial societies there have been moderate increases, but no dramatic changes, in the rates of upward mobility.*

This could change if there is a continued shrinkage in the demand for unskilled manual labor. But, thus far, the proposition maintains that industrialization continues to spell enlarged opportunity. It should be noted, of course, that the massive increases in the material standard of living discussed in the preceding chapter are *not* a function of social mobility. In principle, one could envisage a society with no mobility at all, in which, nevertheless, all classes enormously improve their standard of living. Put differently, the son of a blue-collar worker who remains in his father's occupation, or in one very close to it, may nevertheless be much better off than his father.

Proposition: *In all advanced industrial societies, education has become the single most important vehicle of upward mobility.*

This fact, with its quantum jump in the significance of credentials and certification procedures, has changed the character of social mobility even if its overall rates have not changed dramatically. This too could change as higher education becomes more and more widespread, since, logically, the market value of any degree will diminish as it becomes less scarce.

All these propositions refer to empirical characteristics of the class system as far as these can be objectively discovered by sociologists. As has already been pointed out, the subjective perceptions of all this may vary considerably. In the United States, people tend to have an optimistic view both of the progress made since their parents' time (that is, their own past mobility) and their own chances.[24] (It is interesting to note that the single most optimistic group in this regard are American blacks.) Recently, there has been more pessimism on the chances of the coming generation. Still, the popular view among Americans is that the class system is quite open and that hard work and getting an education are the major factors determining whether an individual "makes it" in terms of mobility. There is very little interest in equality, in the sense of a guaranteed egalitarian outcome of the struggle for success and thus broad disagreement with the common egalitarian criticisms of American society. Most Americans continue to believe that the class system is quite fair. What is more, most Americans are prepared to seek remedies for specific elements of unfairness, such as those based on racial or sex discrimination. In addition to hard work and education, there is also a widespread belief in the importance of sheer luck and a willingness to accept this too as essentially fair, in disagreement with egalitarian critics.[25] As was pointed out above, many Europeans have a less benign or accepting view of the workings of the class system. It should be stressed that the objective data on class and mobility do *not* falsify any of these beliefs; rather, it is a question of subjective value judgments or norms whether one will view the existing situation as fair or unfair. Most Americans, at any rate, continue to feel that the present class system does not, *grosso modo,* violate their standards of fair play.[26]

Proposition: *Industrial capitalism, especially when combined with political democracy, is most likely to maintain openness in the stratification system of a society.*

It will be clear even from the way in which this proposition is worded that "openness" is a relative term. There has never been, and probably never will be, a society in which every individual rises or falls in rank simply as a result of his own abilities and efforts. Of course every society, including the class system of Western industrial capitalism, will appear "closed" or "unjust" if compared with an ideal of perfectly equal opportunity for all (not to mention the egalitarian ideal of equal result). The social sciences are not in the business of idealism; within a social-scientific frame of reference, the question of "openness" must always be one of empirical comparisons. In other words, the question must be: In comparison to what other societies can this or that stratification system be called "open" or "closed"? If the question is thus posed, two comparative procedures suggest themselves: The present class system can be compared with the past of Western societies; or it can be compared with empirically available alternatives in the present. In both cases, it is hypothesized here, the relative openness of industrial capitalism and its class system is manifested.

When compared to the past of Western societies, the modern class system, of course, is much more open. The very presence of an industrial economy, as we have seen, sets in motion a dynamic within the occupational structure that opens up innumerable new avenues of mobility. But also, through the interaction of economic and political forces, Western societies have progressively removed traditional barriers to the advancement of individuals regardless (or, to put it more carefully, relatively regardless) of their social origin. The same opening-up of mobility opportunities can be observed today in Third World societies undergoing initial industrialization. Both comparisons, with the Western past and with contemporary Third World societies, support the contention that modernization activates and mobilizes societies and by the same token liberates individuals from traditional restraints on mobility. Equally important for the proposition, though, is the comparison with the societies of industrial socialism. These societies will be looked at in somewhat greater detail later in this book, but a few preliminary comments about them must be made here if the above proposition is to be given a hearing.

Insofar as these latter societies are also industrial and ipso facto modern, they too have experienced the mobilizing dynamic of an industrial economy. Thus an individual in, say, an industrial city in Soviet Central Asia will have open to him opportunities for mobility that were absent for an earlier generation in that locale, and these opportunities (including the ones opened up by a modern educational system) are quite similar to those that opened up as a result of Western industrialization.[27] Comparing this situation, though, with a similar one in a Western industrial country—that of a relatively traditional region being integrated into a modern society—the differences also become manifest. Compare it with, say, the situation of an individual in a poor, still heavily traditional region of Southern Italy. Many of the prospects and the difficulties for advancement will be similar in the two cases: Are there jobs in the modernized sector of the economy? Are there opportunities for education and training making these jobs accessible to the individual? Does the individual have the ability and the motivation to make use of the available opportunities? But there is an additional and very important element in the Uzbek case that is absent in the Mezzogiornio—the element of pervasive political control over the entire opportunity structure. In the Soviet Union there is the additional factor of political barriers that the aspiring individual must reckon with, questions that do not exist in a Western capitalist society: Is he a party member? What is his political record (and, for that matter, the record of his family)? Whom does he know in the political control mechanisms? With some modifications, this additional factor is present in all societies of industrial socialism—in Moscow as well as in Uzbekistan, and, mutatis mutandis, in all the industrial societies of Eastern Europe (including Yugoslavia, though there in a considerably attenuated—if you will, "Westernized"—form).

One way in which all this can be put in theoretical terms is as follows: Every industrial society creates a structure of opportunities determined by economic, technological, and demographic forces that are cross-nationally similar. This structure is highly developed in the advanced industrial societies, still in the making in societies at less developed stages of industrialization. Industrial capitalism allows the rationale of this structure to work itself out relatively autonomously. By contrast, industrial socialism *superimposes* on this rationale another and quite different rationale, which is political and ideological. The tension between these two rationales explains in large part what goes on in the socialist societies. At the same time, this tension makes these societies empirically *less* open than the societies of industrial capitalism. From the point of view of the aspiring individual, both types of society present him with a modern opportunity game; industrial capitalism allows him to play this game more freely. This simple but decisive difference, of course, is obscured if one simply compares overall mobility rates.

In calling industrial capitalism more open than industrial socialism one must also take into account the previously discussed superior productive power of the former. It is not only that, quite apart from income distribution and social mobility, capitalism has shown an unsurpassed capacity to improve the standards of living of virtually all strata. It is also that the very fact of successful economic growth continues to maintain and to expand the structure of opportunities and to allow both individuals and groups to move up without forcing others to surrender what they have. Put simply, a growing pie allows upward mobility without forcing an equal amount of downward mobility. This not only makes for a more open society—one with permeable boundaries between the strata—but a less coercive one. Whenever one is confronted with the criticisms of economic growth that were so fashionable a few years ago, one does well to remember that most of human history took place in zero-growth situations. One may then also recall that these situations were, in the overwhelming number of cases, characterized by rigid barriers between strata, frozen hierarchies, and near-zero mobility.

The above proposition, however, also refers to political democracy, and that too is an important element in the comparison between the class system of industrial capitalism and its empirically available alternatives. In the following chapter the correlation between capitalism and democracy, and the reasons for it, will be explored in some detail. But a few observations about it are appropriate here: Wherever industrial capitalism is combined with political democracy, the latter has invariably increased the openness of the class system—not necessarily by improving income distribution or the overall amount of upward mobility but by giving greater access to education and other facilitators of mobility to people from the less privileged classes. In this perspective, the entire welfare state, as it has developed in Western democracies, can be seen as a vast mechanism to further open up an already highly dynamic class system. George Will has described this with great succinctness: "The market delivers rough justice. The welfare state takes the roughness out of the justice."[28] This corresponds very neatly with the aforementioned feelings of Americans about the "fairness" of their society. The phrase "democratic capitalism," which has been used with great effect by Michael Novak, suggests that any discussion of contemporary Western capitalism must take cognizance of the political system with which it has come to be empirically linked.[29]

To sum up this matter, industrial capitalism provides a market situation of opportunities. Individuals are given relatively free rein to play this market and to reap the benefits of their successes. Barriers to this free play, either traditional ones rooted in the past or political ones imposed in the present, are relatively weak. Background continues to count, of course, but so does individual achievement and plain luck. What is more, political democracy, which allows individuals from all strata to have some say in the workings of the society, ensures a further weakening of barriers and an equalizing of access to the institutions that facilitate success. It also provides insurance to those who are unable (or, for that matter, unwilling) to succeed in the mobility game. All of these characteristics spell a high degree of openness.

Marx expected capitalism to produce ever greater and sharper class conflict. This expectation has been falsified. Instead of class conflict escalating toward revolution, it has become increasingly institutionalized in Western societies.[30] There are many reasons for this—the increasing material well-being of the lower classes, social mobility, differentiations both within the bourgeoisie and the working class diminishing the degree of polarization, the rise of labor unions, and (last not least) the effects of political democracy and of the welfare state. Yet Marx was probably correct on one important point: At any given historical moment, class conflict is mostly between two antagonists.[31] Marx may even have been correct in his view that those two antagonists were bourgeoisie and working class at the earlier period of industrial capitalism that he lived in, as aristocracy and bourgeoisie were the two antagonists in the final period of the ancien régime. This Marxian insight is very relevant to some recent developments in the class system of Western societies.

Roughly since World War II (although the origins lie farther back) there has been a very significant change in the character of the Western middle classes; it was briefly mentioned earlier in this chapter. It can be summarized by saying that, whereas before there was one horizontally stratified middle class (from upper-middle to lower-middle), there now are two vertically divided middle classes, each one stratified within itself. In other words, there now are two middle classes instead of one. There continues to be the old middle class, consisting of the business community and its professional as well as clerical affiliates. Even at some remove (as, say, with accountants or even dentists), these are people who derive their livelihood from the production and distribution of material goods or services. But then there is a new middle class (recently referred to as the "New Class"), consisting of people whose occupations deal with the production and distribution of symbolic knowledge. Let this be called the "knowledge class."[32]

The economic and technological roots of this phenomenon are not mysterious: Material production has become so efficient that a progressively smaller proportion of the labor force is required to keep it going.[33] In consequence, more and more people are employed in the so-called quaternary, or service, sector of the economy. That covers too much ground, though; after all, services are provided by psychiatric social workers, by hair stylists, by janitors, and by call girls; only the first of these occupations is likely to produce members of the new class at issue. Then there is another category, that of the "knowledge industry," employing large numbers of people in the production and distribution of knowledge.[34] That category, however, is also too broad: It lumps in the psychiatric social workers with all those people in what John Kenneth Galbraith called the "technostructure"—such as nuclear engineers, stock market analysts, brain surgeons—most of whom continue to be concerned with material production and (in the case of the brain surgeons) services of a material kind. That is why the focus here is on the purveyors of *symbolic* knowledge—knowledge that is not directly, or in most cases even indirectly, oriented toward material life. Helmut Schelsky, in his analysis of intellectuals in contemporary society, has described three areas of activity that fairly coincide with the boundaries of the new class suggested here—*Belehrung, Betreuung, Beplanung,* roughly translatable as indoctrination, therapy, and planning.[35] (It should be added that the planning too is of the symbolic kind, as in the area of "quality of life"; it should exclude such activities as planning for the water supply of a metropolitan area or the raw materials needed by the automobile industry.) But even with these restrictions, the category of the knowledge class covers quite a large number of people—in the United States, certainly comprising several million. These are the people employed in the educational system, the communications media, the vast counseling and guidance networks, and the bureaucratic agencies planning for the putative nonmaterial needs of the society (from racial amity to geriatric recreation).

It is important to stress that this knowledge class is a much larger group than the people conventionally called "intellectuals." These people (presumably definable as primary producers of symbolic knowledge) are only a sort of upper crust of the knowledge class.[36] For instance, there are professors of psychiatry or psychology at prestige universities who can reasonably be described as intellectuals. But they share their class affiliation with much larger numbers of people —ordinary practicing therapists, social workers and counselors, and even clerical employees in therapeutic organizations—who also derive their livelihood from the *Betreuung* of their fellow citizens. In other words, the new middle class, like the old one, is stratified within itself; just as there was an haute and a petite bourgeoisie (and, with changes in nomenclature, continues to be), so there is an upper- and a petty-knowledge class. There are tensions between these strata; but they also share common class interests and a common class culture.

Proposition: *Contemporary Western societies are characterized by a protracted conflict between two classes, the old middle class (occupied in the production and distribution of material goods and services) and a new middle class (occupied in the production and distribution of symbolic knowledge).*

The term "class," of course, is used here as it was defined early in this chapter.[37] As soon as this is done, one's attention is drawn to both political and cultural aspects of the matter. Class conflict is always about interests, in the hard material sense. But classes also develop a specific culture or subculture (or, if one prefers, a specific class consciousness). This has always been so, as Marx correctly perceived, and the contemporary situation is no exception. It follows that class-specific cultural traits are symbolic of the class interests in contention —*not* in the sense that they are not valued by people for their own sakes but rather in the sense that inevitably these cultural traits are drawn into the conflict. Thus, in the older conflict between aristocracy and bourgeoisie, each group was attached to forms of etiquette and of aesthetic taste ("aristocratic manners," "bourgeois sensibilities") that by no stretch of the sociological imagination could be described as direct expressions of class interests. But once these cultural traits are established in a class (as a result of whatever historical circumstances), they serve as symbols of mutual recognition and of collective solidarity, and any disagreements over these cultural items become part and parcel of the underlying class conflict. In other words, a *Kulturkampf* is very frequently a concomitant of *Klassenkampf*. The above proposition hypothesizes that this is the case with many cultural divisions in Western society today, such as those over sexual morality, the role of women, the environment, patriotism.[38] The hypothesis would be falsified if the data showed that these divisions do *not* significantly vary between the two classes as defined. Most of this is not directly relevant to the present argument. But one aspect of the phenomenon is very relevant indeed: The new knowledge class tends to be politically and ideologically to the left of the old middle class, and it is ipso facto anticapitalist in overall orientation.

Proposition: *The new knowledge class in Western societies is a major antagonist of capitalism.*

This, once again, is a hypothesis that is open to falsification by data showing the contrary. Anyone, though, who has followed the recent politics of the democracies of North America and Western Europe will understand the reasoning behind the hypothesis. The evolution of the Democratic party in the United States since 1972 or the rise to power of François Mitterand's socialists in France would be especially clear cases of the leftward lurch of any political constituency dominated by knowledge-class people.[39] Now, to the extent that the knowledge class takes its cultural cues from those considered to be "intellectuals" (in addition to which, one may assume, even many members of the petty-knowledge class consider themselves to be intellectuals of some sort), this should not be a surprising statement. The anticapitalist animus of the intelligentsia has long been noted and indeed was elaborated in considerable detail by Joseph Schumpeter and more recently by Daniel Bell.[40] In the American context it has long been part and parcel of what Lionel Trilling called the "adversary culture," in which antibourgeois cultural sentiments had a natural affinity with anticapitalist politics. The interesting sociological question is why this should be so.

As one looks at the societal location of the knowledge class, two interests suggest themselves. The first is an interest in having privilege based on educational credentials, in which this class has an obvious advantage. This interest could well underlie a general antagonism against privilege based on "raw" achievement in economic terms and thus against the capitalist market system that, in principle, is open to anyone regardless of education or other extra-economic certification. But there is also a second interest, which is due to the fact that a large proportion of this knowledge class depends for its livelihood on government payrolls or subsidies. This suggests a built-in vested interest in the expansion of the welfare state, which, of course, is that part of government in which this class finds employment and subsidization. Put differently, the knowledge class has an interest in the distributive machinery of government, as against the production system, and this naturally pushes it to the left in the context of Western politics (whatever "left" may mean in ideological terms, politically it means an expansion of the welfare state in the Western democracies). Incidentally, this second interest may help to explain why the knowledge class in America, still, is less to the left than the same class in Western Europe: In America a larger proportion of this class sells its services on the market and thus may have a larger interest in maintaining a market economy (one may reflect here, in comparing the two continents, on the role of privately owned mass media and private education in the United States).

If the hypothesis about the knowledge class holds, it concerns a very new and rising class. If so, many of the classical Marxian notions about such situations would apply to it: It only has an incipient class consciousness at this point (in Marxian parlance, it is still more of a class-in-itself than a class-for-itself), though one may expect this to change as its culture becomes more distinct and self-confident. Outsiders too still do not quite perceive it as a class, still thinking of it in terms of the older stratification out of which it is emerging (here this means simply thinking of these people as a segment of the upper-middle class, just as the rising bourgeoisie was perceived as the old Third Estate long after that term no longer adequately fitted it). And, like all rising classes, the knowledge class rhetorically identifies its own class interests with the general welfare of society and especially with the downtrodden (just as the early bourgeoisie did in its conflict with the ancien régime). This is especially so because the knowledge class has such an interest in the welfare state, which is ostensibly set up on behalf of the poor and of other disadvantaged groups (such as the racial minorities in America). Politically, this has meant a curious symbiosis (and perhaps a quite objective convergence of interests) between this generally affluent and well-educated group on the one hand and various "underclass" groups on the other hand. The common interest here, of course, is in the distributive and redistributive role of the state. This has also meant a tense relationship with the industrial working class, especially as represented by organized labor, which has very different interests. The possible scenarios in these various relationships are very intriguing but obviously cannot be pursued here.[41]

Capitalism as such can neither be praised nor blamed for class as a social phenomenon nor for the dynamics of modern social mobility. Capitalism, however, can be taken as a causal force (be it approvingly or pejoratively) for the predominance of class over other forms of stratification and capitalism in conjunction with political democracy as a cause for the relative openness of the class system of modern Western societies. However one may view class from a philosophical or ethical point of view, any assessment of class in industrial capitalism ought to include a comparison with empirically available (and possibly also with empirically plausible) alternatives. Barring a return to traditional forms of society, industrial socialism and its stratification system would seem the most relevant basis of comparison. Whatever other attributes those societies may have, and whether one calls them "class societies" or not, they are not characterized by the absence of stratification. Even leaving aside questions of political liberties and individual rights, industrial capitalism comes out of this comparison as having a much more open system of stratification.

If that is a tentative conclusion to this chapter's discussion of class, one may also now formulate some interim propositions on the relationship of capitalism and modernity, and thus of a theory of capitalism and modernization theory. Industrial capitalism is one version of modernity; it is not coextensive with modernity. There are some important characteristics of contemporary Western societies that will probably have to be ascribed to their being modern societies and not to their being capitalist ones. Notable among these characteristics are the patterns of income distribution and social mobility. On the other hand, what in all likelihood can be ascribed to capitalism is the productive power of these societies, as well as the relative openness of their class system. If these propositions hold up empirically, some important steps will have been taken in the theoretical disaggregation of the two phenomena of modernity and capitalism.

# 4

# CAPITALISM AND POLITICAL LIBERTIES

In American popular consciousness there is a taken-for-granted linkage between political, economic, and personal liberties. Anyone interested in verifying this statement might study the different situations to which Americans apply the time-honored phrase "It's a free country!" (Perhaps the National Endowment for the Humanities might sponsor a vast investigation of the distribution and uses of this phrase, which could well be called the American legitimating formula par excellence.) Sometimes the phrase clearly refers to the sphere of political democracy: "You have no political experience whatsoever and you are planning to run for governor? It's a free country!" "You are going to picket the White House? It's a free country!" At other times, the insistence on this being a free country refers to the economic sphere, more specifically to the economic liberties associated with capitalism or to the sphere of personal liberations: "You are going to invest in this risky real-estate scheme?" "At your age, in mid-career, you are going to change occupations?" "You are really going to become a Buddhist monk, in New Jersey no less?" The answer comes back, usually in a tone of pride: "It's a free country!" Now, the fact that these three sets of phenomena are linked in the minds of people need not necessarily mean that they are linked in the empirical world "out there." After all, one does not have to be a Marxist to see that, sometimes, people are in "false consciousness"—put plainly, they may be mistaken about the empirical realities of their society. Thus the linkage between capitalism, political democracy, and the liberties of the individual cannot be assumed a priori but must rather be the subject of empirical exploration.

Throughout this book the overriding concern is to understand the manner in which the economic arrangement known as capitalism interacts with other processes and institutions in modern society. As was explained at the outset, the term "economic culture" is intended to suggest this concern. One could, of course, use other terminologies, suggesting different images. Thus Joseph Schumpeter speaks of the "capitalist engine." One then tries to see it as a gigantic machine, roaring away. Yet other forces intervene in its journey—forces of class, of the state, of culture—and these may deflect it from its course or even (as Schumpeter thought) eventually make it stop in its tracks. Whatever terms or images are employed, the concern is with interrelations, with reciprocities. Arguably one of the most important of these relationships is between modern capitalism and the modern state, and especially the modern democratic state. The modern state, while its origins probably antedate capitalism, attained its fullest development in tandem with the development of capitalism, and this modern state represents the most efficient and pervasive organization of political power in history.[1] Another political phenomenon, democracy, developed precisely in the same Western countries in which modern capitalism unfolded. And modern democracy was clearly one of the historical achievements of the bourgeoisie, the rising capitalist class. This conjunction, of course, was clearly understood by Karl Marx, and to that extent the phrase "bourgeois democracy," as still commonly used by Marxists, is *historically* valid (even if one puts aside its pejorative connotations and the implication that there is another, better form of democracy under socialism).

The term "democracy" has been used in many different senses. Following what is by now a conventional approach of the majority of political scientists, the term is used here in a quite narrow sense as denoting a specific set of *political institutions* or, even more precisely, a specific set of *institutionalized political processes*.[2] The emphasis is, first of all, *empirical;* that is, it concerns empirically available phenomena in society and *not* theories, philosophies, or value systems. (Needless to say, this empirical focus in no way prejudges the question of the extent to which ideas about democracy have influenced its social realizations, but this is a question to be left to investigation and not to be sneaked into the definition.) Such an empirical approach cannot deal with the question of whether there is such a thing as "true democracy," and ipso facto whether any particular democratic structure is more or less "true" than another. Also, the emphasis here is on the *political* area of social life. This implies that questions about "democracy" in other areas of society (say, in the family or in the workplace) are excluded from consideration. As always, the narrowness of a definition increases rather than decreases the scope of possible empirical investigations. Thus, for example, a researcher interested in the distribution of power within the family (that is usually the interest when the term "democracy" is used here) is perfectly free to explore this matter empirically, and the exploration will then also be free to deal with the question of how these intrafamilial processes may or may not relate to the existence of a democratic polity in the overall society. Finally, the term "democracy" is used here to refer to *institutions*— to ongoing patterns that regulate and channel human actions over time. What is excluded thereby are fugitive, transitory events that fail to settle down into such patterns.

Definition: *Democracy is a political system in which governments are constituted by majority votes cast in regular and uncoerced elections.*

It goes without saying that this definition leaves open a good many questions.[3] Thus, for example, it omits the question of the extent of suffrage.[4] But the definition clearly implies the following: There is genuine competition for the votes of the electorate, and those engaged in this competition (whether as individuals or in associations, such as political parties or factions) are free to organize for this purpose. Minimally, this means guaranteed political liberties related to the electoral process, especially freedom of speech and freedom of association. Since it is virtually unthinkable that such liberties are limited in time to election periods, these same liberties must be permanently institutionalized and (at least in a modern society) protected by law. This further means that the legal system guarding political liberties has a measure of independence from the government in power. Also, elections must take place at regular intervals; they must not be sporadic or at the whim of the sitting government. Also, elections must be protected from coercive interference, be it by government or by extra-governmental forces. Finally, a government defeated in an election must actually relinquish power, the elected government must in fact take office, and the power of the elected government must not be just á facade for unelected power-holders. In empirical reality, this or that element of the definition will be in doubt. This fact, however, is not an argument against the above definition; on the contrary, the definition then allows the proposition that, in a particular situation, the democratic character of the polity is questionable.

Another important point should be made about this definition of democracy: It does *not* include the panoply of civil and human rights commonly associated with the democratic tradition of the West and implied by the common phrase "liberal democracy." Once again, this exclusion is precisely intended to facilitate empirical explorations. In principle and indeed in many empirical instances, this conjunction fails to pertain. Take, for instance, the matter of religious liberty. A despotic regime may allow this liberty and a democracy may deny it. More broadly, there are liberal despots and illiberal democratic majorities. In fact, in the contemporary world, there is a very high correlation between religious liberty and democratic governance, but this correlation is to be empirically determined and (if possible) explained, not to be posited *ex definitione*.

Now, even within the narrow confines of the definition of democracy employed here, one fact comes into view: *Democracy constitutes an institutionalized limitation of the power of government.* This presupposes that the political institutions of society are clearly differentiated from the other institutions and are not allowed to coalesce with them. Comparing a modern democratic polity with, say, European feudalism brings home the importance of this presupposition. This separateness of political institutions was intended by the classical distinction between the state and "civil society" and has been an important topic of modern sociological theory.[5] If one now recalls the manner in which modern capitalism and modern democracy developed historically, the above fact points to an intriguing paradox: Capitalism has been associated both with the greatest concentration of political power in history—to wit, the modern state—and also with the most intense effort to limit this power.

Clearly, the modern state can exist without capitalism. The contemporary world is full of states presiding over noncapitalist economies.

The question that must be considered, however, is whether modern democracy is possible without capitalism. Within the logic of the present argument, this question may be further specified in terms of extrinsic and intrinsic linkages: Are there in fact noncapitalist democratic polities? And, to the extent that democracy is empirically linked to capitalism, is this linkage simply the result of historical accidents (such as the fact that both capitalism and democracy are products of Western civilization), or can it be ascribed to built-in structural features of these two institutional configurations?

The question of premodern democracies, if any, may be left aside here (such as, say, of yeomen republics in the early days of the Swiss Confederation). In terms of the contemporary world, the empirical correlations can be summed up as follows: *All democracies are capitalist; no democracy is socialist; many capitalist societies are not democracies.*

These three statements, of course, are based on the foregoing definitions of democracy, capitalism, and socialism. It goes without saying that a different definition of "democracy" would permit very different statements about the empirical distribution of the phenomenon (indeed, very few regimes in the contemporary world, including the totalitarian states of the Soviet bloc, describe themselves as anything but "democracies"). The above statements are based on the conceptualization of capitalism and socialism developed in the earlier chapters of this book. Thus (following Marxist practice) these two types of socioeconomic organization were defined with reference to *production* (in Marxist parlance, of the "mode of production") and *not* in terms of the redistributive activities of the modern welfare system. It follows that Western democracies, such as the Scandinavian countries, that have developed extensive welfare systems while retaining a largely market-oriented and privately owned economy, should *not* be designated as "socialist" (a conclusion that is very much shared by the Marxist critics of those societies). The question of the range of the welfare state and of its effects on the economy is, to be sure, a very important one; it is the major domestic issue dividing right-of-center and left-of-center parties in Western democracies. But it is a *different* question from the one about capitalism and socialism. Different capitalist societies may vary greatly in their welfare-state provisions, but there is no necessary linkage between a socialist "mode of production" and a highly developed welfare state; thus it is doubtful whether the socialist societies of Europe provide better health or disability services, for example, than the welfare states of the West. Whether the burden of an elaborate welfare system eventually cripples the productive power of the economy is equally relevant for capitalist and socialist societies.[6]

If one concedes the empirical association between capitalism and democracy, both historically and in the contemporary world, the question arises as to why this should be so. One possible answer is that the association is merely the result of historical accident—namely, the common Western provenance of the two phenomena—but that there is no necessary or intrinsic linkage between them. This was essentially Joseph Schumpeter's position.[7] Schumpeter believed that, in principle, democracy was possible under both capitalism and socialism, though he believed that a socialist democracy, because of the pervasive controls it would have to maintain over society, would not be conducive to personal freedom. In other words, Schumpeter thought that democracy (which he too defined narrowly in terms of political processes) was possible under socialism, but that it would probably *not* be *liberal* democracy. When Schumpeter wrote about this, the only socialist society in existence was the Soviet Union; he was speculating about socialist possibilities in other societies (he did not, of course, look on the Soviet Union as a democracy). In the intervening years many more socialist societies have sprung up in different parts of the world, by no means all being simple extensions of the Soviet model. In the light of this much ampler empirical evidence, there is no reason to question Schumpeter's belief in the illiberal character of socialism; there *is* reason to doubt his view that socialism and democracy as a purely political arrangement could coexist.

Another possible answer is that the association does indeed exist but that it is not what it seems. More specifically, it is argued that democracy is a pretense designed to obscure the real power relations in society, which are determined and dominated by the capitalist class. Or, put somewhat differently, democracy may not be a complete sham, but it operates in such a way as to further the interests of capitalist domination. Different versions of this interpretation, of course, are held by all Marxist analysts of Western societies, and some non-Marxist analysts have expressed similar views.[8] Criticism of this interpretation would entail a detailed empirical examination of the relations between the democratic state and capitalist interests in all the relevant societies. All that can be said here is that there is a heavy burden of proof on those who must argue, by their own logic, that most of what appears as democratic politics is in fact an illusion. To say this does not deny that capitalist interests do indeed exercise power in various ways outside the democratic process or even that there may be societies (especially in the Third World) where the Marxist interpretation applies quite adequately. But an empirically oriented perspective on politics and government in the advanced capitalist societies of the West is very unlikely to provide support for this interpretation.

There is a methodological problem here, stemming from the fact that these Marxist (and *marxisant*) interpretations are essentially conspiracy theories: Lurking behind the Potemkin villages of formal government and of the democratic process is the *real* power, which is the octopus of capitalist domination. Conspiracy theories are notoriously difficult to falsify. After all, by definition, conspiracies are hidden, below the surface. The only viable course of testing such theories is to examine, society by society and case by case, how government actions and how the outcomes of the democratic process do or do not further capitalist interests. This cannot be done here. It can only be proposed that such empirical analysis, at least in the advanced capitalist societies of Western Europe and North America, strongly tends to falsify the Marxist thesis of the illusionary or ancillary character of democratic governance. Right-of-center politicians and business spokesmen complain all the time how a vast array of government actions serve to weaken the capitalist economy and the interests of the business community. A close examination of democratic politics in these societies would seem to bear out this complaint.

There is, on the contrary, the view that "economic freedom" (that is, a capitalist economy) is necessarily linked to "political freedom" (that is, democracy) because both are expressions of one and the same impulse of individual autonomy against the coercive power of the state. Milton and Rose Friedman have called this "the fundamental proposition that *freedom is one whole,* that anything that reduces freedom on one part of our lives is likely to affect freedom in the other parts."[9] There is much to be said for this proposition. However, it cannot be postulated a priori. After all, there are some liberties that would clearly *not* seem to be part and parcel of "one whole"—say, the liberty to vote in elections and the liberty to choose any conceivable sexual life-style (there are sexually "repressive" democracies and sexually libertarian societies that never had an inkling of democracy). In other words, if political liberties are indeed intrinsically linked to the economic liberties of capitalist enterprise, then this linkage must be explained by the empirical workings of the social institutions at issue.

Such an explanation, as it were, can be made in positive and negative terms. Positively, one can seek to explain how capitalism and democracy "fit" under modern conditions, and negatively, how socialism fails to "fit" (which, incidentally, points up the fact that a theory of capitalism requires a theory of socialism as a tree necessarily casts a shadow). The positive argument is that the modern state has the innate tendency to project its power further and further into society, *unless* it meets up with institutionalized limits. Capitalism, by providing a social zone relatively independent of state control, facilitates this limit. Put differently: The modern state, even in its democratic form, represents the greatest agglomeration of power in human history—not because of any malign totalitarian ideology somehow inherent in modernity but because of the immense technological resources available to governments for purposes of control. Conversely, a capitalist economy, even when subjected to all sorts of governmental interventions, creates its own dynamic that confronts the state as a relatively autonomous reality. Whatever else the government then controls, it does not fully control this zone, which ipso facto limits state power. The "fit" between capitalism and democracy is the consequence of this.[10]

This explanation is greatly enhanced when one augments it by a negative argument concerning socialism. Whatever else socialism may mean as a utopian vision, *empirically* it has consistently meant an immense expansion of state power, indeed amounting to a quantum leap of this power. The zone of economic activity is incorporated into the sphere of the state in a much more complete manner than characterizes even the most interventionist, or *dirigiste,* government that still allows an independent capitalist dynamic. The term "command economy," often applied to socialism by its critics, expresses this fact very well, though the less pejorative term "planned economy" indicates the same political consequence. The political controls over the economy dictated by the socialist project must be, by their very nature, permanently institutionalized; thus they are very difficult to relax (let alone remove) once established. Put differently, empirical socialism has meant a pervasive bureaucratization of the economy; quite apart from the economic malfunctions this brings about (malfunctions that go a very long way in explaining the low efficiency of socialist economies), the all-embracing bureaucracy makes the expression of political liberties very difficult if not impossible.[11] Now, to be sure, the modern corporation is also a bureaucratic institution, and many analysts have pointed out the effects of *its* bureaucratization on capitalist economies. But there is an essential difference between these two types of economic bureaucratization: No capitalist corporation, however powerful, controls the economy as a whole, and at least in no advanced capitalist society does the corporation have the full coercive power of government at its beck and call. By contrast, the socialist state functions as a monopoly of economic-political power, being able at any time to bring the full force of modern government to bear within any area of economic activity. Put simply, capitalism creates "escape hatches" from political power; socialism makes such escape very precarious if not impossible.

This understanding of the political effects of capitalism and socialism has been propounded in the work of F. A. Hayek, and at least to date it has been amply confirmed by the empirical evidence.[12] To the extent that socialism, in addition to replacing market forces by a political-bureaucratic decision-making process, *also* has entailed the abrogation of property rights over the means of production, the explanation of its incompatibility with democracy gains additional weight. Socialist revolutions bring about radical expropriations; *that* indeed is one of their foremost ideological purposes. But, human nature being what it is, new forms of property (de facto if not de jure) keep emerging anew and thus keep threatening the socialist character of the postrevolutionary society. Therefore, if the socialist project is to be maintained, *expropriation must be a permanent process.* It is very difficult indeed to see how such a process could be kept going under a democratic polity; some form of dictatorship would seem to be necessary.[13] All of this has far-reaching implications for a sociopolitical theory of socialism: For the moment, these considerations can be tentatively summarized by saying that, while capitalism does indeed "fit" with democracy, socialism would appear to have a built-in totalitarian (or, minimally, authoritarian) tendency. The contrast with capitalism can also be put in historical terms: As modern society emerged from the old feudal order, the political and the economic institutions of society became much more differentiated. Socialism tends to revoke this differentiation; it establishes a renewed unity of the political and economic spheres. In this perspective, the socialist vision takes on a curiously "reactionary" quality (once again, a point that will be taken up later in this book).

These reflections all tend toward a simple but far-reaching hypothesis: *Capitalism is a necessary but not sufficient condition of democracy.* [14]

As pointed out before, the proposition refers to modern conditions only. It goes without saying that a theory of democracy (as distinct from a theory of capitalism) will have to be vitally concerned with those *other* conditions that may be deemed to be sufficient for the democratic phenomenon; indeed, most recent theorists of democracy have dealt with precisely this issue. As to falsification of the above hypothesis, the most convincing one would be the emergence, in empirical reality rather than in the realm of ideas, of even one clear case of democratic socialism. That such a society will emerge in the future is, of course, the fondest wish of democratic socialists. The future is always open, and social science is not capable of making definitive statements about it. It is clear, though, that the above hypothesis implies that the future emergence of a democratic socialism is very improbable.

Of more immediate empirical concern is the question of "mixed economies." As has been pointed out repeatedly in the foregoing pages, there are no "pure" cases of capitalism and socialism in existence; to that extent, *all* empirically available economies are "mixed." If capitalism "fits with" democracy, the question is what degree of admixture of political intervention in the economy would tilt a society into a nondemocratic polity. Conversely, if socialism is intrinsically correlated with nondemocratic forms of political organization, there is the question of the degree of modification of a socialist economy by market mechanisms that would tilt such a society into a readiness for democracy. Present knowledge is inadequate to allow for an answer to either question. The experience of Western societies would seem to indicate that a greater degree of political intervention is possible, with democracy remaining intact, than some procapitalist theorists have thought (including perhaps Hayek). The resistance to the introduction of market mechanisms in socialist societies by the party and bureaucratic elites also suggests that there is a tilting point in the reverse direction. In other words, all those apparatchiks have very good grounds for worrying that, if the socialist system is modified beyond a certain point by market mechanisms, the new entrepreneurs will become uppity and start demanding political liberties that would undermine the control of the party.

One could indeed formulate two rather vague hypotheses: *If a capitalist economy is subjected to increasing degrees of state control, a point will be reached at which democratic governance becomes impossible.*

(It should be clear that this hypothesis refers to state control over the *production* process, *not* to the welfare system and its redistribution policies—leaving open the question, as not properly pertaining to a theory of capitalism, whether the latter too might eventually endanger democracy.)

*If a socialist economy is opened up to increasing degrees of market forces, a point will be reached at which democratic governance becomes a possibility.*

("Possibility" here meaning, of course, that a necessary but not a sufficient condition for democracy would prevail.)

Needless to say, these hypotheses are of little *practical* use unless or until they can be made more specific as to the character of the two "tilting points."

It is clear that there can be capitalism without democracy. This raises the question of what other factors, besides a capitalist economy, are required to make a democratic polity possible. It is worth noting that, following the end of dictatorial regimes in Spain, Portugal, and Greece, all the cases of nondemocratic capitalism are found (at the time of writing) in the non-Western world. Thus the role of European civilization, with its rich heritage of libertarian and individualistic ideas and institutions, cannot be discounted as a historical factor; indeed, the same factor figures significantly in the hope of some (including the so-called Eurocommunists) that a democratic socialism, if anywhere, would be realizable in a Western country. It is also worth noting that Third World societies that are drawn into the "world system" of international capitalism are ipso facto drawn into an international culture centered in the capitalist "metropolitan" societies of

Europe and North America—societies that are characterized by the ideas and institutions of democracy. Put graphically, if a Third World society imports the hardware of capitalism, it will find it difficult to avoid the software of democracy. Those who want Western technology without the "spiritual pollution" of Western ideas, be they Muslim fundamentalists or recalcitrant Maoists, have discovered that this is a very frustrating business. Conversely, Third World societies that take a socialist direction and seek separation from international capitalism are led, by the political logic of the contemporary world, into closer relations with the Soviet bloc—and ipso facto with the totalitarian ideas and institutions of the latter. These geopolitical, cultural, and ideological factors make the search for intrinsic linkages more complicated.

Nevertheless, it is plausible to argue, precisely from cases in the non-Western world (such as South Korea or Taiwan), that *successful* capitalism generates pressures *toward* democracy. It is quite clear that so-called development dicatorships do work in the earlier, or "take-off," stages of capitalist development (this does *not* mean that dictatorship is *necessary* for capitalist "take-off"). Where this is so, the social psychology of the process is fairly clear: People who are just escaping from an economic existence of harsh subsistence and who can see, in their own lives and in assessing the prospects of their children, that a better life is at hand are likely to be less interested in political liberties. This acquiescence is likely to disappear with the maturation of a new generation which no longer remembers the earlier period of grinding poverty, which takes economic progress for granted, and which therefore is able to develop "finer" aspirations, such as the aspiration for political liberties and personal liberation. At that point the legitimations for a "development dictatorship" begin to lose plausibility.

Also relevant to this issue is the distinction between two quite different types of nondemocratic regimes in the modern world—between authoritarian and totalitarian regimes.[15] An authoritarian regime is one that does not tolerate political opposition but is prepared to allow institutions and sectors of society to function free of the state provided they do not engage in political activity. A totalitarian regime is one that seeks to impose state control over every institution of society, regardless of whether it engages in political activity or not and with the intention, finally, of integrating society as a whole within an all-embracing political design.[16] The contemporary Third World has a large number of authoritarian states with capitalist economies. All presently existing totalitarian states, however, are in the socialist sphere.[17] The various movements of liberalization in the socialist countries of Europe (notably Hungary, Czechoslovakia, Poland, and, most important, Yugoslavia) indicate, minimally, that a movement from totalitarianism to authoritarianism within a socialist framework is conceivable (thus one may argue that the movement in the first three cases would have succeeded in the absence of Soviet hegemony over the region and that the movement *has* succeeded in Yugoslavia). Nevertheless, the socialist project in itself contains a totalitarian tendency, since it necessarily precludes the autonomy of the economic sector of society vis-à-vis the political structure. By contrast, capitalism presupposes such autonomy and, by the same token, inhibits totalitarian developments. The question of the political dynamics of socialist societies will have to be taken up in a later chapter.

For the moment, on the basis of the foregoing considerations, there is a prima facie case for the following hypothesis: *If capitalist development is successful in reaching economic growth from which a sizable proportion of the population benefits, pressures toward democracy are likely to appear.*

Very probably, as theorists of democracy have frequently argued, this is related to the emergence of a middle class, which will want political participation as one of the prizes of its economic success.

Democracy, as it has been defined here, is a procedure by which governmental power is limited by means of popular participation. This definition is careful in narrowing the concept to the political area of society or, more precisely, to the formal political institutions. But it is important not to lose sight of the fact that popular participation in social life, and specifically in the decision-making processes of society, is not confined to the political area proper. Thus there is a great variety of, as it were, subpolitical institutions through which people participate in the life of the larger society and (to use a favorite phrase of so-called participatory democracy) through which they "participate in the decisions that shape their lives." These are the institutions that stand between the individual and the mega-structures of society. Institutions, such as extended kinship, clan or tribe, village, religious community, exist in traditional societies but are frequently carried over with modifications and adaptations into periods of modernization. And then there are new, modern institutions, such as organized interest groups, cooperatives, labor unions, occupational groups and voluntary associations for all sorts of local or regional purposes. All these institutions, though their goals may vary widely, serve as "mediating structures" —that is, they mediate between the individual and the larger society (including the large institutions of the economy and the state), and they serve as bridges between private and public life.[18] It has been argued, ever since Edmund Burke and Alexis de Tocqueville, that such intermediate institutions are essential if democracy is not to degenerate into tyranny but also essential for a stable democracy to emerge in the first place. Now, most of these institutions have little to do with capitalism or even with economic interests of any kind. However, for the same reason that capitalism is inimical to totalitarianism, capitalism favors mediating structures. It "leaves room" for them, precisely because it creates a highly dynamic zone that is relatively autonomous vis-à-vis the state. By contrast, socialist societies are much more prone to try to control, or to integrate politically, all these groupings which, by their very existence, threaten the overall rational design of a "command economy."

By comparison with socialism, capitalism is uncontrolled, turbulent, "messy." This quality has an intrinsic affinity with spontaneous institutions of participation. Such institutions, however, function as "schools for democracy." The individual who has learned to participate in decision making on the level of a village council or a farmers' association learns the skills that will eventually pay off in the formal processes of democratic politics. It has also been argued that such subpolitical participation is a precondition for capitalism itself.[19] Be this as it may, the positive affinity between capitalism and mediating structures may serve to explain, at least in part, the foregoing hypothesis that successful capitalism creates pressures toward democracy.

If there is a correlation between capitalism and democracy, there is also a correlation between democracy and respect for human rights.[20] The second correlation is not *logically* necessary. Nondemocratic regimes may respect human rights and democracies may violate them. *Empirically,* however, democracy appears to serve as the most reliable guarantee for human rights. Nor are the reasons for this mysterious: The *same* institutional mechanisms that make political democracy possible—all the limits on government power to permit political oppositions to function—*also* serve to protect human rights over and beyond political liberties. Thus, for example, a government that is limited in its power to control the free expression of dissenting political views is likely to be so limited in its power over the free exercise of religion. Democracy *need not* be liberal, and despotisms *may* be liberal. Empirically, though, despotic regimes tend to become illiberal sooner or later, while by contrast liberal democracy is the most likely outcome of the institutionalization of democratic politics.

This correlation between democracy and human rights is, of course, one of the major legitimations of democracy, and it is an important issue for an empirical theory of democracy. It is also relevant for a theory of capitalism. The argument that there is a direct, intrinsic relationship between capitalism and human rights is not persuasive; such an argument, while frequently part of the rhetoric of capitalist ideology, should not be made within an empirical theory of capitalism. Nevertheless, capitalism does have a relationship with human rights— *indirectly,* via the affinity with democracy. An additional indirect relationship, via specific cultural affinities, will be taken up in the next chapter.

One of the most fundamental traits of modernization is a vast movement from fate to choice in human affairs.[21] Modern technology ensures this by immensely increasing the ability of human beings to control their environment, thus diminishing those aspects of life that were previously experienced and perceived as unalterable destiny. The paradox here is that modern technology *also* supplies the means by which powerful institutions can control the lives of individuals. Thus the totalitarian state is made possible by modern technology. The great drama of modernity is this dynamic tension between liberation and re-enslavement.

Modern capitalism too has been a liberating force. The market in and of itself liberates people from the old confines of subsistence economies. It opens up choices, options, that were unheard of in traditional societies. These new choices are not merely economic and technological. Historically and empirically, there is a correlation with social and political choices, and even with choices on the level of consciousness. Thus the modern city, itself a creation of capitalism, has been a liberating force. The old German adage put it succinctly—

*"Stadtluft macht frei"* (city air liberates). One may paraphrase: *"Kapitalistische Luft macht frei"* (the air of capitalism liberates). *That* is the empirical justification of the ideological proposition that there is an intrinsic connection between economic freedom and all other liberties (even if, as the foregoing considerations suggest, the connection is more indirect and possibly extrinsic). However, it does not follow from this that the liberating effects of capitalism are inevitable or irreversible.

On the contrary, capitalism as a liberating force creates tensions and countermovements on all levels—economic, social, political, and on the level of consciousness. The same antinomy has been pointed out by theorists of democracy. It is inherent in the precarious balance between political liberties and the effectiveness of the state. The fragility of this balance is not simply due to capitalism. Thus, if one imagines a democratic socialism, it would certainly be marked by the same if not (as the present argument would suggest) an even greater fragility. But capitalism creates specific tensions of its own, potentially threatening its liberating character. Joseph Schumpeter has spelled some of these out very persuasively.[22] The very core of liberating capitalism is the free entrepreneur. As capitalism develops, however, the rise of the corporation hems in this type of entrepreneurship. Marxists have analyzed this in terms of "monopoly capitalism," an agglomeration of economic and political power that undermines the free operation of market forces. Undoubtedly there is some validity to this analysis, though it tends to overlook the continuing pressure of market forces on the corporation and the emergence of countervailing forces by way of political democracy. But Schumpeter analyzes the process by which entrepreneurship declines more in sociocultural than economic terms. Mature capitalism fosters the bureaucratization of economic activity, thus pushing forward a managerial type of individual quite different from the free entrepreneur. Also, mature capitalism creates an adversary class (as discussed in the previous chapter), thus "digging its own grave" in a way unimagined in the Marxist scheme. Put simply, Marx and his followers thought that capitalism was doomed because of its economic and political failures; Schumpeter came to the same conclusion, but because of the very success of capitalism in purely economic and political terms. In other words, he believed that the liberating force of capitalism would be self-liquidating.

One need not assent to the full-blown Schumpeterian thesis in order to concede that these disintegrative forces are indeed at work. The capitalist corporation does infringe on the free operation of the market, it does create a bureaucratic milieu that differs greatly from the earlier "spirit" of entrepreneurship, and the very affluence and political liberties made possible by successful capitalism have indeed brought into being the new knowledge class that is deeply antagonistic to capitalism. These developments may not be as inexorable as Schumpeter thought, but they do exist and, potentially at the very least, they are a threat to the empirical linkage between capitalism and democracy.

There is more. Probably intrinsically, the modern democratic state is also a welfare state. And the economic requirements of the welfare state have the strong propensity to increase ever more massively. To meet this ongoing clamor for revenues (even leaving aside the massive economic requirements of national defense), the Western democratic state is pushed toward massive interventions in the economy. To be sure, these interventions are incremental and generally designed not to destroy the capitalist character of the economy. But they do raise the question (posed very sharply by Hayek and others), at what point capitalism as such will have become a legal fiction. In other words, there is the process pejoratively described as "creeping socialism" and, if the argument of this chapter holds up, this leads ipso facto to the question of whether there is a point at which this ever-expanding state must cease to be democratic.[23] The very political liberties guaranteed by democracy further foster this process. As has just been argued, capitalist democracy allows the development of all sorts of intermediate or mediating institutions. That is, it creates a society marked by social and political pluralism. By their very nature, many of these institutions coalesce into political pressure groups, whose major purpose is to pressure the state to guarantee and fund their favored entitlements. The modern democratic state, by its very nature, is a gigantic mechanism handing out entitlements. Thus modern democracy favors the growth of what Mancur Olson has aptly termed "distributional coalitions."[24] Olson has argued that this phenomenon is causally related to decreasing economic productivity: The state intervenes ever more deeply in the economy in order to satisfy the demands of the "distributional coalitions"; this results in reduced economic efficiency and in reduced national wealth; as the reduced wealth makes it more difficult for the state to fund the established entitlements, the state intervenes even further in the economy. And so on. Again, one need not consider Olson's analysis as leading to the conclusion that democratic capitalism must eventually collapse in order to concede that these forces threaten the precarious balance on which this particular political-economic system depends.

It follows that the argument made here concerning the linkage between capitalism and democracy is by no means an argument for the inevitable future survival of this empirical conjunction. Both capitalism and democracy are historical constellations that have "come together" for empirically available reasons. Like other historical constellations, they have a beginning, a course of development determined by both intrinsic and extrinsic causes, and built-in forces that serve to undermine them. Neither can be indefinitely projected into the future as inevitable.

# 5

# CAPITALISM AND PERSONAL LIBERATION

WHEN PEOPLE from non-Western countries first come to the West and are asked what has impressed them most, almost invariably the answers contain a reference to Western "individualism." Needless to say, this impression is not always favorable. Very often this Western "individualism" is castigated as selfishness, lack of community, lack of binding moral standards. But at least with equal frequency the same "individualism" is celebrated as an experience of personal liberation. It is evidently possible for a single individual to have both reactions and even to have them more or less simultaneously. Very commonly this ambivalence becomes a permanent feature in the consciousness of non-Western people who have come in contact with Western civilization, regardless of whether they take up residence in a Western country or return to their home society. When large numbers of people experience a social reality in the same way, it is very likely that they perceive something important about it. Thus the experience of Western societies as "individualistic" and the concomitant ambivalence about this may be taken as containing valid perceptions.

Nor is it very difficult to describe what is meant by this term, despite the wide variety of its usage within the history of Western thought.[1] When, say, a student from India studying in America describes the latter as "individualistic," what he means by this is quite clear: In America he is by and large responded to as an individual, without reference to his family, caste, or language group. Even more importantly, when someone does *not* respond to him in this way but rather in terms of collective stereotypes of one sort or another, this is castigated by other Americans as "prejudice." He notes that Americans, compared to him, interact freely with people of widely different backgrounds, are relatively free of family allegiances, and change friends with remarkable ease. Before long he discovers that the same freedoms are available to himself. He too is encouraged to do things of which his family at home would have greatly disapproved, to choose friends from the most unlikely backgrounds, and in the end he may confirm the worst fears of his parents by marrying a woman totally outside the pale of his religion and caste. Let the question be bracketed here as to whether he is happier for all this (chances are that the answer to that question will be as ambivalent as his original perception of American "individualism"). The point is, quite simply, that his experience of American society as liberating has been a real experience, and this liberation is adequately indicated by the term "individualism."

If one tries to further clarify this term, in the light of this type of experience, one easily discovers several characteristics pertaining to it: It is not simply an idea, but it refers to processes in society and in the consciousness of individuals. Put differently, "individualism" is not just a theoretical construct (say, of philosophers, jurists, or novelists), but it refers to human conduct and to highly pretheoretical contents of human minds. Thus the person who "discovers himself" as someone distinct from his family or his caste is not simply discovering a new idea. And when, in consequence of this "self-discovery," he marries someone disapproved by his family and impure by the laws of caste, he is certainly not engaged in a theoretical exercise. Also, this "individualism," even to the extent that it *is* an idea (and, of course, it is *also* an idea), has both a cognitive and a normative aspect: It purports to make a statement about the nature of human beings—they *are* individuals, over and beyond any collective identifications. But it also proposes that there are moral consequences to this fact—human beings have rights *as* individuals, not only apart from any collectivity to which they may belong but even (indeed, especially) *against* this collectivity. Neither the cognitive nor the normative aspect is universally taken for granted; on the contrary, these notions are highly peculiar innovations of Western modernity. For most of human history, most human cultures held that an individual human being *is* his collective identifications (a member of his clan or tribe or caste, and so on), and that morality (say, *dharma* in the Hindu context) consists precisely in acting out the performances prescribed by these identifications.

Since the common term "individualism" suggests primarily an idea, it is probably better to replace it with some term less suggestive of theoretical cerebration. The meanings elucidated in the preceding paragraph are more or less aptly caught by a different term, that of *individual autonomy.*[2] Minimally, this term refers to three spheres of reality. It is, to be sure, *an idea.* Thus there is a long history of thought in Western civilization pertaining to the nature of man and to its ethical implications, eventuating in the modern Enlightenment with its emphatic and indeed revolutionary proclamation of the rights of the autonomous individual. But the term also refers to *a psychic reality*—or, if one prefers, to *a particular experience of identity:* Thus modern people, even those who have never read a serious book and are blissfully ignorant of the aforementioned history of ideas, experience themselves as autonomous individuals and make passionate moral demands on the basis of this experience. Again, if one wants to get a good sense of the range of this experience, at least in America (which, by general agreement, represents a particular profiled case of Western "individualism"), the following exercise would be useful: Make a list of all the projects commonly legitimated by the phrase "It's a free country!" Each of these projects (from changing one's religion or "sexual preference" to choosing an unconventional occupation to keeping large numbers of pets in one's basement) implies an affirmation of individual autonomy both as a fact and as a moral entitlement. Finally, however, the term also points to *a set of institutions in society*—to wit, all those institutions that make the experience of individual autonomy possible. Most obviously, these are legal and political institutions (including, of course, the institutions of political democracy discussed in the preceding chapter). Thus an American embarked on one or another of the projects just mentioned (including the project of converting his basement into a private zoo) will almost certainly mobilize both lawyers and politicians if anyone should dare to interfere with this expression of his inalienable rights. But other institutions are crucially involved as well, beginning most importantly with the institution in which these experiences of self are first socialized—namely, the sort of family that rears children who grow up to become autonomous individuals. In sum, individual autonomy and the personal liberations it implies is a reality on at least three levels—the levels of ideas, of identities, and of institutions.[3] Or, more succinctly, personal liberations require a liberating culture.[4]

Now, capitalism has been both praised and castigated for the individual autonomy that is so central to Western civilization. Today the proponents of capitalism almost always refer to its alleged linkage with individual liberty, not just in the sense of political democracy (which, as was pointed out, need not always be liberal) but precisely in the sense of allowing and fostering the free unfolding of the individual person. On the other side, critics of capitalism routinely blame it for the alleged excesses of "rampant individualism," for selfishness and personal greed, and for the disintegration of community. Both the praise and the blame go back a long way. Adam Smith saw the virtue of capitalism (even if he did not use the term) precisely in its linkage with human freedom. And Karl Marx condemned capitalism because, on the contrary, it made impossible that "leap into freedom" toward which history moved and substituted for it a false, morally debilitating individualism.[5] It is by no means only Marxists or critics on the left who criticize capitalism in these terms. The very word "individualism" was first used, in an emphatically pejorative sense, by a very conservative thinker, Joseph de Maistre, writing in France in the 1820s.[6] De Maistre thought that this individualism fatally weakens all authority. Our Hindu student, trapped in the wild freedom of an American university, would agree with him. Both are quite right. The question is whether they are also right in blaming capitalism for this aberration.

It has been a commonplace of Western social thought, at least as far back as the eighteenth century, to contrast individualistic modernity with the putative communalism of medieval Europe. Indeed, a good case could be made that many of the formative ideas of modern sociology came out of this assumed contrast, such as Ferdinand Toennies's notion of the movement from *Gemeinschaft* to *Gesellschaft* or Emile Durkheim's of the evolution from "mechanical" to "organic" solidarity. A by-now classic statement of this alleged change from medieval communalism to modern capitalist individualism is that of

Karl Polanyi, in his study of early capitalism in England: "To separate labor from other activities of life and to subject it to the laws of the market was to annihilate all organic forms of existence and to replace them by a different type of organization, an atomistic and individualistic one."[7] In other words, the theory of capitalist modernity presupposed a sort of theory of the Middle Ages as a noncapitalist, nonmodern, and, of course, nonindividualistic culture.

The irony is that, while social scientists of different ideological persuasions continue to use the Middle Ages as such a foil, medieval historians have begun to dismantle this theoretical edifice, Gothic brick by Gothic brick. Typical of this very inconvenient revisionism (inconvenient, that is, to social scientists) is the recent work of Alan Macfarlane.[8] This radically challenges the idea that England was a "peasant society" until the sixteenth century, when the great revolution was supposed to have begun. Based on his research into English village records of all sorts, Macfarlane argues that England was *not* a "peasant society" at least as far back as the mid-thirteenth century—and he is not at all sure that it was that even earlier, but his records do not go back any farther. The evidence for this revisionist view of the English Middle Ages is based on both behavior (notably in terms of land ownership and social mobility) and on what he calls "sentiments" (expressions of values and emotions). Macfarlane states categorically that English individualism was a social and psychic reality long before the advent of modernity: "Within the recorded period covered by our documents, it is not possible to find a time when an Englishman did not stand alone."[9]

Macfarlane believes that England was an exceptional case (he even contrasts it with Scotland and Ireland). This may be questioned. Recent research into the history of the family and the household suggests that similar "individualistic" patterns prevailed elsewhere in Northern and Western Europe.[10] The differences, then, are not so much a function of time as of space: Southern and Eastern Europe had different patterns all the way back into the medieval period. But, quite apart from the question of English "exceptionalism," the English case is surely the most important, since it is in England that both modern capitalism and the Industrial Revolution had their most dramatic developments. And here Macfarlane argues a total reversal of the conventional notion of causality: It is not modernity that has caused individualism, but, on the contrary, the individualistic patterns of medieval England made it possible for modernity to arise there. The roots of capitalism and of the Industrial Revolution must then be sought in medieval English structures of ownership and household, as must the roots of the modern English history of equality and liberty.

As far as Western individual autonomy is concerned, though, it did not require recent reinterpretations of the Middle Ages to come to the conclusion that it could not be simply understood as a product of modern capitalism. After all, Western civilization, when contrasted with other great civilizations, notably those of Asia, has always been perceived as having given unusual importance to the individual. When Hegel looked upon history as the history of freedom, he was right to the extent that the statement is made to refer to *Western* history. What is more, the reasons for this must almost certainly be sought in the very origins of European civilization on the two opposing littorals of the eastern Mediterranean—that is, in the world-transforming experiences of ancient Israel and ancient Greece. Here took place the two great "leaps in being," as Eric Voegelin called them, that created the civilization of the West. These two ruptures with archaic, mythologically grounded culture were certainly different from each other in very significant ways. The first was grounded in a totally new religious experience, the second in a new discovery of the power of reason. Yet each, in its own way, made for the emergence of sharply profiled individuals. The Israelite experience of the one transcendent and personal God almost inevitably created the counterpoint of the solitary human individual engaged in a strange battle of wills with this God. That is why the Hebrew Bible abounds in highly individual vignettes —think here of David, or Solomon, or Elijah—as against the mythological beings of the literature of the surrounding cultures. David's encounter with the prophet Nathan may be taken as a paradigm of this peculiarly Israelite individuation, as is the sentence pronounced by the prophet in order to convict David of the crime of murder—"Thou art the man"—which one might change slightly, while remaining within the meaning of the text, into "Thou art *a* man": That is, David cannot take refuge in the prerogatives of kingship and its communally sanctioned roles, but he must accept responsibility *as an individual* for his actions. Socrates before his accusers may serve as a paradigmatic illustration of the other, the Hellenic experience of individual autonomy, based now not on the encounter with a terrible God but on the (perhaps equally terrible) discovery of the autonomous power of human reason. And both paradigmatic figures have much earlier antecedents.

Modern historical scholarship cannot uncover the first roots of these developments. Who knows just what took place in the Sinai wilderness where a few wandering tribes made a compact with a God different from any other? And who knows what prompted those anonymous Greek artists who first shaped human figures standing free, having stepped out, so to speak, of the friezes of the earlier representations? To stay within the last image, Western history has been a continuing process of this "stepping out" of the collective bonds so aptly represented by the frieze. Seen in this light, modern individual autonomy is but a further step—no matter that its radical character would have been equally inconceivable to an ancient denizen of Jerusalem or Athens.[11] Looking at Western history in this way is very much to follow in the footsteps of Max Weber, who also looked for the origins of modernity in very ancient events, especially in ancient Israel. The much more recent events that he took to be causal factors for modernity, including the Reformation and its "Protestant ethic," were seen by him to have very deep roots in the past.

The historical debate about all these matters is far from over (if one can imagine that it will *ever* be so). Yet the foregoing considerations allow some hypothetical formulations: *The roots of individual autonomy in Western culture long antedate modern capitalism. Further, this premodern "individualism" of Western culture engendered the particular "individualism" associated with capitalism.*

The modern entrepreneur, that paragon of Western individualism, thus stands in a long lineage going back to prophets and philosophers, hermits and heroes, none of whom would have shown the slightest interest in capitalist enterprise (and, for that matter, in just about any other modern activity). None of this changes the fact, though, that this entrepreneur is a very distinctive figure. Giving up the notion that individual autonomy or "individualism" is the product *tout court* of modern capitalism by no means does away with the question of how the latter is linked to the distinctively modern versions of this phenomenon. In other words, whatever its ancient roots, what is the relationship of *modern* individual autonomy to *modern* capitalism? Any discussion of this question must delve into the culture of that class which was the historic "carrier" of capitalism, namely the bourgeoisie. Capitalism and bourgeois culture developed in tandem over the centuries of the modern era, and it can be argued that both developments were crucially related to the genesis of individual autonomy in its distinctive modern Western form.

The bourgeoisie, like any other class, had from the beginning both specific class interests and a specific class culture. The interests follow logically from the social location of a class, that is (in accordance with the definition of class discussed in an earlier chapter), from its relation to the production process of its society. It follows that class interests can be deduced, more or less rationally, from an understanding of the social location in question. Class culture is almost always a more complicated matter. A certain kind of "vulgar Marxist" analysis would deduce class culture from class interests in a direct and rational manner, and in certain cases, it should be conceded, such an analysis can be persuasive. For example, if a military aristocracy, whose power depends on armed force, develops a culture that extols heroism and other martial virtues, it is plausible to argue that this class culture is a direct and highly rational expression of class interests. However, it is quite possible that this same class adopted a style of erotic etiquette that has nothing whatever to do with martial activities. It could then be said that "it so happened" that this erotic style came to be adopted by this particular class; or, to put it differently, this element of culture happened to be "picked up" by this class in the course of its historical trajectory. An attempt to analyze this accident of history in terms of class interests would, therefore, fail. In such cases, though, there would still be an indirect but finally quite rational connection with class interests: The style of erotic etiquette, once established in this class, becomes an indicator of class affiliation. It then becomes part and parcel of the body of symbols by which members of the class can recognize each other ("sniff each other out," if you will)—and, very importantly, recognize those who do *not* belong. At that point, quite obviously, the class culture is functional in terms of the overall class interests, which certainly include some mechanisms by which the boundary between insiders and outsiders can be established. The same analytic logic pertains to the case of bourgeois culture. It would be futile to try and explain every single item of this culture in terms of the hard class interests of the bourgeoisie, yet it makes very good sense to ask which elements of the culture did relate to bourgeois class interests or, put differently, which elements of the culture helped the bourgeoisie "do its job" as a class.

It is once again useful to recall that bourgeois culture, at least from the seventeenth century and into its triumphal nineteenth century, developed in sharp and conscious distinction from the culture of the aristocracy, the earlier ruling class *against which* the bourgeoisie had to establish its ascendancy.[12] The ideal of the bourgeois gentleman *(bourgeois gentilhomme)* was deliberately counterposed to the older ideal of the gentleman, which, of course, was an aristocratic ideal. And, needless to say, the aristocracy was first amused and irritated, then annoyed, and finally profoundly threatened by this new ideal.

The bourgeois extolled rationality and an overall "methodism" of life (what Max Weber called "life discipline")—this against the aristocrat's reliance on "healthy instinct" and spontaneity. It followed that the bourgeois knew that his life-style was a matter of self-cultivation; the aristocrat always believed (falsely, one may point out) that his was the result of genetic inheritance or, as he would say, of "breeding." It also followed that the bourgeois respected learning, while the aristocrat, at least insofar as it was "book learning," despised it. The bourgeoisie was, virtually from the beginning, a literate class; the aristocracy, well into the eighteenth century, contained many individuals of noblest lineage who were proudly illiterate (after all, they could always hire a clerk to read and write for them). It goes without saying that this particular difference had enormous implications for the status of women and of children in the two classes: Bourgeois women played a key role in the education of their children, and one naturally looks differently on a child perceived as an object of cultivation as against a child perceived as the accomplished product of a long genetic process.

The bourgeois believed in the virtue of work, as against the aristocratic idealization of (genteel) leisure. The bourgeoisie differed in different countries in its style of consumption (in Protestant countries it tended toward a style of *in*conspicuous consumption), but it is a fair generalization that the deliberate display of wealth was an aristocratic rather than a bourgeois trait. The bourgeois emphasized personal responsibility ("conscience," especially in its Protestant form), while the aristocrat relied on the mandates of "honor," a much more collectivistic concept. Perhaps one could even generalize that the bourgeoisie created a culture of conscience, in counterposition to the aristocratic culture of honor; thus bourgeois culture was individuating at the core of its moral worldview. Also, the bourgeoisie went in for "clean living," both in the literal and the derived (moral) sense. This theme (epitomized in the maxim that "cleanliness is next to godliness") carried into the minutiae of daily conduct—the manner of dress and speech, habits of personal hygiene, the appearance of the home.[13] Bourgeois children were already well scrubbed and well spoken and careful not to disturb the meticulously maintained furniture, while their aristocratic contemporaries were still allowed to disport themselves in spontaneous slovenliness. Just one small vignette on this point: When Frederick the Great of Prussia built the palace of Sans Souci, which was to be a magnificent rival to Versailles, he found it necessary to post a notice on the great portico requesting the gentlemen of the court not to urinate on the stairs. And one small postscript: The great palace of Schoenbrunn, summer residence of the Habsburgs, did not have indoor toilets at the outbreak of World War I.

As the bourgeoisie established its ascendancy, its culture spread beyond itself, both upward and downward. The upward diffusion was probably effected above all by the intermarriage of aristocratic men and bourgeois women (the typical bargain by which the latter obtained a title for themselves and their children, while the former were rescued from bankruptcy by the dowry bestowed on daughters by doting bourgeois fathers). The epic of these bourgeois women and their *mission civilizatrice* among the aristocratic barbarians remains to be written.[14] The downward diffusion probably did not happen until the nineteenth century. Its major missionaries were schoolteachers and social workers, who inflicted the bourgeois virtues on the more or less recalcitrant masses of the working class. With the coming of compulsory and universal education, the triumph of bourgeois culture was complete, with only pockets of resistance remaining. Now it was working-class children who were made to wash their hands, tuck in their shirts, and, last not least, to stop "talking dirty." Once again it was women, in the main, who carried out this mission.[15]

The relationship of capitalism and cultural values (notably religious ones) was at the core of Max Weber's work, beginning with his classical essay, *The Protestant Ethic and the Spirit of Capitalism*. He argued that the Protestant Reformation, inadvertently rather than deliberately, fostered attitudes that were highly congenial to capitalist enterprise. Lutheranism began to do this by transforming the notion of "vocation" from a religious to a secular one: Whereas formerly one had a "vocation" to be a priest or a member of a monastic order, now any lawful occupation in the world should be looked upon as a "vocation" in which one must try to do God's will. But, in Weber's view, it was Calvinism and its various offspring denominations (especially in the Anglo-Saxon countries) that made a crucial contribution to the development of the "spirit of capitalism" (a phrase that, without violating Weber's intentions, might well be translated as the "economic culture of capitalism"). The Calvinist doctrine of "double predestination," holding that God has decided before all time began as to who will be saved and who will be damned, naturally led to a pervasive anxiety concerning one's own fate in this highly depressing scenario. Calvin himself and the other early Calvinist reformers (such as John Knox in Scotland and Cotton Mather in New England) believed that the Christian must learn to live with this anxiety and (awesome demand!) must serve God faithfully even if, in the end, he will be counted among the damned. Ordinary people, not surprisingly, found this to be intolerable; they wanted *to know*. And one way to find out, they thought, was to have God's blessings on their activities in the world—especially economic activities: After all, would God bless those destined for perdition? For Weber, the prototype of this vulgarized Calvinist was the Puritan businessman, who worked very hard, enjoyed himself very little if at all, and in consequence fashioned himself into a successful capitalist entrepreneur. The constellation of values and attitudes of this prototype was given the name "inner-worldly asceticism" by Weber, sharply differentiated from the "*other*-worldly asceticism" of the Catholic monk or nun: Like the Catholic monastic, the Puritan was ascetic—he led a life of self-denial and discipline; unlike the monastic, this Puritan asceticism was directed toward activities in this world and especially toward economic activities. Theologically speaking, this was an immense misunderstanding of the Calvinist view of salvation, but this in no way diminished its historical importance.

After Weber's "discovery" of inner-worldly asceticism in Western history, he set out to explore other cultures to see whether this ingredient could be discovered elsewhere. He believed that it could not and that this absence helped to explain (he never claimed that it explained everything) why modern capitalism originated in the West rather than elsewhere. Thus, for example, he argued that the asceticism of Hindu and Buddhist cultures was always other-worldly, while the definitely inner-worldly attitudes of Confucianism never developed asceticism. Neither other-worldly asceticism nor hedonistic inner-worldliness (or this-worldliness) were conducive to the "spirit" of modern capitalism; *ergo,* India and China, despite their grandiose cultural achievements, provided infertile cultural soil for capitalist economics.

It is now about eighty years since Weber's essay on Protestantism was published; it has had very great influence in several disciplines, and the debate over its central thesis continues seemingly without end. Much of the debate has to do with the question of whether Protestant morality was really as crucially important for the development of Western capitalism as Weber made it out to be. It is possible that Weber underestimated the vigor of capitalist developments in non-Protestant countries. Thus, for an important example, French Catholics did not do quite as well economically as their Protestant compatriots, but they did manage to create a bourgeois ethos of their own.[16] What is more, the capitalist success stories of Japan, beginning with the Meiji Restoration, and other East Asian societies in this century strongly suggest that Weber was mistaken in his view of the economic consequences of Confucian and Buddhist cultures. It is likely that some of Weber's *answers* must be discarded; his *questions,* about the relationship of capitalism and culture, remain as relevant as ever. Equally relevant are his insights to the effect that most historical events are unintended and unforeseen, and that it is the vulgar rather than the "high" versions of ideas that have the most historical efficacy.

One of Weber's insights that has remained widely accepted is this: The capitalist entrepreneur is a very distinctive type of human being, and not all cultures are equally congenial to the emergence of this type. What has here been called individual autonomy has been an important trait of this type, at least in the development of capitalism in the West. It would follow that cultures fostering this type have (to use an economist's term) a "comparative advantage" in successful capitalist development. As far as the history of capitalism in the West is concerned, even critics of Weber tend to agree that Protestantism provided such a "comparative advantage," especially in its Calvinist version, though these critics will then add that this cultural fringe benefit of the Reformation was *not* the condition sine qua non of successful capitalism.

Philip Greven has recently given us a vivid picture of childrearing in New England during the period (from the seventeenth to the early nineteenth century) when the Calvinist ethos was still virulently alive in that region.[17] Greven distinguished three patterns of childrearing in his materials—those of groups he called, respectively, "Evangelicals," "Moderates," and "The Genteel" (the differences between them, as indicated by the categories, were both in terms of religion and of class). The Evangelicals, of course, were the group in which Calvinism was most unbroken and who, to the end of the period studied by Greven, were mindful of Jonathan Edwards's winsome view of children: "As innocent as children seem to be to us, yet if they are out of Christ, they are not so in God's sight, but are young vipers, and are infinitely more hateful than vipers."[18] The most bloodcurdling example in Greven's study of the practical consequences of this view is an account, published in a Baptist magazine in 1831, of how one Reverend Francis Wayland (a Baptist minister and president of Brown University) disciplined his fifteen-month-old son.[19] The child, characterized as "more than unusually self-willed," had thrown a temper tantrum. He was put in his room, without food and drink, and left strictly to himself—except for periodic visits by the father, who offered him food on condition of repentant behavior. This regime was maintained for two days and the intervening night. By the afternoon of the second day, as noted by his loving father, "the tones of his voice in weeping were graver and less passionate, and had more the appearance of one bemoaning himself." The child, not surprisingly, finally surrendered and allowed himself to be held by his father, who observed that "so entirely and instantaneously were his feelings towards me changed, that he preferred me now to any of the family. As he had never done before, he moaned after me when he saw that I was going away."

This sort of socialization was known as "breaking the will" of a child, but the end result of it was, perhaps paradoxically, the emergence of peculiarly strong-willed and self-directed individuals. The psychology of this need not overly concern us here, though it begins to make sense when one reflects that the purpose of the whole exercise was not subservience of the child to the father but rather to the values (notably responsibility, discipline, and industriousness) that the father embodied. (In the case in point, the end result was eminently successful: Young Wayland became, like his father, both a Baptist minister and a college president.) The Moderates and the Genteel employed considerably less draconian methods of childrearing, but it is significant that very similar values were to be inculcated. A good case can be made that these basic values survived for a long time the demise of classical Calvinism in New England: the Puritan personality long outlived any Puritan theology. Perhaps one may even say that the American personality to this day has been the result of a universalization of the "Moderate" style, with the value of individual autonomy still squarely at the center of the socialization process.

Proposition: *Bourgeois culture in the West, especially in Protestant societies, produced a type of person strongly marked by both the value and the psychic reality of individual autonomy.*

(The important point is that here were people who not only *believed* in individual autonomy as some sort of ideal but actually experienced themselves as, indeed *were,* persons characterizable as autonomous individuals.)

If the above proposition can be sustained, many of the developments in the intellectual life of Western civilization since the bourgeois ascendancy make sense in *sociological* terms—that is, these developments can be related to specific social and institutional processes, notably those of class.[20] What we now know as modern Western culture has been crucially influenced by the values and the psychic configuration (the "psychology," if you will) of the bourgeoisie, and this goes especially for both the ideal and the empirical reality of the autonomous individual. What is conventionally described (and correctly perceived by non-Western observers) as the "excessive individualism" of modern Western culture means an intensive interest in individual subjectivity—that is, a perception of the individual as enormously complex, endowed (or perhaps afflicted) with profound depths, and because of all this of very great worth (the "sanctity of the individual," in the common American, quasi-creedal phrase). The process by which this conception of the individual has been established is the one aptly called "subjectivization" by Arnold Gehlen.[21]

The ramifications of this process are vast. Historians of modern

Western philosophy have spoken of the "turn to the subjective," referring to that great shift of interest, beginning with Descartes, from the outside world to the workings of the human mind. This would appear to be a valid characterization of what indeed has been the major focus of philosophical reflection over the centuries of the modern era. But the ramifications of "subjectivization" on the level of intellectual life go far beyond the history of philosophy. Very obviously, the modern discipline of psychology, notably all the schools derived from Freud's work, would be inconceivable without it. But equally inconceivable, in the absence of "subjectivization," would be much of modern literature. A very large segment of the latter, and especially that segment that represents the development of the novel (the modern form of literary expression par excellence), has been endlessly concerned with the complexity and the depths of the individual's subjective reality.[22] In all these cases—philosophy, psychology, literature—the "turn to the subjective" represents a replication on the intellectual or theoretical level of an underlying social and social-psychological process of "subjectivization," without which all these writers would have been engaged in an incomprehensible undertaking.

Now, there are aspects of this Gehlenian "subjectivization" that have little if anything to do with capitalism (and Gehlen himself does not discuss capitalism at all). In this as in other matters under discussion in this book, it is very important not to ascribe to capitalism processes that properly pertain to the larger phenomenon of modernity; that would be to repeat the fallacy of *pars pro toto* with which Marxism was reproached in an earlier chapter. And, for that matter, the concept of "subjectivization" covers more than individual autonomy. Thus even the *non*autonomous individual, as he has been described and decried by many culture critics (one may think here of Karen Horney's "neurotic personality of our time" or David Riesman's "other-directed man"), can be understood as a product of the global "subjectivization" process. All the same, that aspect of "subjectivization" that is the emergence of individual autonomy, as an ideal and as a social-psychological reality, *does* have its roots in bourgeois culture. Ipso facto, because this culture is the product of the class that brought capitalism into power in Western societies, the emergence of individual autonomy *is* related to capitalism and is, therefore, a necessary concern for a theory of capitalism. Other aspects of "subjectivization," which can be related to other characteristics of modern Western societies (such as technology, urbanism, or the pluralization of social life-worlds), need not be pursued here.[23]

As one looks at the historical development of bourgeois culture and at the "bourgeois self" that emerged from it, one is struck by a curious ambiguity. On the one hand, bourgeois culture liberated the individual —not only from the constraints of birth and status on which the preceding aristocratic order was based but also from the determinisms of lower-class existence (such as the "idiocy of village life," as Marx put it). The bourgeois ideal of individual autonomy embodied this liberation in tangible form. On the other hand, though, bourgeois culture imposed new disciplines on the individual, precisely in order to make him into this kind of autonomous actor. This has been the "repressive" (in Freudian terminology) or even downright tyrannical aspect of bourgeois culture (the picture of Puritan socialization presented by Philip Greven certainly suggests the adjective "tyrannical"). This ambiguity has overshadowed bourgeois culture from its beginnings. Insofar as bourgeois culture is linked to capitalism, the latter phenomenon too is marked by the same ambiguity: It liberates and oppresses at the same time. Nor is this an extraneous perception only: Both bourgeois culture and capitalism have been perceived in these ambiguous terms by large numbers of people who have never bothered their heads with theories or with intellectual analysis. This was true in Europe and North America in earlier periods of history, but the same ambiguity can be noted today in Third World countries as new populations are being swept into the "creative destruction" (Schumpeter) of capitalist modernization. Thus the vast urban agglomerations of the Third World, veritable cauldrons of modernization, are beacon lights of liberation to the masses migrating there from the hinterlands —and, at the same time, these gigantic new cities become symbols of oppression to many of the same people.

Typically, there are two responses to this ambiguity. One is conservative, backward looking, "reactionary": The new culture of individual autonomy is compared pejoratively with an older, often idealized culture in which the individual was more securely embedded in various communal solidarities. Or, alternatively, the oppressive qualities of the new culture are in the forefront of attention, and the liberation sought is precisely *from* the new culture of individual autonomy. Both responses constitute "escapes from freedom" (Erich Fromm), though, of course, with quite different social-psychological and political consequences.

The second response has frequently taken the form of what may be called "hyper-individualism."[24] Here bourgeois culture is perceived as oppressive in a particularly sharp manner and the goal is liberation from all its disciplines. The ideal is an individual free from all "repressions." In America, logically enough, this ideal has always defined itself in opposition to the Puritan heritage of American culture. Throughout Western civilization, at least since the early nineteenth century, this hyper-individualism has characterized all so-called bohemian movements among artists and intellectuals.[25]

The contrast between bourgeois and bohemian individualism has been succinctly described by César Graña in his study of nineteenth-century French literary life: "The bourgeoisie had created a society of individualized goals and, in that sense, made possible and even invited literary individualism. But while bourgeois individualism had economic and political targets and looked on the world as something concretely to be measured, governed, and used, literary individualism was wholly centered on the person as an intellectual and imaginative reality. The literary individualist, therefore, was bound to find the mundane boundaries of bourgeois effort and ambition intolerable."[26]

In the American context, with reference to Emerson, this ideal has been described as "the affirmation of the possibility of an imperial separateness and timelessness" of the individual.[27] Given this ideal, it is hardly surprising that, from its origins, it has also been marked by a strong anticapitalist animus. The new situation in the second half of this century, as we have seen earlier in our discussion of the new knowledge class, is that there are now millions of largely affluent people animated by this ideal, as against a handful of penniless writers and artists clustering in places like Montmartre. There has been a great inflation of bohemian types.

To repeat: The effects of modernization on the social psychology of individuals are wider than the effects of bourgeois culture and capitalism, and not every element of bourgeois culture can be directly related to its capitalist matrix. However, it should be possible now to isolate those elements of bourgeois culture that have been directly relevant to Western capitalist development. Put differently, it should be possible to describe the "identity kit" (as Erving Goffman called such things) of the Western type of entrepreneur.

At the core, clearly, is the "individualism" or individual autonomy just discussed. Persons shaped by this "ego ideal" are liberated from strong communal ties, directed by an internalized "conscience" (David Riesman's "inner-direction") that, if necessary, gives them the psychic resources to stand up not only against outsiders but against their own group. In very practical terms, such persons can be "enterprising," going out to seek new opportunities and try out new courses of action without the constraints of collective traditions, customs, and tabus. Further, in the process of socialization by which individual autonomy is inculcated, these persons acquire a strong sense of personal responsibility (that relentless bourgeois conscience must be steadily satisfied), and ipso facto they will be persons upon whom others (such as business partners) can rely; they are "men of their word." This clearly involves a strong discipline, precisely those traits that Max Weber called "inner-worldly asceticism." Both parts of this phrase are important. This type of individual is concerned with the affairs of this world, is pragmatic and geared to action, as against the more contemplative or sensitive values. But he is also self-denying, prepared for "delayed gratification," as against someone who immediately spends all he makes. As Weber correctly pointed out, it is this "asceticism," rather than acquisitiveness, that distinguishes the modern entrepreneur from other types of economic actors: Men have always been "greedy"; what distinguishes the capitalist is systematic and prudent "greed." Needless to say, this is a virtue directly relevant to saving and thus to capital accumulation.

Also, this is an individual marked by a high degree of rationality —not in the sense of philosophical or even scientific reason but by functional rationality, by a sober, no-nonsense, problem-solving attitude to life in general and, of course, to economic life in particular. This set of attitudes is sharply marked off against tradition and magic; both, in the mind of such an individual, are denigrated as "superstition." Put differently, what we have here is a "calculating" individual —not, or not necessarily, in the sense that all human relations are perceived in terms of some sort of economic costs/benefits analysis (that is an anticapitalist sterotype)—but rather in the sense that specific sectors of life, and notably the sector of economic activity, are approached in a rationally calculating and planning manner.[28] This individual is also animated by a strong sense of ambition and the goals of this ambition are to be reached by way of competitive achievement.[29] Finally, here is an individual who is open to innovation, as against one bound by the past. Indeed, there is a tendency within this individual to regard anything as better just because it is new. This trait, of course, is highly relevant to the "creative destruction" of capitalism.

There should be little doubt that the social-psychological gestalt just described has indeed been associated, probably importantly so, with the development of modern Western capitalism. Further, it is very plausible that individual autonomy must be seen as an important component within this overall gestalt. The matter becomes much less clear when one asks whether the gestalt in general and the component of individual autonomy in particular should be understood as intrinsically or only extrinsically linked to capitalism. Anyone familiar with modernization theory will likely hypothesize that at least some of the aforementioned features, and perhaps even individual autonomy itself, should be primarily ascribed to modernization, no matter whether the latter occurs within a capitalist or noncapitalist economy.[30] Even if one concedes that Western capitalism had its roots in a premodern Western "individualism," it does not follow from this that capitalism elsewhere must have a similar sociocultural matrix. But, conversely, even if one supposes that there could be a non-"individualistic" capitalism in non-Western society, it does not necessarily follow that Western individual autonomy could survive the demise of capitalism.

In the West itself, it can be plausibly argued that the decline of entrepreneurial "individualism," and its widespread replacement by a managerial-bureaucratic ethos, has created a threat to the survival of a capitalist economy and has made a socialist future more probable.[31] Such an argument suggests the hypothesis that, at least in the West, the linkage between capitalism and individual autonomy is an intrinsic one. On the other hand, the emergence in recent decades of a successful East Asian capitalism puts a serious question mark behind the notion that this linkage holds cross-culturally. As will be discussed in a later chapter, a number of East Asian countries, notably Japan, have developed highly successful capitalist economies on the basis of emphatically non-"individualistic" cultures, though the evidence is as yet inconclusive whether the traditional cultures of these countries are being changed in an individuating direction by these capitalist successes. And then there are the industrial socialist societies, which are characterized by a strong denial of individual autonomy both in theory and in practice. It may again be argued that their economic weaknesses can at least in part be ascribed to the way in which their polities suppress the individual and thus negate the economic benefits stemming from the creativity of individual enterprise.

Proposition: *Given the social and cultural bases of Western civilization, capitalism is the necessary but not sufficient condition for the continuing reality of individual autonomy.*

The question of what additional conditions may be necessary would lead one into a variety of areas, including the theory of democracy and various reflections about the social-psychological dynamics of major cultural institutions.

*Certain components of Western bourgeois culture, notably those of activism, rational innovativeness, and self-discipline, are prerequisites of successful capitalist development anywhere.*

This hypothesis does not imply that non-Western societies embarked on capitalist development must become culturally Westernized, but rather that, even if they reject such Westernization, they must find "functional equivalents" in their own cultural traditions that are capable of supplying the aforementioned prerequisites.

But, for the moment, let us return to the West. As Georg Simmel argued many years ago, the development of the capitalist money economy went hand in hand with the liberation of the individual— or, perhaps one could say more accurately, with a whole set of liberations of the individual.[32] In an ingenious reversal of the Marxian view of money as an instrument of "reifying" oppression, Simmel argued that the very abstraction of money (which becomes generalized in a money economy) frees the individual from the bondage of concrete social allegiances. As we have seen before, capitalism allowed individuals to purchase, with "cash on the barrel," not only commodities but status and status symbols that had previously been nonpurchasable accoutrements of noble birth or royal favor. This meant liberation, socially and economically and, eventually, politically as well. Once again the archaic Greek frieze may be taken as a paradigm of non-"individualistic" existence—the individual embedded firmly in the collective structures. Capitalism liberates the individual by letting him step out of his particular frieze—provided, of course, he acquires the money to do so. Money, with its great power of abstraction, makes it possible to convert all socially relevant phenomena (goods, services, statuses, even identities) into units of specific monetary worth. The individual too can be so converted. The American phrase "What is he worth?" illustrates this monetary conversion very graphically. Often this phrase has been cited as evidence of the "dehumanizing" effects of capitalism. Maybe so, depending on one's ideal of "humanity." But the same phrase illustrates the liberating effect of capitalism. To assess a man's "worth" in terms of the money he possesses ipso facto puts in brackets whatever "worth" he may have by way of congenital and collective ascription: Nobody chooses his parents, but anyone, in principle, can accumulate capital. And just as the capitalist market transcends old boundaries of clan, tribe, and even nation, so the individual in a capitalist society can continuously transcend the boundaries of his biographical starting point. If Simmel is right, individual autonomy developed in Western civilization in a dialectical interaction with the autonomy of market forces. The necessities of the entrepreneur become the rights of the individual, and vice versa.

The critics of capitalist modernity, both from the right and the left, have nevertheless been quite correct in claiming that this liberation from collective solidarities has been costly. The cost is precisely what Marx called "alienation" and Durkheim *"anomie."* It is the emergence of individuals severed from communal moorings, thrown upon themselves, interacting with other equally isolated and mobile individuals. If those costs are not somehow minimized, the emerging constellation is the one earlier labeled as "hyper-individualism"—which, not surprisingly, is perceived as *the* pathology of contemporary Western societies by both non-Western observers and critics of those societies from within (where we find a curious agreement between Marxists and ultra-conservatives). Durkheim, following Henry Maine, believed that a major institutional concomitant of this liberation of the individual was the proliferation of contractual relations between people.[33] A contract specifies what is required in any particular relationship between individuals: A owes B *this*, no more and no less. The contract, in other words, spells out all rights and obligations in a precise and exclusive manner. This stands out in sharp distinction from the imprecise, diffuse networks of rights and obligations that characterize most if not all premodern societies. The capitalist market, of course, could not exist without a mature development of contract law. But there is a carry-over from the market to all other human relations. One may speak, then, of the "contract society" as a hyperbole of market individualism.

It is thus not surprising that hyper-individualism today is expressed in a proliferation of contractual arrangements. All individual claims become codified in entitlements. The rise of the welfare state, of course, has greatly fostered this process. But it can also be observed throughout the private sphere. The notion of the marriage contract, as advocated by feminists, is an example of this, and so is the burgeoning movement of "children's rights." Where there are contracts, there must be lawyers. The astronomical increase in litigation in American society is, at least in part, due to its becoming more and more a "contract society." To a lesser extent, though, the same "juridification" of social life can be observed in other Western societies as well. The presupposition for all this is that older, more imprecise and diffuse rights and obligations decline. Less and less can be assumed to be "understood"; therefore, more and more must be contractually, legalistically spelled out.

Hyper-individualism and the "contract society" can properly be understood as fruits of capitalism. But their relationship to capitalism, as Daniel Bell has pointed out, constitutes a "cultural contradiction."[34] Individual enterprise, on which Western capitalism has depended, requires innovation and mobility, a freedom from collective ties. A system of entitlements, however, reconstitutes a new system of collective ties, all spelled out in contracts, codified in law and relentlessly expanded by all those lawyers. Such a system of entitlements contradicts the freedom of enterprise. Thus it is not surprising, even if it is paradoxical, that the movements of hyper-individualism and entitlement-enhancement tend to be anticapitalist in effect if not in original inspiration.

Take, for example, an American businessman, one whose success could plausibly be traced to old-fashioned individual entrepreneurship. What are his complaints? Of course he complains about the burden of innumerable laws and regulations imposed on his business by various levels of government, forcing him to expend time and energy on bureaucratic activities that are uncongenial to him—and quite possibly forcing him to hire bureaucratic types (accountants, tax lawyers, and the like) who tell him how to run his business. All of this acts as a brake on his entrepreneurship, as do various institutions of the welfare state (such as those dealing with employee rights of one kind or another). But now, in addition, he will probably complain about additional constraints deriving from seemingly ever-expanding entitlements—affirmative action constraints to safeguard entitlements based on race and gender, protections of consumers (with every one of whom he is now supposed to have complex contractual relations), protections of the environment (or, more precisely, various individuals and groups upon whose environment he is presumed to impinge), and so on. And as his luck would have it, he may come home to be accused by his wife to have violated this or that provision of their marriage contract, his children will clamor for *their* rights (perhaps, who knows, with the support of a "children's rights advocate"), and his mistress may slap him with a "palimony" suit. Such a man may be forgiven if he feels that he has misunderstood the meaning of a "free society."[35]

Now, if one imagined these "contradictions" operating without countervailing forces, one would certainly predict the collapse of capitalism along with the final demise of bourgeois culture. The empirical reality, however, is that there are countervailing forces of considerable strength in Western societies. Individual autonomy depended historically on a subtle balancing act between liberties and responsibilities, between liberation from communal ties and security within communities. This balancing act was not simply an individual feat; rather, it was grounded institutionally. Put differently, individual autonomy depended upon *balancing institutions,* whose function it was to provide the individual with a secure "base" to venture out into the turbulent public world created by capitalist modernity, as well as to mediate between the private world of *Gemeinschaft* and a public world dominated by "cold" contractual relationships. That is why these balancing institutions may also be called "mediating structures."[36]

There is no mystery as to the nature of these institutions. Most important among them were family and religion. Nor has this changed, despite all (highly premature) obituaries for these two institutions. The family in question here, of course, is not just any form of kinship pattern but the *bourgeois* family. This family was decisively legitimated and sustained by religious values, in all Western societies (though in the Protestant societies these values were particularly congenial to capitalist culture). At least in the Anglo-Saxon countries, and especially in America, these two central institutions were further assisted in their balancing and mediating functions by an array of voluntary associations, which allowed the individual to stake out a zone of liberties and at the same time provided a social base from which to sally out into the turbulent world of capitalist enterprise.[37]

What is at issue here is quite simple. The world created by capitalism is indeed a "cold" one. Liberating though it may be, it also involves the individual in countless relations with other people that are based on calculating rationality ("What is this person worth *to me*?"), superficial (the "personalizations" of salesmanship), and inevitably transient (the very dynamics of the market ensures this). Human relations too become subject to the "creative destruction" of capitalism. There is, therefore, an overriding need for a world of "warmth" to balance all this "coldness." Family, church, private friendships, and freely formed associations have provided this balance throughout the development of bourgeois culture; they continue to do so today, despite the tensions and "contradictions" of this culture. Those who overlook these balancing institutions misperceive essential qualities of these societies in question.[38]

Proposition: *Capitalism requires institutions that balance the anonymous aspects of individual autonomy with communal solidarity. Among these institutions are, above all, the family and religion.*

At least in Western societies, this requirement is reciprocal. Threats to the bourgeois family and to the religious values underpinning it are ipso facto threats to capitalism, because such threats undermine the social setting in which individuals geared toward enterprise can emerge. Conversely, the capitalist economy provides the context within which personal liberties can thrive and institutions fostering these liberties, including the bourgeois family and organized religion, can function without pervasive state controls.

In sum, liberation and "alienation" are the reverse sides of the same capitalist coin. The liberation of the individual, which capitalism in the West has fostered, must be "contained" within structures of community if it is not to liquidate itself, be it in the anarchy of hyperindividualism or in a network of ever more constraining entitlements. Capitalism depends on this balance. Progressive anarchy, with each individual out "on the make" by and for himself, undermines capitalism, because it deprives it of the fabric of trust and value without which it cannot function effectively. On the other hand, the imposition of collective controls on the individual by authoritarian or totalitarian polities, quite apart from other costs, also incurs economic costs and finally makes capitalism impossible, because such polities cannot permit that free enterprise upon which capitalism depends.

# 6

# CAPITALISM AND DEVELOPMENT

CAPITALISM has become a global phenomenon. From the enclaves of capitalist enterprise, superimposed on the centuries-old feudal and subsistence economies of Europe, it first conquered those economies and then thrust out beyond them—through trade, imperial expansion, and cultural penetration—until today it has reached virtually every part of the world not ruled by Communist regimes (and even there its outposts are to be found). Capitalism has been one of the most dynamic forces in human history, transforming one society after another, and today it has become established as an international system determining the economic fate of most of mankind and, at least indirectly, its social, political, and cultural fate, as well. Yet, evidently, contemporary capitalism has different faces in different parts of the world. Its image, everywhere, is that of the horn of plenty that heaped such immense material wealth on the countries in which it originated. This image contrasts sharply with the reality of many other countries that have become part of the international capitalist system. There the dynamism of capitalist economics coexists with perduring and, in some cases, increasing poverty. The capitalist horn of plenty is an image of hope, a promise of wealth and well-being. When the reality fails to catch up with the image, when the promise remains unfulfilled, the dream easily turns into bitterness and hatred. The dialectic of hope and disappointment is the great drama of the so-called Third World (an ambiguous but nonetheless useful shorthand term for the poorer countries of Asia, Africa, and Latin America).

The coexistence of capitalist wealth and Third World poverty is one of the most common and the most trenchant impressions of travel in those parts of the world. The promises are proclaimed most graphically by advertising—billboards and commercial media messages offering all the wonderful goods and services coming from Europe and North America. But a way of life enriched by these goods and services is also held up by mass communications that do not overtly try to sell anything—motion pictures, television programs, and illustrated stories in print media that suggest that this way of life is both real and attainable. Beneath the billboards and out of the range of television cameras swirls the everyday life of millions of people for whom grinding poverty continues to be the overwhelming reality. The traveler from the "metropolitan" countries of capitalism is shielded from this reality as long as he stays within the carefully protected envelope of international tourism, but if he is sensitive at all to what goes on around him, he understands how fragile that envelope is. He moves quickly by car or train through crowds making their way slowly on foot, in animal-drawn vehicles or on bicycles. He steps from an air-conditioned car into air-conditioned hotel lobbies or offices; they stay in the heat of the streets. He drinks purified beverages; they get their water from leaky and hygienically dubious pipelines. He uses his internationally respected credit cards; they painfully count out the few coins in their pocket. Most important, he comes and goes; they stay on.

The term "development" has been used in different senses and, of course, there have been controversies about how, if at all, it is to be used. Yet in the minds of ordinary people the meaning of the term is really quite simple: *Development is the process by which people in the poorer countries are to reach the levels of material life achieved in the countries of advanced industrial capitalism.*

Understanding the term in this commonsense manner immediately suggests two implications: Economic growth, clearly, is the condition sine qua non of development. And economic growth (be it in Gross National Product or in GNP per capita) is relatively easy to measure. But economic growth per se, equally clearly, does not yet constitute development. It is, after all, possible that only a very small minority of people benefit from this growth, while the mass of the population remains imprisoned in poverty. The commonsense notion of development necessarily implies a *distribution of the benefits of growth.*

Thus, moving from the commonsense level to a slightly more refined conceptualization, development may be defined as *a process of ongoing economic growth by which large masses of people are moved from poverty onto an improved material standard of life.*

To understand development in this way is not to brush aside the question of what nonmaterial costs this process may or may not exact —such as costs in terms of cultural meanings, human rights, or political liberties. Nor is it to imply that poor people in the Third World are only interested in improving their material living conditions. But when most people, anywhere, speak about development, *that* is what they have in mind.

A theory of capitalism must necessarily address the question whether and to what extent capitalism as an economic system favors development in the contemporary world. Put simply, the question is whether capitalism can realize the expectations contained in the notion of development. As soon as one asks this question, one must recall that, of course, all the countries that today constitute the "metropolis" of advanced industrial capitalism were once poor, "underdeveloped." In terms of all the obvious indicators of poverty—infant mortality, life expectancy, caloric intake, housing conditions, standards of education and health care, and, last not least, cash income—every single country of Europe and North America was a "Third World" country two hundred years ago, and several were very poor indeed much more recently. Capitalist history in these countries, as discussed in earlier chapters of this book, has been a story of development in precisely the sense just suggested. If so, the question about capitalism and development can be further refined: *Is it plausible to assume that the story of development as it took place in Europe and North America will repeat itself in the poor countries of the Third World?* If the assumption holds, the outlook, of course, is optimistic. It makes sense then to look at, say, India today through the eyes of England in the earlier days of the Industrial Revolution, with the prospect being that India farther down the road will increasingly resemble contemporary England in its material standards of life (if not also in other ways). One will then ask what *stage* of development any particular country is in at any given point in time, with the implication that underdevelopment, however painful at the moment, is a temporary and even necessary condition in a predictably upswing process.[1]

It is fair to say that the optimistic assumption generally prevailed when social scientists first turned their attention to the issue of Third World development in the years following World War II, especially in the 1950s and early 1960s. A paradigmatic and at the time very influential statement of this position was that by W. W. Rostow.[2] Britain is here presented as the first society experiencing modern economic growth (no one, of course, will question that), but it is also presented as the exemplar that other societies will have to follow. These other societies will pass through the same stages (though, of course, within different time spans). It would be wrong to read into Rostow the notion that this sequence of stages is rigidly determined, or that it cannot be modified by policies or events. All the same, in his view it makes very good sense indeed to look at any given Third World society today and place it on a trajectory corresponding to the history of modern Britain. First is the stage of "traditional society," covering a great variety of economic and sociopolitical cases, all of them having one all-important characteristic in common—no or very limited growth. Rostow was particularly interested in the preconditions for development from this first stage; in Europe, these were both technological and sociopolitical; in other parts of the world, the conditions were largely brought about by European intrusions. If the preconditions for development are present, there occurs the second stage of the "transitional society"—the condition of a large number of Third World societies when Rostow was writing. The third stage is that of "take-off," when modern economic forces come to dominate a society and growth becomes a sustained process. The fourth stage is that of "maturity," as attained by the advanced industrial societies of the West. Rostow believed that this stage is generally reached after some sixty years following take-off, related to what he called the "powerful arithmetic of compound interest" (in other words, to the dynamics of capital accumulation) and to the capacity to absorb modern technology.

The general assumption of Rostow's approach was shared by a much larger group of authors.[3] Later on this approach was castigated as ethnocentric, as reflecting a Western bias. That charge is quite unfair.

The approach was not so much ethnocentric as optimistic: It assumed that the basic course of development was set and that, if due attention is paid to its inherent logic, the outlook for all the developing countries is bright. It is worth noting that this optimistic viewpoint was not limited to academia but also animated those concerned with making policy in the Western democracies. Thus, for example, the Alliance for Progress, by which the United States was to assist Latin America on the road of development, was very much inspired by these optimistic ideas. And while many later criticisms of this approach had merit, it is important not to overlook the positive sides of the approach. It was very broad, combining an attention to economics with an awareness of social, political, and cultural factors. It had a strong sense of history. And it provided a theoretical framework for comparing societies with each other. A more balanced criticism of these authors would be that they too easily identified modernization with development, assuming that the technological and economic transformations of modernity led in a more or less natural way to certain desired ends, including the important end of material standards comparable to those of the affluent West. Perhaps it would already then have been possible to state the relation of modernization and development as a *hypothesis* rather than some sort of law of history, in which case it would have been (as it still might be today) a hypothesis for which a pretty good case could be made.

Beginning with the late 1960s, this approach to development came under increasing fire and was increasingly replaced by viewpoints much less optimistic about the prospects of the Third World within the international capitalist system. Both within Western academia and within the portion of the Western policy community concerned with these issues, not to mention Third World intellectual and political elites, an outlook much farther to the "left" came to dominance in a surprisingly short period of time. Today it has become the conventional position in sizable parts of the intellectual world, and it requires close attention. It should be pointed out, though, that the optimistic outlook sketched above was subjected to earlier criticisms, most of them precisely caused by skepticism about its optimistic forecasts.[4]

The new position, when confronted with the question of whether contemporary Third World societies can be expected to run through the "stages" experienced by England and other Western capitalist economies, supplies a clear reply: *No.* Today this position is often designated as "dependency theory" (more on this in a moment). It is not a monolithic approach, there are different strands within it, and not all can be called Marxist or even socialist in orientation. Yet its basic conceptual apparatus does derive from Marxism, as does its strongly anticapitalist animus.

The most important historical source of this new position is Lenin's theory of imperialism—a work of rather mediocre and unoriginal quality intellectually, which nevertheless has had vast influence since its original publication in the midst of World War I.[5] Lenin, heavily influenced by earlier writers (especially John Hobson and Rudolf Hilferding), maintained that imperialism is the *necessary* expression of capitalism at an advanced stage of its history, specifically at the stage of "monopoly capitalism"—when market competition has supposedly been largely replaced by large, powerful cartels. Two different reasons were given for this alleged necessity by Marxist thinkers who influenced Lenin—the search for markets and the search for investment opportunities for "surplus capital."[6] Both in turn were the result of the decline of competition due to the concentration of capital in giant corporations. Either the domestic market for goods or for financial investment then dries up, and, inevitably, capitalists have to look abroad for new markets and/or investment opportunities. Imperialism is the political-military instrument to secure these economic goals. Since Marxism has always regarded the state as the executive arm of the capitalist class, it was easy, within the Marxist frame of reference, to understand the colonial expansion of the European states as a direct expression of economic necessities: The establishment of the Western colonial empires was a direct consequence of the "contradictions" of advanced Western capitalism.

It may be observed in passing that the Leninist interpretation of imperialism, over and beyond its supplying a Marxist interpretation of Western colonial expansion, also helped to solve two vexing problems of Marxist theory. One, alluded to in an earlier chapter of this book, was the problem posed by the unfortunate fact that Marx's immiseration thesis failed in its prediction concerning the Western working class: Far from becoming progressively impoverished, the "proletariat" of the advanced capitalist societies became progressively better-off. The immiseration thesis could now, as it were, be exported: The peoples of the colonial countries could be perceived as an "external proletariat" (the phrase was coined by Rosa Luxemburg), and it was this latter vast population that could now be seen as subject to the immiseration process. The struggle between capitalist class and proletariat could then be reinterpreted as a struggle between colonizers and colonized, with the working classes of the imperialist countries being co-opted by their respective bourgeoisies. Thus the immiseration thesis, so central to the Marxian drama of revolutionary redemption, is saved by being globalized. And two, the new theory of imperialism helped to assuage the disappointment that, again contrary to Marx's prediction, the working classes of Western Europe and North America became not more, but less revolutionary, and thus increasingly unpromising recruitment fields for the Marxist revolutionary movements. It now became possible to argue that this was only to be expected (the rise of Marxist revisionism, of social democracy, and of the labor unions, and the concomitant establishment of the modern welfare state, being all part and parcel of the great co-optation process). Most important, this theory justified the strategy, absolutely essential for Lenin, of working for revolution on the periphery rather than in the center of the capitalist world. Thus the theory of imperialism first legitimated the Bolshevik revolution in Russia, and later on (to this day) the idea that the future of socialism lies in the Third World.[7] Thus it is not surprising that this theory has loomed very large in Marxist thought over the last half-century or so.

The thesis of imperialism as a necessary consequence of advanced (or, as Marxists prefer to say, "late") capitalism has been a matter of intense discussion among Marxists of various orientations.[8] The different modifications of the thesis within the Marxist camp need not be pursued here. Non-Marxist economists have questioned the thesis on various grounds.[9] Most important, they have questioned the interpretation of the dynamics of capital accumulation on which the imperialist necessity is allegedly based: It is not at all clear that advanced capitalism faces an insurmountable problem either in terms of finding domestic markets for manufacturing goods or domestic investment opportunities. Also, the thesis has been questioned on strictly historical grounds, because the actual development of modern imperialism cannot be adequately explained in terms of economic interests only but rather must be explained in a combination of these with economically "irrational" motives of national power and national myth.[10] Indeed, historians now disagree on whether the great colonial empires, such as those of Britain and France, constituted economic assets or economic liabilities in the aggregate. In other words, it is possible that, over time at least, the colonial empires cost the "mother countries" more than they were worth in terms of economic advantage.

But another question is more important for the present argument —namely, the question of the effects of "metropolitan" capitalist penetration of societies on the "periphery": Whatever may have been the driving forces and the results of imperial expansion in the countries of advanced capitalism in the West, what have been the consequences in the Third World societies which have been the targets of this expansion? This has been the focus of so-called dependency theory. Its central thesis has been that the development of the periphery has been distorted or even prevented by this penetration ("dominance") by the forces of international capitalism. In exploring this thesis, it is important to distinguish the *facts* of "dependency" from the *alleged nefarious consequences* of this condition. Few observers would question that something reasonably called "dependency" comes about when very powerful economies impinge on much weaker ones: When, say, United States corporations powerfully intrude into a small Central American country, it is plausible to say that the latter comes to be "dependent" on the United States economy. But is this dependent condition necessarily bad for the people of the Central American country and specifically for their chances of development?

Dependency theorists have answered this question affirmatively, for several reasons: Decisions on national economic policy are now made outside the country and for the benefit of others. The national economy is "distorted," because its course is dictated by external needs and not by its indigenous logic. National enterprise is smothered, often to the point of "industrial infanticide"—that is, domestic industrial development is arrested in the interest of the foreign enterprises dominating the national economy. Last not least, the indigenous population is pauperized (immiserated), with the exception of the so-called comprador class—the local groups who become agents of foreign enterprise.[11] This view of the effects of capitalist penetration has been brilliantly summed up in a phrase coined by Andre Gunder Frank, himself an important dependency theorist—the "development of underdevelopment."[12] In other words, the underdevelopment of the Third World is not a condition preceding the advent of international capitalism in those countries but rather is a condition *brought about* by this international capitalism, and necessarily so.[13]

In terms of current discussions of these issues, dependency theory is more important than the older Leninist theory of imperialism, which (and even then with modifications) tends to be limited to the more orthodox Marxists. This should not obscure the fact that it supplied the intellectual presuppositions even for those versions of contemporary dependency theory that disavow the designation of Marxist. The root presuppositions are: that the capitalist system has a built-in need to penetrate, by whatever means necessary, the less developed countries; and that the consequences of this penetration are damaging to the development of these countries. The transition from the old to the new theory of imperialism took place, of course, in a greatly changed world. Lenin wrote his influential essay at a time when, despite the war, the great European colonial empires were fully intact; indeed, at the conclusion of that war, some of the colonies simply changed hands. By contrast, dependency theory originated at a time when these empires had been almost completely dismantled and replaced by a large number of independent states. If the object of the old theory was colonialism, that of the new came to be "neocolonialism." The term itself points to the great disappointment that political independence was not necessarily equivalent to economic independence, or even economic development in a dependent position. The disappointment in events in what was soon to be called the Third World then happened to coincide in the late 1960s and early 1970s with the strong revival of neo-Marxism among Western intellectuals. For reasons that have very little if anything to do with what was happening in Third World countries, the cause of the Third World became an important rallying point for significant numbers of Western intellectuals.[14]

Yet dependency theory had its most important protagonists not in the newly independent countries of Asia and Africa but rather in Latin America.[15] The 1950s had been a period of high hopes in Latin America. There had been the widespread expectation that the major countries in the region (notably Brazil, Argentina, and Mexico) were ready for successful "take-off." Instead, what occurred were mounting economic, social, and political problems. The concept of "dependency" arose *not* from Marxist dogma but from concrete attempts to understand specific situations. This is very much the case with the two major figures in the emerging theory, the Brazilian Fernando Henrique Cardoso and the Mexican Pablo González Casanova.[16] Neither was a Marxist. But both were increasingly convinced that the development theories of the 1950s (that now came to be pejoratively called "developmentalism," or *desarrollismo*) were not adequate in explaining what was happening. Of the two authors, Cardoso was the more important —more than anyone else the "father" of dependency theory and with an influence far beyond Latin America itself.

Cardoso insisted that one cannot understand the Latin American situation on economic grounds alone nor as a replication of European and North American development. Rather, one must undertake concrete analyses of political interest groups, both in their internal workings and in relation to external forces (that is, the forces of the international capitalist system as they impinged, not always in the same way, on Latin American countries). The latter analysis resolved itself into an understanding of the interrelation of international business (especially the new multinational corporations), foreign governments, and local classes or interest groups. Very important in all of this was a consistently cross-national perspective (until then, most Latin American social scientists had dealt with their own countries in isolation) and a brilliantly executed combination of economic, political, and sociological (especially class) analyses.

Cardoso always put his conclusions in reasoned, even moderate language, and distanced himself from the strident vulgarizations to which his approach was soon subjected.[17] But such are the hazards of the theoretical life. Dependency theory continues to exist in more modulated forms. It has also become popular internationally in more radical and explicitly Marxist forms.[18] It is to date the subject of intense study and discussion in "left" circles in Europe and the United States. In Europe, where there has never been too much interest in Latin America, it came to be applied in Marxist analyses of other Third World regions.[19] In the United States it linked up with the "world systems" approach of Immanuel Wallerstein and others (discussed earlier in this book). It also came to be associated with the criticisms of multinational corporations, which, of course, are major villains in this view of the world.[20] Thus the Spanish term *"dependencia"* has become a password among radical students as far away from Hispanic culture as the universities of India, Indonesia, and South Korea (a professor in Seoul has recently written of *"dependencia* fever" among his students). Even among explicitly nonradical economists and other development experts, who are frustrated by the failures of various development policies, two key presuppositions of dependency theory have gained considerable credence: that capitalism makes Third World countries dependent and that it perpetuates their poverty. Both in its moderate and its Marxist versions, dependency theory has become an important element of what by now can be called a "Third World ideology," routinely expressed by spokesmen of the so-called Group of Seventy-seven (the caucus of less developed countries) within the United Nations system, where it has also been useful in undergirding the demand for a "New International Economic Order."[21] A central element in all of this is that the root causes of underdevelopment are sought *outside* the national societies, in the workings of the international capitalist system.

It is questionable to what extent even the Latin American situation can be adequately interpreted in the dependency perspective.[22] The focus here will be on the more general question of the adequacy of this approach in understanding the relation of capitalism to development. In terms of the first overall presupposition of the theory, that capitalism has an intrinsic need to expand into the less developed countries, it is doubted by most economists not affiliated with the "left."[23] The Third World continues to be important for the "metropolitan" economies—for markets, investment opportunities, and, last not least, raw materials—but these economies are much more geared to each other than to the "periphery." One may leave aside the question of raw materials (especially oil), since this question occupies a very minor place in dependency theory—and, if it did, would have to be dealt with as a *reverse* dependency. Apart from raw materials, the possibility that the entire Third World might become economically inaccessible would be less dislocating to, say, the United States than the inaccessibility of any one of the other major advanced capitalist societies. For the present argument, as already observed, another presupposition of the theory is more important—to wit, that capitalism is bad for development in Third World countries. This presupposition is very dubious, to say the least. The presupposition can be broken down into two parts—that capitalist penetration was responsible for underdevelopment in the *past* and that it is so in the *present*. The second part of the presupposition will be discussed for the rest of this chapter, and, needless to say, it is theoretically possible that there has been a change in the effects of capitalist penetration as between past and present.

Yet, even limiting oneself to the past, the presupposition is dubious.[24] It may be stipulated that in some specific cases the effects of capitalist penetration on the "periphery" have indeed been nefarious. For example, there is a good case to be made that it was deliberate British policy to throttle the Indian textiles industry because the Indian market was desired for British textiles.[25] And even in the postcolonial situation, similar cases can be made, for example for the operation of some United States corporations in Central America or for the role of French capital in West Africa. But to argue that, *in the aggregate,* capitalist penetration has done economic harm to Third World countries is very difficult indeed. Taking Africa as an important test area, countries *least* affected by colonialism (such as Ethiopia) are in the worst economic condition, while countries *most* affected by it (such as Kenya) are in a much better state. Even in cases where one might plausibly speak of colonial "exploitation," the colonial regimes left behind physical infrastructures (such as railroads and highways) and social institutions (such as a modern bureaucracy and an educational system) that can only be regarded as assets for development in the postcolonial period. And even if the argument could be made (which it probably cannot) that the wealth of the erstwhile colonial powers (notably Britain, France, and the Netherlands) can be explained, at least in part, by "exploitation" of the colonies, such explanation fails completely for some of the major industrial countries whose colonial history is comparatively insignificant (notably the United States, Germany, and Japan). Finally, one should observe that, even if dependency were an economically debilitating condition, this would not be in itself an indictment of capitalism: If the international capitalist system contains all sorts of "inequalities," there is no reason whatever to believe that an international socialist system would be any more egalitarian; indeed, this point need not be made speculatively, since the Soviet Union and its industrialized allies in Europe have indeed established such an international socialist system, in which both "inequality" and "dependency" are important features.

In the manner in which dependency theory is used today, there are two major actors to whom reference is frequently made—the multinational corporations and Third World governments. The overall bias is that the actions of the former are inimical to development, while the latter are to be fostered as agents of development. Again, one should not be one-sided or doctrinaire on this subject: There *are* multinational corporations whose actions inhibit development, and there *are* Third World governments whose policies are conducive to development. In the aggregate, however, the reverse formulation is more persuasive. Multinational corporations, whatever sins they may have committed here and there, are the most important vehicles for the transfer of capital and technology to Third World countries, for training of indigenous personnel in modern economic occupations, and, last not least, for reliable tax revenues into Third World treasuries.[26] On the other hand, a much better argument can be made that a large number of Third World governments are *obstacles* to development.[27] Often their policies have the direct effect of perpetuating underdevelopment—such as economically destructive socialist experiments, regulations that favor urban populations by artificially depressing farm prices and thus discourage agricultural development, persecution of economically productive minorities (such as the Indians in East Africa or the Chinese in Southeast Asia), and policies that discourage enterprise and international trade through excessive regulation and licensing. At other times, even if government policies are not directly inimical to development, the latter is hindered by widespread government ineffectiveness (what Gunnar Myrdal has aptly termed the "soft state") and by pervasive corruption (P. T. Bauer has coined the word "kleptocracy" for this, alas, common feature of many Third World governments). Thus both the antimultinational and the statist biases of dependency theory as currently used have very little empirical justification.[28]

Dependency theory today, both in its more moderate and its more radical version, has become part of a vague but nonetheless potent ideology of "Third Worldism."[29] This has its advocates among intellectuals all over the world, including those employed in elite academic institutions in Western countries. It is, for obvious reasons, a particularly attractive ideology for Third World politicians, government officials, and intellectuals. Its statist bias directly serves the vested interests of political elites. Beyond those vested interests, however, it serves a very useful psychological function: If the roots of under-development are to be sought *outside* one's own society, one is spared often painful (and personally embarrassing) self-examination and one is provided with very convenient external scapegoats. This combina-tion of political and psychological motives is sufficient to explain the popularity of this viewpoint in the Third World; its acceptance by many intellectuals in Western countries requires more complex explanations.[30]

But back to the presupposition that capitalism has been bad for development in the Third World: The empirical basis for this allega-tion is generally very shaky. There is one very important case, though, which undermines the presupposition in a decisive manner. *The devel-opment of the capitalist societies of East Asia is the most important empirical falsification of dependency theory.*

These societies, which constitute a "second case" of modern indus-trial capitalism, will be looked at in greater detail in the next chapter. But their place in the present argument should be stated now. Here are the preeminent "success stories" of development since World War II—Japan, of course, as the most significant case, but followed now by the so-called Four Little Dragons (South Korea, Taiwan, Hong Kong, and Singapore) and now possibly being followed by at least some of the other Southeast Asian countries (notably Thailand, Malaysia, and Indonesia). These are not only "success stories" in terms of economic growth (which, of course, has been phenomenal over a sustained period of time) but also in terms of development precisely in the aforementioned sense—with masses of people being lifted from poverty into a comfortable and in places highly affluent standard of life, with the virtual eradication of the common indicators of Third World underdevelopment, and with comparatively egalitarian income and wealth distributions. None of this makes any sense whatever in terms of dependency theory. Japan alone makes this point. If ever there was a victim of imperialism, it was Japan. Its first great miracle of development took place during the Meiji period—the direct result of an act of naked imperialist aggression, when Commodore Perry of the United States Navy steamed into Tokyo Bay in 1853 and, at gunpoint, forced the opening of Japan to Western capitalist penetration. The second miracle, of course, took place after World War II—following devastating military defeat at the hands of the Western powers, after two atomic bombs had been dropped on the country, and (an epitome of "neocolonialism") under American military occupation. The dramatic development of the Four Little Dragons is equally inexplicable in dependency-theory terms. All four could be cited as textbook cases of "neocolonial" dominance, by the United States and Britain—and one, Hong Kong, remains under colonial rule to this day.

If these were some small countries with little international importance, one might dismiss them as special cases of no theoretical significance. This is not feasible here. Together they contain large populations and they have made a great difference in the world economy. And one, Japan, has become one of the major industrial powers in the contemporary world, directly competing in many areas with the old "metropolitan" countries of the West. The theoretical significance of East Asia for the immediate argument can be simply stated: One cannot go on doing dependency theory while ignoring this region of the world, but its development cannot be explained from within the theory.[31]

If the explanations of the relation between capitalism and development of both the older and the more recent imperialism theorists must be rejected, a general counterproposition should now be formulated. Its empirical plausibility will be argued for the rest of this chapter.

Proposition: *The inclusion of a Third World country within the international capitalist system tends to favor its development.*

Again, of course, this proposition is to be taken as hypothetical. What is good for the goose of dependency theory must be good for the gander of this contrary position: A few less important cases will not falsify the hypothesis, but it could not be maintained if it fails to hold for important regions in the world. Now, it should be stressed that the hypothesis does *not* imply that inclusion within the global capitalist system guarantees development, let alone that such development has already been achieved wherever the inclusion has occurred. Either implication would be patently absurd. Rather, it is implied that the inclusion releases forces that, in tendency, foster development. Quite deliberately, the issue of dependency is brushed aside here. In other words, it is implied that the degree of dependency of a national economy is not relevant to the question of development. This is not to prejudge the question of whether there may be *nondevelopmental* costs to dependency—in terms of political weakness, cultural deterioration, or plain frustrations of national pride. Such costs may be important, even decisive, in some cases. But their discussion does not belong here, not only because they are irrelevant to the issue of development but also because they have nothing to do with the issue of capitalism. Thus, for example, the question here is not whether United States economic power in Latin America makes this or that country in the region a pawn of foreign power politics or whether it serves to subvert Hispanic culture or whether it is just a great annoyance to have all those *gringos* marching about the place. The question is, very sharply, whether this capitalist economic power, in the aggregate if not in all individual instances, tends to improve the material lot of most of the people. The hypothesis is to the effect that it does.[32]

There is widespread agreement today, from Chile to China, that an economy allowing market forces the fullest feasible sway will perform better than one in which all decisions are centrally administered. The term "perform" here, it should be noted, refers to the strictly *economic* processes, notably growth, productivity, and innovativeness within the economy proper. In other words, people might share in this agreement and nevertheless favor a limitation (or even an elimination) of market mechanisms for noneconomic reasons, be it for the sake of a vision of community, of equality or equity, or of political purposes. Antagonism to market forces because of communitarian ideals or because of political interests need not be discussed at this point, but a very important issue for the present argument is whether an economy dominated by the logic of the market provides improved material benefits to all and whether it does so with some measure of "distributive justice."

This issue, of course, was discussed in some detail earlier with regard to the capitalist societies of the West; what must be discussed now is whether the "horn of plenty" of capitalist economics in the West continues to manifest itself in the Third World today. The term "capitalism," of course, is shunned by many who sing the praises of market mechanisms; one may only mention here the ingenious (or, possibly, disingenuous) ways in which the current leadership in China describes its radical modifications of a socialist economy in language full of Marxist terminology and conceptualizations. This is very interesting, but there is no need to use such circumlocutions here. In fidelity to the earlier definition of capitalism precisely in terms of market mechanisms, it is appropriate to formulate an explicit hypothesis here despite the aforementioned widespread agreement (after all, the agreement may fall apart in the future or, more important, new evidence about the economic performance of socialist systems might emerge).

Proposition: *The superior productive power of capitalism, as manifested in the advanced industrial countries of the West, continues to manifest itself today wherever the global capitalist system has intruded.*

Some words of caution are necessary here. It would be a serious error to understand this proposition as implying that *only* capitalism can generate economic growth. In recent decades the overall world economy has grown phenomenally and virtually *all* countries have registered positive economic growth.[33] The latter statement definitely includes the less developed countries (LDCs) as a group. Thus between 1955 and 1970 the aggregate of these LDCs experienced 5.4 percent growth in Gross National Product and 3.1 percent in GNP per capita; between 1970 and 1980 the LDCs registered 5.3 percent growth in GNP and, once again, 3.1 percent growth in GNP per capita (the major reason for the difference between GNP growth and growth in GNP per capita, of course, is population growth). Economic growth of similar proportions continued in the early 1980s, despite a worldwide recession, and the growth of the LDCs was, in many individual countries, greater than the growth of Western economies. From 1955 to 1980 world output (that is, the sum total of all countries' GNPs) tripled in real terms (that is, measured in constant dollars, so as to control for inflation). In the same quarter-century world GNP per capita doubled, despite the fact that the world population rose from about 2.8 to about 4.4 billion.

This is an awesome spectacle. There is no way in which capitalism alone can be credited with it. Modern technology as such, operating in virtually any economic system, will result in a vast increase in productive power and thus necessarily in increased economic growth. Indeed, one may argue that any country that has access even to a modicum of modern technology and nevertheless *fails* to grow must strain considerably to do so: Nongrowth represents a sort of political achievement.[34] The argument, then, is *not* that only capitalism can provide economic growth. Rather, it is that capitalism provides economic growth on a more secure and sustained basis and also that the economic performance of capitalism has a much more dynamic quality in terms of innovation and versatility. And the reasons for this, again, are not mysterious at all. They all go back to the unique capacity of the market in stimulating and rationalizing economic activity.

All the same, one should concede to the critics of capitalism that economic growth per se, or for that matter any other indicator of economic performance by itself (including the aspects of innovation and versatility), should not be identified with development. On this, the critics of *desarrollismo,* or "growthmanship," were quite correct: It is possible to have a highly dynamic economy operating amid widespread misery. For example, an observer in the 1970s described Brazil as a Sweden superimposed on an India—a modern, highly technologized, and affluent sector coexisting in the same country with some of the worst poverty to be found in the world. This is why the two equity questions must be addressed in assessing the relation between capitalism and development: How are the living standards of the mass of the population affected by the economic growth? And how are the benefits of this growth distributed? As was detailed earlier, the two questions are by no means the same. The first refers to absolute standards of material life, the second to income distribution.

An awkward but useful phrase has been introduced into the development discussion by Roman Catholic theologians—the "preferential option for the poor." The phrase denotes a moral principle, to the effect that the test of any human society should be its treatment of the poorest groups in the population. The religious and ethical rationale for this principle is beyond the present scope, but it is very useful in providing a yardstick for assessing development. If development means anything beyond the mechanical adding-up of economic indicators, it means that the poor are better-off than they were before—perhaps not *all* the poor, but *most* of the poor. In this sense, the "preferential option for the poor" can readily be translated from the language of Christian ethics to that of the social sciences. It is precisely in this sense that the equity questions are considered here.

An important element of "Third Worldism" is the opinion that the condition of the poor in the less developed countries is deteriorating.[35] This view is closely linked to the notion of a "widening gap" between developed and developing countries. Once again, there are ideological aspects to this matter. There are also methodological problems of a severe sort. There are huge discrepancies in data on poverty supplied by different national governments and international organizations and even between different branches of both of these.[36] If one reflects that there have been intense debates over the scope and nature of poverty in the United States and other Western democracies in recent decades, it becomes quickly evident that it is very naive indeed to look at all data coming from Third World countries as a reliable basis for analysis. National governments in these countries frequently collect data in a very inefficient and incomplete manner, and they often lack the statistical machinery and techniques to collate the data they do collect. To this must be added the simple fact that a considerable number of governments (especially, but not only, dictatorial ones) will sometimes deliberately distort data on the condition of their people, making it seem better or worse than it is, depending on what policy objectives are to be served. As to international organizations (the World Bank is an important exception), their usual practice is simply to accept the data supplied by national governments.

Some years ago an American visitor was led through the statistical department of an agriculture ministry in a Third World country. His guide, an employee of the department, was showing a row of brand-new computers, just received from the development aid program of a Western country. Data were being busily fed into the computers by a small army of technicians, and office messengers picked up huge piles of printouts, evidently carrying them off to the higher reaches of the department where policy was being made. The visitor said that he was impressed. The guide smiled and commented, "We have the newest machines here. They look as if they came from the twenty-first century. That's just as well, since the data are pure science fiction." This simple but commonly overlooked fact also accounts for the typically different view of the condition of the people from the capital (where the statistical departments are located) and from observers in the field. Typically, the former view is more pessimistic than the latter. Richard Critchfield, who has made it his life work to study village life in different parts of the world, has observed that he has repeatedly found dramatic improvements in the condition of peasants that were unregistered (and disbelieved) by analysts in the capital cities. Thus he concludes a recent book summing up his field researches as follows: "There is a much happier ending than I ever expected to write when I set out ten years ago. Then, I had a squishy and conventional sense of apocalypse. . . . I've since found that cheery inconsequence wears better."[37]

What can one do about this, apart from being skeptical about the "squishy sense of apocalypse" that continues to be conventional in a sizable segment of the community of development experts? Nick Eberstadt, a demographer, has suggested that a study of the poor ought to focus on the "physiology" of development—that is, on basic demographic changes derived from census data rather than on the usual economic data.[38] The reason is that demographic census data are at least *relatively* reliable if compared with, for example, data on the average income of the poor. Specifically, data on life expectancy and infant mortality allow some reasonably confident deductions on the condition of the people to whom the data refer. Also, there is some reason to believe that these raw census data, if available at all, are less likely to be deliberately distorted than economic data. This is particularly true of income data. As Bauer has pointed out, a decline in mortality appears as a *negative* economic indicator, since, obviously, with every person added the per capita figure derived from dividing GNP by population will become smaller: "The birth of a child immediately reduced income per head within the family and also that in the country as a whole. But do the parents feel worse off? Would they feel better off if they would have no children or if some of them died?"[39]

Eberstadt compared capitalist and socialist societies in the Third World in terms of these basic demographic data. As far as life expectancy and infant mortality are concerned (the latter typically determining the former), the main fact is these have improved virtually everywhere. The reason for this, again, lies with modernization as such rather than with any particular socioeconomic system. Elementary hygiene, better nutrition, access to even rudimentary methods of modern child care and medicine, water purification—these factors can have a dramatic impact on demographic data even in the very short run, and this has indeed been the case in most less developed countries. If, however, one wishes to explore how the poor fare under different socioeconomic systems, one must see whether a particular system falls above or below the general rising curve of demographic improvement. As to life expectancy (the demographic measure par excellence), there is no evidence that the socialist countries do better. For example, life expectancy in Cuba *declined* in the immediate postrevolutionary period, 1960–69; since then, there has been improvement but less so than in other Caribbean countries. Eberstadt believes that postrevolutionary improvement in life expectancy could have been projected from the prerevolutionary data: Cuba was one of the healthiest countries in the region in the 1950s; the revolution retarded its health development briefly (for whatever reasons), and then allowed the curve to continue its upward secular trend. This is not in itself a bad record, but it hardly substantiates the extravagant claims for what the revolution is supposed to have done for the health of the poor. For another (and much more important example), China clearly suffered terrible demographic costs in the wake of the so-called Great Leap after 1958; since then, life expectancy has improved—in a development very similar to that of India (not to mention the vastly superior performance of Taiwan and the other capitalist societies of East Asia). For a final example, if one compares the two Koreas, the record on life expectancy in the South is better, despite the better starting point of the North at the time the country was divided.

In any discussion of the condition of the poor in the Third World, the question of hunger looms very large indeed. Eberstadt argues plausibly that infant mortality is the best available indicator of the presence of hunger, since young children are its most immediate and numerous victims. There has been a sharp decline in infant mortality in some less developed countries (for example, Mexico, the Philippines, and Thailand). Even India and Indonesia (hardly top performers in demographic improvement) have experienced a drop of more than half since the 1950s. The data for Cuba, not surprisingly, reflect the abovementioned data on life expectancy—after a hiatus in the immediate aftermath of the revolution, Cuba continued to improve its record— but no more so than a number of other countries in the Caribbean (for instance, Jamaica) and no more so than could have been projected from prerevolutionary trends. China, as is now known (and admitted by the Chinese government), suffered massive famines in the early 1960s, as a direct consequence of the follies of Maoist agrarian policy. As against this, there has been an agricultural miracle in India, which can be directly related not only to the so-called Green Revolution (a technological event not necessarily linked to any particular socioeconomic system) but to the fact that Indian agriculture has remained organized as an almost purely capitalist enterprise in sharp distinction to the industrial sectors on the Indian economy.[40] One of the most dramatic changes in China in recent years has been the freeing of agriculture from the constraints of the socialist system. The result has been a rapid and enormous increase in agricultural productivity, from which, by all available accounts, the rural poor have profited directly and substantially.[41]

To sum up, the performance of socialist Third World societies in improving the material condition of its peoples (most of whom, of course, were poor to begin with) is hardly remarkable and certainly does not substantiate the extravagant ideological claims made in this regard. It is no better than the performance of many Third World societies with capitalist systems. Even more important is that all the socialist societies have been dramatically out-performed by a number of successful capitalist countries, especially in Asia. Finally, as particularly shown by the agricultural developments in India and China, the move from socialist to capitalist agrarian strategies dramatically improves the condition of the rural poor. This is all the more important in view of the widespread agreement (including development experts on the "left") that agriculture is the key to development and thus to the fate of the urban as well as the rural poor.

The following hypothesis may then be formulated: *Capitalist development is more likely than socialist development to improve the material standards of life of people in the contemporary Third World, including the poorest groups.*

(Needless to say, this proposition does *not* imply that capitalist development has this effect automatically and in all places; the proposition is phrased in probabilistic language.)

It is safe to say that most poor people are much more interested in the improvement of their condition than in comparing themselves with other groups. It is the intellectuals rather than the poor who tend to have an interest in "equality." This is why, given the yardstick for development supplied by the "preferential option for the poor," it is much more important to look at absolute standards of material life than at the relativities of income distribution. Still, the latter issue must also be addressed, not only because it looms large in contemporary debates but also because extreme inequalities of income, even if these do not necessarily preclude an improvement in the condition of the poor, tend to generate social and political tensions inimical to development. There is a widespread assumption that, in the choice between capitalist and socialist development models, there is a trade-off between growth and equality.[42] In other words, it is conceded, even by socialist theorists, that capitalism is better for the achievement of economic growth, but it is then maintained that the cost of this greater economic efficiency is a high degree of inequality. Let the question be put aside here whether, in view of the effects of economic growth on material standards of life, the price of inequality may not be well worth paying. Rather, the question at the moment is whether the trade-off does indeed prevail.

Everything said above on the unreliability of Third World statistics, of course, applies to the data on income distribution, especially as "equality" is an officially proclaimed ideal in many Third World countries (not only the explicitly socialist ones), so that the temptation to skew data in order to show progress toward that ideal is very great. Conversely, if specific countries are to be criticized for their development policies or on any other grounds whatever, there is the temptation to dwell on alleged inequalities. Among economists there is a very widespread (though not completely undisputed) belief that the Kuznets effect discussed earlier in this book in terms of Western history holds in the Third World today (with the possible exception of some East Asian countries, of which more in the next chapter). In other words, the majority of economists believe that their data show that inequality in income increases in the earlier stages of economic growth and then levels off at a later stage.[43] Belief in the Kuznets effect has led to the argument that redistributionist government interventions are necessary to offset the inequalities that would otherwise occur "naturally." An important question, then, is that of the basic mechanisms of equalization and their susceptibility to government intervention: What economic processes make for a more equitable income distribution and to what extent can these processes be influenced by government policies?

Gustav Papanek, an economist who has spent many years in cross-national studies of income distribution, argues for the primacy of the wages of unskilled labor in any process of equalization.[44] The assumption here is that, as these wages rise, income distribution becomes more equal. If one is interested in "equality," one ought then to focus on how different development strategies affect the wages of unskilled labor. Statistically, the question is whether unskilled labor income improves more rapidly than per capita income nationwide (a sort of neat statistical correlate of the "preferential option for the poor").

Unlike Eberstadt, Papanek disregards the fully socialist societies. Instead, he differentiates between three strategies in other Third World societies: a growth-oriented private-enterprise strategy or, if one prefers, a capitalist strategy *tout court* (for example, the "Four Little Dragons" of East Asia, and Indonesia and Pakistan in the 1960s); "modified capitalism"—that is, heavy government interference through wage and price controls (for example, Indonesia and Pakistan in the 1970s and many African countries); "populist strategies"—even heavier government interference, both through nationalization and regulation (for example, India and Tanzania). The result of Papanek's investigations is quite unambiguous: In terms of the income of the poor, as measured by the wages of unskilled labor, the "populist" strategies are worst; "modified capitalism" is better; an all-out growth strategy is best.

Papanek is not satisfied with noting these effects; he is also interested in explaining them. He argues that redistributionist government policies tend (unintentionally, of course) to make for inequality, not only because they inhibit growth but because they introduce political distortions into the economic process. Specifically, they tend to create a "protected sector" (mostly consisting of urban skilled labor), which benefits from the policies, and then ipso facto tends to generate economic hardships in the other sectors of the society.[45] The same government policies tend to set artificially low prices for agricultural products, thus depressing the income of the rural population (which, of course, is the large majority in most Third World countries). When government intervention takes the heavier "populist" course, there tend to be the additional aggravating factors of unprofitable nationalized industries and heavy investment in capital-intensive "big projects" —with negative results for the income of unskilled labor.

It should be stressed that this analysis by no means leads to the conclusion that government can do nothing to improve income distribution. Among equality-inducing policies cited by Papanek are education, improving asset ownership among the poor (this means, above all, land ownership), fostering investment in labor-intensive projects, moving away from primary exports only (that is, fostering industrialization), and removing legal or social barriers to opportunity (this applies, very importantly, to the status of women, also to discrimination against groups on the basis of race, caste, or religion). But the general point here is that government policies designed to control economic growth in the pursuit of equality typically produce the opposite effect from the intended one. "Populist" strategies slow down economic growth, which in turn reduces the number of jobs. The impact of this is heaviest on the poor, *both* in terms of absolute living standards *and* of relative income. And, while Papanek does not do this, the same argument can be applied a fortiori to full-blown socialist strategies. The "preferential option for the poor" here translates itself to an option for capitalist development strategies.[46]

Proposition: *Capitalist development leading to rapid and labor-intensive economic growth is more likely to equalize income distribution than strategies of deliberate, government-induced income redistribution.*

Once again, this is a hypothesis, carefully put in probabilistic terms. Capitalism can no more *guarantee* greater equality than material prosperity. Every development strategy is uncertain, threatened by unforeseen disasters of every kind, and liable to have severe unintended consequences. What this means is that the probabilistic character of all social-scientific prognoses has its logical correlate in the situation of the policymaker, who is constrained to gamble. Every development strategy is a gamble. What the considerations of this chapter suggest is that capitalism is generally the better bet. There is some reason to think that this insight is spreading in the Third World today.

# 7

# EAST ASIAN CAPITALISM: A SECOND CASE

Visual images help define the way in which Western people have come to perceive Japan (and, to a lesser extent, the other capitalist societies of East Asia): skyscrapers festooned with neon lights blinking messages in Japanese characters; old ladies in kimonos emerging from high-speed electric trains; the centuries-old calm of Buddhist monastery gardens enclaved within the vast urban landscapes of Tokyo or Seoul or Taipei. These are images of *juxtaposition* —modernity, even hyper-modernity, superimposed upon a civilization that continues to be emphatically different from that of the West. Precisely this juxtaposition defines the theoretical problem to which this chapter must address itself (a theoretical problem, let it be quickly added, which has enormous practical implications). Simply put: Japan is the first non-Western country that has achieved the status of an advanced industrial society. What is more, it has done so with an economic system which, despite various important differences from the Western model, is indubitably capitalist in character; indeed, Japan has become an important actor in the "world system" of industrial capitalism. These facts alone dictate that any theory of capitalism must pay serious attention to Japan. But Japan is no longer alone in this theoretically significant status. There are also the so-called Four Little Dragons—South Korea, Taiwan, Hong Kong, and Singapore—each an economic success story in its own right, both amplifying and modifying the insights to be obtained by the Japanese example. And it now seems that the economic dynamism of East Asian capitalism is penetrating beyond Singapore (which, because of its ethnic composition, is a sort of East Asian outpost in Southeast Asia) into other countries of the ASEAN (Association of Southeast Asian Nations) region, notably Malaysia, Indonesia, and Thailand. In other words, the phenomenon at issue is one of imposing geographical and demographic scope.

The position taken here is that this new East Asian capitalism is sufficiently distinct to be called a "second case." That is, East Asia has generated a new type, or model, of industrial capitalism.[1] Looking at the phenomenon in this way allows one to compare, item by item, the similarities and dissimilarities between the Western and East Asian cases. To be able to do this constitutes a very great intellectual gain. It is analogous to the gain obtained by, say, a zoologist who has been studying a certain species in one environment and who suddenly comes on a second environment in which the same species is flourishing: Minimally, the zoologist will now be in a much better position to decide which characteristics are species-specific and which are due to peculiarities of the one or the other environment. Now the social scientist is coming to be in a better position to decide which characteristics of Western societies are intrinsic to the species "industrial capitalism" and which are, as it were, accidents of Western history and Western culture. One must try to understand East Asia in order to better understand the West and, for that matter, to understand and perhaps to predict the development of other non-Western societies in which industrial capitalism is emerging.[2]

There is widespread agreement on some salient features that are common to East Asian societies.[3] They have developed fully modernized industrial economies of a capitalist type. They have sustained high growth rates, even during periods of recession (as after the oil shock of the early 1970s)—between 1955 and 1975 from 7.8 percent to 9.5 percent growth in GNP and above 5 percent in per capita GNP. Further, these societies have succeeded in virtually eliminating the type of poverty associated with the Third World, as evidenced by their "physiology" (meaning by this, as in earlier chapters, the material conditions of life of even the poorest strata). Also, these societies have developed economies heavily geared toward manufacturing exports (though in this the Four Little Dragons outdistance Japan, which during its highest growth period, because of its large domestic market, was less dependent on international trade than some of the economies of Western Europe). While there are important political differences between these societies, they are all characterized by a very active role of the state in shaping the development process.[4] With the exception of education, these societies have an underdeveloped welfare state (though this is changing in Japan). Related to this, they have relatively low tax rates. In terms of individual economic behavior, finally, these societies are characterized by high savings rates (encouraged by the tax laws), high productivity (especially in blue-collar work), and a very positive work ethic.

The word "model" was used earlier. It is worth noting that this word has a double meaning. On the one hand, it means a specific pattern or type; on the other hand, it means an example to be emulated. Both meanings of the word have been much in evidence in recent discussions of East Asia, but it is important to see that one meaning does not necessarily imply the other. The features of these societies just enumerated may be deemed sufficiently distinct so as to justify speaking of an East Asian "model" of industrial capitalism, in the sense of a pattern or a type different from that of the West. It does *not* necessarily follow that this "model" could be successfully transposed to other parts of the world, be it because of unique historical circumstances or unique sociocultural properties of East Asian development. The appropriateness of the term "model" here cannot be assumed; it can only be assessed a posteriori as this "second case" comes to be better understood.

The "economic miracle" achieved by Japan in the period following World War II is well known.[5] In brief, it began about 1948, only three years after the shattering defeat and devastation of the war, while the country was still under military occupation. By 1953 Japan reached the economic level, in terms of GNP, of the prewar period. High growth rates have been maintained ever since. Between 1952 and 1963 the GNP almost tripled, with growth at 9 percent per annum; during the same years, the volume of manufactured goods quintupled and consumption doubled. Between the beginning of this economic triumphal march and, say, 1970, Japan succeeded not only in establishing itself as a formidable industrial power, challenging the West in key economic areas, but also in virtually eliminating grinding poverty and providing a standard of living for its people that compares well with the more affluent Western countries. The term "economic miracle" is quite appropriate for this history. But it will be recalled that precisely the same phrase was used, during precisely the same period, for the rapid development of West Germany. These two cases are very comparable indeed—economic giants reemerging from the ashes of war and defeat. In other words, neither country embarked on its *Wirtschaftswunder* completely de novo; both countries had undergone their primary industrial revolutions in the nineteenth century. Indeed, between 1890 and World War II, Japan's growth was among the highest in the world, at about 3.5 percent per annum. Thus, remarkable though it was, the economic recovery and upsurge of Japan in the wake of World War II is *theoretically* less interesting than its original embarkation upon modern economic development. The most important phenomenon for the theoretical questions at issue here is the "Meiji model of development" (if one may call it that)—that is, what happened in Japan between 1868 and 1912.[6]

These events deserve the label "miracle" as surely, if not more so, as the more recent history of Japan. Three dates serve to highlight the rapid pace of this development: 1853—the little flotilla of Commodore Perry sails into Tokyo Bay, forcing Japan to open itself to trade with the United States and, subsequently, with the other major Western countries; 1868—the so-called Meiji Restoration, a more or less bloodless coup, overthrows the feudal Tokugawa regime and inaugurates a hectic modernization process; 1905—Japan defeats Russia, one of the most powerful military nations, both on land and on sea. The year 1912 is more arbitrary as marking the end of this revolutionary period (it just happens to be the year in which the Meiji emperor died), but certainly by the outbreak of World War I Japan had essentially completed its initial transformation.

The Meiji period was indeed one of revolution—a swift and deliberate move from feudalism to capitalism.[7] An interesting question is to what extent the principal actors in this drama, the great oligarchs of the Meiji elite, were conscious of just what they were doing. Certainly the originally proclaimed purpose of the coup was not exactly the installation of modern capitalism. Rather, it was to build up military strength in order to safeguard the independence of the country and to avoid the fate of China in the face of Western imperialism. The slogan was *"sonno joi."* (revere the emperor, expel the barbarians). This sounds more like an *anti*modernizing slogan than a clarion call to modernization. Perhaps this is a particular instance of the recurring historical irony that one can only resist the "barbarians" by becoming more like them oneself. Be this as it may, one of the most fascinating aspects of the Meiji revolution is the deliberate manner in which it was engineered by a highly intelligent and reflective political elite. One of the most dramatic episodes of the period is the mission of Tomomi Iwakura to the West, during which this large and carefully selected group of officials visited one Western country after another in order to see which institutions in each country might be suitable for Japanese emulation. The Iwakura mission was very enthusiastically received in the United States (President Ulysses Grant gave a glittering reception for the exotic visitors), and there was much friendly interest in Britain and France. But it was Bismarck's Germany that most impressed the emissaries, and some of the advice that the Iron Chancellor personally gave to Iwakura was very influential when the mission returned home (such as the suggestions that Japan should generate its own capital and avoid foreign indebtedness, and that the Japanese constitution should safeguard the autonomy of the emperor and not give too much power to the parliament).

The revolution was political, legal, and social, as well as economic. Fiefdoms and all other feudal privileges were abolished. But the aristocratic class thus deprived was compensated—in cash and in bonds, which had to be invested. In an ingenious way (or an incredibly lucky one, depending on one's interpretation of the social-engineering consciousness of the Meiji elite) two problems were thus solved simultaneously: An old ruling class was divested of its privileges but sufficiently rewarded for the sacrifice so as not to become a permanently dangerous opposition to the new regime (there were, of course, some flurries of opposition), and (perhaps in fidelity to Bismarck's avuncular advice) investment capital was accumulated domestically for the new industrialization. One may observe also that in the same process of defeudalization, there took place a kind of land reform, foreshadowing the one that was to occur after World War II and perhaps confirming the widely held view that an agrarian society cannot modernize without changing its system of land tenure (or, if one prefers, successful capitalism moves from the countryside to the cities and not the other way around). At the beginning of the new industrialization, the government developed its own enterprises—model factories and shipyards, operated as national industries, largely under the management of foreign experts. Here could have been the beginnings of a "Meiji socialism," a development that, one might argue, would have been more in tune with Japanese collectivist traditions than Western-style capitalism. But this is not what happened. As soon as enough Japanese nationals had been trained to operate the new industrial enterprises, the government sold them off to private entrepreneurs at very low prices. The new industrial corporations were born. This is not, of course, what it was called, but in effect the government served an "R & D" function for the new capitalists, then (very wisely) stepped back from direct involvement in the production process. Again, it is arguable to what extent the Meiji oligarchs followed their intellectual insights into modern economics or some sort of intuitions—or, again, to what extent they may have just been lucky.

The abolition of feudalism, as in Europe centuries before, created a free labor market almost overnight. People of all classes were now free to change their residence or occupation. In effect, what took place was what today one would call a civil rights revolution—not, of course, in the sense of democratic liberties but in the sense that private property and private economic enterprise were now legally protected against the arbitrary power of the old aristocracy. And finally, while there was no interest in developing a welfare state along the lines of Bismarck's Germany, the government massively intervened to create a system of universal education. The Imperial Rescript on Education of 1890 should thus also be marked as an important moment in this revolutionary drama.

Japan had long had a merchant class, centered in Osaka. But it was precisely this old merchant class that, with a few exceptions (for example, the important house of Mitsui), was suspicious of the new industrial enterprises. A new entrepreneurial class was rapidly formed.[8] It was recruited from different population groups, including enterprising farmers and craftsmen, but a very important group within this new class consisted of lower-status samurai, those who had already been "demilitarized" in the preceding Tokugawa period (as power became progressively centralized, there was no more room for wandering swordsmen). There is disagreement among historians as to the relative proportions of ex-samurai in the new capitalist class.[9] What seems quite clear, though, is that the *new business ethos* was derived from the traditional samurai code—an ethos of dedication and discipline, now transposed from a feudal-military to a capitalist-entrepreneurial context of behavior.

The economic historian Kamekichi Takahashi describes the Meiji period as a "capitalistic revolution."[10] It was indeed that. Originally, some foreign capital was imported, but on the whole reliance was placed in indigenous capital. This may have delayed the "take-off" somewhat, but it made it much more reliable when it occurred. From the beginning of the industrialization, though, Japan had very high savings rates, and in consequence capital accumulation took place quite rapidly. Indeed, given the scope of the revolution, it is hard to see how it could have occurred any more rapidly than it did.

As stated above, Japan no longer stands alone as an "economic miracle" in East Asia. One may still argue about the development status of several of the Southeast Asian countries, but there can be no doubt about the NIC (newly industrialized countries) status of the Four Little Dragons. Their history since World War II is, again, one of staggering economic and social success.[11] Now, it is noteworthy that two of those countries (South Korea and Taiwan) were ruled by Japan until 1945 and that all four underwent their economic transformation during the same period that Japan became the prime industrial power in the region. Thus it may be argued to what extent these four little "economic miracles" can be looked at independently or as extensions of the Japanese case; this question, though, can be left aside for the purposes of the present argument.

The four records are almost monotonous in their relentless onward-and-upward thrust; a reader steeped in the frequently depressing literature of Third World development/nondevelopment almost hopes for some respectable calamity to interrupt the triumphalist recitals of East Asian economic achievements. Take South Korea: Between 1963 and 1974 the GNP was tripled, growing at an annual rate of 10 percent.[12] During the same period, per capita GNP doubled. Much more so than in Japan, this growth was fueled by manufacturing exports. During the same years, exports grew from less than $10 *million* to over $4 *billion*, with a growth rate of 55 percent per annum. Again very interestingly, a radical land reform took place in South Korea in the very early stages of the industrializing push.[13]

Take Taiwan: Here too the big growth began in the early 1960s.[14] At the close of World War II per capita income was about $70 annually; by 1980 it was $2,280. This incredible increase in income occurred despite a population growth that was at the high rate of 3.5 percent in the 1960s (though it fell to 2 percent later). Its GNP grew at an average rate of 9.2 percent in the three decades after World War II; it doubled every seven years after 1963; in 1980 it was eleven times that of 1952! Here, too, as in South Korea, a radical land reform took place soon after the Kuomintang regime moved to Taiwan from the mainland,[15] also in the early stages of rapid industrialization and urbanization. And here too, after an initial import-substitution phase, there was a radical shift to an economic strategy geared to export and to an openness to foreign investment. Unemployment decreased from 6.5 percent in 1952 to 1.2 percent in 1979. After 1968 there occurred a rapid rise in wages.

The comparison of little capitalist Taiwan with the giant of mainland China is particularly illuminating in the context of the present argument. In mid-1978 Taiwan's population was 17.1 million, or *1.8 percent* of that of the People's Republic of China. Its per capita GNP was *six times* that of the People's Republic. This simple comparison, all by itself, may serve as a nucleus for a theory of capitalist productivity. (One may add that informed individuals in the People's Republic have been pondering this comparison for some years now, possibly with very direct policy implications.)

South Korea and Taiwan are both nation-sized economies, with both rural and urban areas. The two city-states in the Little Dragons platoon are, obviously, very different cases. They are also quite different from each other—Hong Kong, still a British colony, with its fate uncertain after 1997, when the People's Republic will reassert its sovereignty over it, and Singapore, an independent republic, though with less than half the population of Hong Kong, located precariously between the much less developed and vastly bigger nations of Malaysia and Indonesia. Yet the economic success stories here too are staggering.

In Hong Kong the take-off also occurred in the 1960s, though the city was already important as a light manufacturing center in the

1950s.[16] In the 1970s the GNP grew at an annual average of 8.9 percent, with the staggering high point of *18.8 percent* in 1976. However, both in the 1960s and 1970s there were erratic ups and downs both in GNP and per capita GNP, probably reflecting both Hong Kong's vulnerability to international trade fluctuations and the ebb-and-flow of refugees coming in from the mainland. Still, despite a huge increase in population (annually at about 2.9 percent), per capita GNP grew at an average rate of 7 percent per annum in the two decades from 1960 to 1980. During the same period, real wages have *doubled,* while population increased *about 50 percent* (so much for "immiseration"). There is also evidence to the effect that unskilled labor benefited as much, if not more, than skilled labor from this upward movement of wages. And Hong Kong has had very low unemployment throughout this period.

The basic figures for Singapore are quite similar.[17] Between 1955 and 1974, average GNP growth was 8.3 percent per annum, and per capita GNP growth was 5.7 percent. And, even more so than Hong Kong, Singapore transformed itself into a modern, increasingly high-technology economy. Like all the other Little Dragons, its economy has been marked by rising wages and very low unemployment.

It hardly needs emphasizing at this stage of the present argument that high productivity and growth alone do not suffice to establish "success." One must also ask who benefits from these economic achievements. This is why, in East Asia as in the West, one must explore material standards of living, income distribution, and the dynamics of class. More specifically, one must here raise the question if and to what extent the "second case" of East Asian capitalism modifies the patterns found in these areas in the West.

In an earlier chapter it was indicated that there is considerable disagreement among historians as to the effects of the Industrial Revolution in England on the condition of the poor. The same is true of Meiji Japan.[18] There appears to be a majority of historians (as there had been in the case of England, at least until recently) who believe that the early industrialization of Japan led to growth at the expense of the lower classes—that the material condition of the poor did not improve, but possibly deteriorated, in the early stages of the development process. There is also dissent from this view. But even those who maintain that the material consumption of the lower classes improved with economic growth concede that, very likely, income distribution became more unequal during this period.[19] Thus it is likely that the Japanese experience from the 1880s to about 1925 *confirms* the Kuznets thesis on the relation between growth and inequality in the early stages of economic modernization. After 1925, due to depression and to the militarization of the economy in the 1930s, there appears to have been a fall in consumption levels.

The picture, not surprisingly, is much clearer for the period since World War II.[20] There has been an enormous and very rapid rise in consumption on virtually all levels of Japanese society—a dramatic improvement in material standards of life. As to income distribution, in 1955 it was roughly the same as in the United States. Again, the period of rapid economic growth in Japan in the postwar period *confirms* the Kuznets thesis: Between 1956 and 1971 the income share of the lowest 20 percent in the population *decreased* from 7.2 percent to 3.8 percent, while the share of the highest 20 percent *increased* from 39.6 percent to 46.2 percent. Put bluntly, the rich benefited from growth at the expense of the poor. Since then, however, there has been a leveling effect—again in conformity with the Kuznets thesis. Today Japan compares favorably with advanced Western societies in its income inequalities. In 1977 the ratio of the highest to the lowest 20 percent income groupings in Japan was 4.1. By way of comparison, in the United States it was 9.5 (1972), in Sweden 5.6 (1972) and in the United Kingdom 5.4 (1979). To give an idea of how Japan stands in comparison with the less developed countries in Asia, suffice it to cite the ratio for the Philippines (1971)—it was 14.6. In terms of an overall understanding of the dynamics of income distribution, Japan certainly supports the proposition that income distribution is "driven" by forces that can only be moderately influenced by public policies (the comparison with Sweden and the United Kingdom is particularly relevant here—Japan does better than either one, despite the virtual absence of redistributionist policies).

Not surprisingly, the economic upsurge of the postwar period affected the Japanese class system in significant ways.[21] There occurred massive and rapid urbanization, with the concomitant decline of traditional forms of social organization. Before World War II Japanese cities tended to be composed of tightly knit "neighborhood villages"; these declined in the postwar period (though, if compared with the West, the neighborhood continues to be a social reality even in the largest Japanese cities). The traditional large household, or *ie,* declined, as Japanese lived increasingly in nuclear families. But many analysts insist that the solidarity commanded by the *ie* came to be transferred to other social institutions, notably in the workplace. Japanese have come to feel that they are living in a "mass society," also (for a large majority) that they belong to the middle class (Japanese sociologists have coined the phrase "middle-mass society" to describe this phenomenon). As to social mobility, its rates in Japan today are very similar to those in Western countries.

Thus, leaving aside the controversial question of what happened during the Meiji period, contemporary Japan does *not* suggest any major modifications in the earlier propositions concerning the dynamics of income distribution and class under industrial capitalism. As far as the former item is concerned, the Four Little Dragons present more interesting evidence.

South Korea is a sort of in-between case.[22] It certainly has a more equitable income distribution than other developing countries—in 1976 the aforementioned ratio between the highest and lowest fifths was 8.0—worse than Japan, better than the United States. But there are strong indications that income inequality *declined* in the period between 1968 and 1972—that is, relatively early in the rapid-growth phase. The record of income distribution in South Korea appears to be affected by considerable fluctuations. A major problem was the gap between urban and rural areas. This income gap was *widening* up until 1970; it was *eliminated* between 1970 and 1974. Two reasons have been given for this rather remarkable change—large-scale migration to the urban areas (especially Seoul and Pusan) and to the higher-wage labor market in those areas with some income being sent back to the rural area, and government policies raising farm incomes through price supports for agricultural products.

The South Korean experience does not support the Kuznets thesis; it can be chalked up as a sort of weak disconfirmation. A much more important case for this issue is that of Taiwan. Here one finds the strongest and best-documented instance of an *anti*-Kuznets effect.[23]

In the 1950s income distribution in Taiwan was similar to the unfavorable situation generally found in less developed countries. There then occurred a substantial improvement in the following two decades of rapid growth. In the period from 1964 to 1979, the income share of the poorest 20 percent of families *increased* from 7.7 percent to 8.6 percent, while the share of the richest 20 percent *decreased* from 41.1 percent to 37.5 percent. Put simply, contrary to the Kuznets thesis, the poor were getting richer faster than the rich were getting richer in the very period of rapid growth when the opposite was supposed to occur. By the late 1970s income distribution had become fairly stable, following the pattern of industrial societies. The ratio between highest and lowest fifths was now oscillating between 4.2 and 4.3— very similar to that in Japan, and thus better than that in the major Western countries.

The elimination of severe, Third-World-type poverty in Taiwan is also well documented. Life expectancy increased from 58.6 years in 1952 to 70.7 years in 1979. Illiteracy decreased from 55 percent in 1946 to 11.2 percent in 1978. There have been similarly dramatic improvements in terms of caloric intake, the quality of housing and the distribution of modern household facilities. While much of this change can be plausibly ascribed to the "economic miracle" in and of itself, a number of government policies contributed to it. Land reform was one of the most important. It created a new class of owner-farmers, with important consequences for the distribution of property (which fairly quickly affected the distribution of income). Thus agricultural families owning medium-sized farms increased from 46 percent in 1952 to 76 percent in 1960, while tenant families decreased from 38 percent to 15 percent. During this period of agricultural revolution, the government encouraged the formation of farmers' associations and provided aid in research, technology, and credit. Through tax incentives and other means, government policy fostered labor-intensive industrialization. And, as in all the East Asian countries under discussion, the government pushed a system of universal education, based on strict meritocratic principles. Social mobility has been high, as compared with other countries of comparable levels of industrialization, with education an unusually high factor in determining mobility chances.[24]

The anti-Kuznets data from Taiwan are obviously intriguing and have been much commented upon. Analysts sympathetic to the Taiwan regime have, of course, given the latter credit for the comparatively high degree of income equality and for the combination of rapid growth with improving equity. The comparison with South Korea certainly suggests that land reform, accompanied by various other policies designed to improve rural conditions, must be given some credit. But the comparison with the two city-states, where there was no land to be reformed, makes this interpretation more questionable. For both city-states show similar anti-Kuznets effects.

Take Hong Kong: Between 1966 and 1976 (that is, during a very high growth period), the share of the lowest 20 percent increased from 4.7 percent to 5.3 percent, while the share of the highest 20 percent decreased from 58 percent to 50.1 percent.[25] The general picture is one of a continuous decline of income inequality during the highest growth period, followed by a leveling off, a clearly anti-Kuznets picture. There have been the usual East Asian dramatic improvements in life expectancy, health, education, and housing—some undoubtedly encouraged by government policies (for example in housing, where the government built enormous housing estates to absorb the mass of indigent refugees and other poor people in the colony). But there has also been very high social mobility, with large numbers of people entering manufacturing and a concomitantly higher wage labor market, thus reducing income inequality quite apart from government policies.

Take Singapore: Between 1966 and 1973 (again, a very high growth period), there was a decline in the Gini coefficient (the conventional measure of income inequality) of between 8.2 percent and 9.1 percent —once again, a clearly anti-Kuznets picture.[26] Reasons given for this are very similar to the ones cited in the case of Hong Kong—a mix of government policies (the Singapore government has also undertaken a giant housing effort; indeed, by now the majority of the population lives in public housing estates) and economic developments quite apart from any government actions.

The Four Little Dragons provide evidence on the relation of economic growth and income distribution which forces some modifications of earlier generalizations derived from Western history. At this stage the question cannot be answered as to the extent to which government policies can be credited for this. One thing is quite clear: It was certainly not policies of deliberate redistribution that led to this effect; none of the four governments pursued such policies, and indeed all four societies are characterized by a very underdeveloped welfare state. There are other government policies that are candidates for the role of causal factors—in land reform, housing, and education in particular. Supply-side economists can point, with some plausibility, to the tax policies of these regimes, all tending to encourage saving and investment. Certainly all four societies provide a benevolent climate for capitalist enterprise. But it may also be that, at the end of the day, one will have to attribute causal efficacy to social and cultural factors that are beyond the reach of government actions. All these societies (and now including Japan, as well) are in the orbit of Sinitic civilization, with a number of common traditions and institutions that may be highly relevant to the economic evidence. This possibility will be discussed shortly.

For now, however, a number of propositions may be formulated, as contributions to the overall body of hypotheses of this book:

*East Asia confirms the superior productive power of industrial capitalism.*

*East Asia confirms the superior capacity of industrial capitalism in raising the material standard of living of large masses of people.*

*East Asia confirms the positive relation between industrial capitalism and the emergence of a class system characterized by relatively open social mobility.*

*East Asia disconfirms the proposition that early economic growth under modern capitalist conditions must necessarily increase income inequality, though it confirms the proposition that income distribution stabilizes as this economic growth continues.*

In terms of the last hypothesis, it is important to stress what it does *not* propose: It does *not* negate the Kuznets thesis as it has been supported by evidence both from the West and from countries in other parts of the world, *nor* does it negate the explanation of the Kuznets effect in terms of economic and demographic factors built into the industrialization process. In other words, the East Asian evidence does not make it necessary to scrap the well-supported idea that, *in general,* modernization brings with it first an increase in income inequality, followed by a leveling off. But the East Asian evidence provides *an intriguing exception* to this otherwise valid generalization. Shirley Kuo, a Taiwanese economist, puts this quite carefully: "It is possible for economic growth to be compatible with an improved distribution of income during every phase of the transition from colonialism to a modern developed economy."[27] To say that "it is possible," of course, immediately raises the question whether it might be possible *again* — possible, that is, in other parts of the developing world. The answer to that question hinges on how one explains the East Asian exception —be it in terms of government policies, sociocultural factors, or happy accidents (to employ a Chinese phrase) governing the point in time in which the economies of these societies were ready to plunge into international trade.

The question of whether the East Asian "economic miracle" could be repeated elsewhere in the non-Western world is one of the most important questions in current development thinking. It is not only academics who ask this. Statesmen and politicians in various Third World countries (such as Prime Ministers Datuk Seri Mahathir Mohamad of Malaysia and Edward Seaga of Jamaica) have spoken in glowing terms of "looking east" for models of development—that is, looking to Japan and the other flourishing economies of East Asia rather than to the economies of the West. The assumption here is, clearly, that there could be repeat performances of the East Asian "success stories." It is frustrating that the assumption cannot be unambiguously supported *or* falsified at this point. A number of arguments against it (which means, conversely, arguments in favor of the exceptional status of the East Asian experience) have been made. Thus it is argued that the 1960s were a period of unusual openness in the international economy, with room for aggressive newcomers, but that this stroke of good fortune is unlikely to be repeated any time soon. Indeed, the very existence of the East Asian economies may now provide an obstacle for putative newcomers—there may simply be no more room in the international economy for "more Taiwans," that is, for new, export-oriented, manufacturing economies of the East Asian type. Other reasons have been brought forth for an East Asian "exceptionalism": stable governments imposed or supported by the United States in the post-World War II era (Japan, South Korea, Taiwan) or left behind as a legacy of British colonial rule (Hong Kong and Singapore). In this connection it has been stressed that at least the three non-city-states in the region were of great strategic importance to the United States at the time of their take-off, in the wake of the Korean War, and thus received generous economic benefits (including aid) from the United States. It has also been pointed out that all these countries faced serious external threats at the time of their take-offs: Japan from Western imperialism in the nineteenth century; South Korea, Taiwan, and Hong Kong from the powerful pressure of Communist imperialism; and Singapore from being surrounded by much poorer but more populous neighbors. Thus a Toynbean "challenge" was present, stimulating energies in the quest for survival. Last not least, there is the argument (standing Weber on his head) that East Asian cultures (because of Confucianism or some other religioethical traditions) are peculiarly suited for modern development. In that case, attempts by countries outside the region to emulate the East Asian example may well be futile: One may export the economic policies of, say, Taiwan to an African country, but one can hardly expect Africans to adopt Confucian morality.

These arguments for an East Asian "exceptionalism" are not fully persuasive. Very few of them apply to Meiji Japan, the first non-Western case of successful modernization and thus arguably the most significant one. But even looking at the events since World War II there are good reasons to doubt that the East Asian experience is unrepeatably unique. Windows of opportunity in the world economy recur periodically, and other countries may take advantage of them. Thus the economies of all the capitalist countries of Southeast Asia (with the depressing exception of the Philippines) have been doing reasonably well in recent years while increasingly "looking east" for their development models. So have scattered countries in other parts of the world (for example, Sri Lanka and the Ivory Coast). Stable government is not necessarily an East Asian prerogative, and other countries have received large doses of foreign aid. The argument from external threats rather begs the question: Many Third World countries have faced all sorts of threats, but only some have responded successfully to the "challenge." Perhaps the most serious argument is the one from culture. East Asian societies do indeed have very distinctive cultural characteristics (as will be discussed a few pages hence), and it is certainly illogical to assume that these could possibly be exported to other countries. Yet people in very different societies have managed to mobilize cultural traits of their own for successful economic performance or possibly have *changed* their cultural traditions sufficiently to allow such performance. For examples, one may cite here Hindu and Sikh peasants in the Punjab, who in recent years have achieved an "economic miracle" of their own (an agricultural one, this time), Buddhists in Thailand and Sri Lanka (Theravada Buddhists at that), or the Ibos in Nigeria. To say the least, the position of statesmen like

Mahathir of Malaysia or Seaga of Jamaica that the East Asian model is worth emulating has a fairly solid empirical warrant. By the same token, as far as the argument of this book is concerned, the cases of Japan and the Four Little Dragons provide strong support for most of the propositions about the nature of industrial capitalism developed in the earlier chapters.

The East Asian "second case" is also relevant to the treatment of political factors, international as well as domestic, within a theory of capitalism. It must first of all be pointed out that the development of these societies is very difficult indeed to fit into any Marxist or neo-Marxist ("dependency theory") frame of reference, though, of course, some have tried to do so.[28] The modernization of Japan in the nineteenth century was the direct consequence of Western imperialist intrusion; Japan proved that it is possible to respond to such intrusion ("dependency," if you will) in such a way that, within one generation, one becomes a major player in the same international power game. The post-World War II development of Japan began under the military tutelage of the United States and at no point involved either an opting-out of the capitalist "world system" or the creation of a noncapitalist system domestically. Most important for any comparisons with contemporary Third World societies, each of the Four Little Dragons can easily be described as "dependent"—South Korea and Taiwan overwhelmingly so upon the United States (economically as well as politically and militarily), Hong Kong as a British colony, and Singapore as a very small actor in the international capitalist system that thoroughly penetrates its economy. To call the situation of these societies "dependent development" is a verbal legerdemain that only serves to underline their disconfirming weight upon dependency theory. The basic fact here is that "dependency," as defined within that theory, has clearly not prevented these societies from developing beyond the dreams of most Third World countries, in the process lifting masses of people from abject poverty to a decent standard of living and doing so with an income distribution that compares favorably with the most exemplary social democracies.

The following proposition, then, can be stated boldly: *The East Asian evidence falsifies the proposition that successful development cannot occur in a condition of dependency upon the international capitalist system.*

A further clarification may be in order here: The East Asian evidence on "dependency" is weightier than the evidence on the Kuznets effect. As observed before, there is wide cross-national support for the Kuznets thesis *except for* the Four Little Dragons. Consequently, East Asia is proposed as an important exception to an otherwise valid generalization. By contrast, as was discussed in an earlier chapter, there is no such cross-national evidence for the various Marxist and neo-Marxist theories of underdevelopment. Consequently, the East Asian case can be proposed as a definite falsification of these theories, rather than as a merely interesting exception to an otherwise valid generalization.

East Asia, to put it bluntly, is bad news for Marxists. But East Asia is also not very comforting to ideologists of capitalism who still adhere to some laissez-faire notions to the effect that state interventionism is bad for economic development. All of these societies are characterized by massive state interventions in economic life. They are heavily *dirigiste* and have been so from the beginnings of their respective modernization processes.

Once more, Meiji Japan supplies a paradigm for the subsequent East Asian development pattern. Its economic processes were tightly controlled and to a large extent planned by the oligarchs who constituted the new political elite.[29] As noted above, the government quickly (and wisely) got out of the business of running enterprises directly—an early and highly successful instance of "privatization"! But what the government did do was anything but laissez-faire. It was government, of course, which carried through the "civil rights revolution," which in a series of legislative acts dismantled the feudal system, freed human resources from the traditional constraints, and made all Japanese active participants in the new economic processes. Using twentieth-century language, one could say that the Meiji government executed both a massive "civil rights act" and an equally massive "agrarian reform." Further, it created the legal and administrative framework (including a modern tax system) for capitalist enterprise. And, perhaps most important of all, it brought about a well-functioning system of universal education. Throughout the Meiji period there was very close cooperation between government officials and the new entrepreneurial class. This cooperation was first facilitated by the fact that many individuals in both groups shared a common samurai background; this was later replaced by a common educational background. Put differently, a meritocratic elite, spanning government and business, replaced the old aristocratic elite. What has remained as a paradigm is an interlocking elite, political as well as economic, animated by the same ethos and similar patterns of social interaction.

Despite the introduction of Western-style democracy, this paradigm continues to hold for post–World War II Japan.[30] This by no means implies that the democratic processes are somehow unreal or only a facade for the real power. Rather, democratic politics is superimposed upon the interlocking elite; indeed, democratic politicians (at least those of the predominant party) are members of this elite. There are a number of distinctively Japanese institutions fostering this relationship between government and business, such as the networks of graduates from the most prestigious educational institutions (especially Tokyo University), the practice of "descent from heaven" *(amakudari)* whereby retired government officials take positions in business (since the retirement age in government is fifty-five, this is far from providing sinecures for these individuals), the practice of "administrative guidance" whereby government officials counsel business, and, last not least, the formulation of "industrial policy" by government agencies. The most important of these agencies is the Ministry of International Trade and Industry (MITI), which some analysts have credited with a high measure of responsibility for the economic success of postwar Japan.[31]

The Four Little Dragons are characterized by similarly interlocking directorates as between government and business.[32] Even Hong Kong, often cited as a surviving paradise of laissez-faire government, has an informal government-business elite that does not really break the general East Asian pattern.[33] Chalmers Johnson has suggested the term "developmental state" to describe this phenomenon—different from both the "regulatory state" of the West and the command economy of Soviet-type socialist societies.[34] Ambrose King, referring to the political system of Hong Kong, has used the term "synarchy" to describe it.[35] Whatever term is used, there is here a specifically East Asian model of government-business symbiosis which, while clearly linked to a capitalist economy, is very different from any Western pattern.

Proposition: *The East Asian evidence falsifies the idea that a high degree of state intervention in the economy is incompatible with successful capitalist development.*

An important caution here: This proposition is *not* to be construed as an argument for a "mixed economy" as advocated and to some degree practiced by Western social democrats—the East Asian economies under consideration are much more unambiguously capitalist. Nor is the proposition to be understood as embracing *any* type of state intervention in economic affairs. East Asian governments are highly *dirigiste* in some areas, quite reluctant to interfere in others. It cannot be the present concern to unscramble "good" and "bad" forms of state intervention; this would lead into details of economic policy far beyond the scope of this book. What is important is that the East Asian experience forces a modification of all theories of capitalism that seek to salvage a doctrinaire *laissez-faire* approach to the role of the state in a capitalist economy.

Still within the realm of the relations between political and economic institutions, one must also ask the question of whether, or to what extent, East Asian capitalism has fostered democracy. On the face of it, the question would seem to be easily answered. Japan today is a Western-style democracy by any reasonable criterion but that democracy was imposed by the victors after World War II and Japan was certainly not a democracy in the initial stages of its modernization. And none of the Four Little Dragons could, at the time of writing, be described as full-fledged democracies, though there are democratic developments in each. On that level, then, all that one can say is that East Asia does not falsify the earlier hypothesis that capitalism is the necessary but not sufficient condition of democracy under modern conditions. *That,* however, is not a terribly interesting contribution to the present theoretical enterprise. A more interesting question, though, is whether the East Asian experience supports another hypothesis— namely, that successful capitalism generates pressures toward democracy.

Curiously, Japan, despite the fact that it is the only full-fledged democracy in this group of societies, provides the least clear evidence in this matter. Japan is indeed a crucially important case for a theory of democracy: Along with India, it provides strong disconfirmation of the thesis that democracy cannot be successfully established in a non-Western culture; and, along with West Germany, Japan disconfirms the widely accepted notion that democracy cannot be imposed by force of arms. But neither of these two results tell much about the relation between democracy and capitalism. Again, the earlier period of Japan's modernization may be theoretically more significant than the more recent one. Despite the careful measures by which (more or less along Prussian lines) the Meiji oligarchs tried to limit the powers of parliament, there were strong demands for popular participation from early on in the Meiji period.[36] But it is difficult to assess to what extent these demands were based on a democratic impulse as such or rather on the feeling that, along with other Western-derived institutions, Japan needed to acquire parliamentary democracy in order to become a respectably modern nation. The democratic developments, of course, were squelched with the rise of military authoritarianism in the period leading up to Pearl Harbor. But when the American occupation regime imposed democracy on Japan, there were some indigenous democratic tendencies that could be worked with (though clearly less so than in Germany). It is also possible to argue that democracy has become ever more firmly anchored in Japanese public opinion in the years since then, to the point where it is not easy to imagine a return to authoritarianism. Again, however, it is difficult to assess the role of capitalism in this development.

The record of the Four Little Dragons in this area is more readily accessible (it is shorter, of course, and well documented) and perhaps somewhat more helpful in testing the hypothesis. There do indeed appear to be pressures toward democracy in each of them, and these pressures have escalated in at least three of them (Hong Kong being the exception) in tandem with the increase of affluence—with the increasing participation of all population groups in the successes of capitalist development. South Korea and Taiwan are particularly instructive here. In both, authoritarian regimes, while repressing attempts to organize formal political opposition, have permitted the growth of participatory institutions centered around nonpolitical (primarily economic) concerns and, subsequently, have opened up the formal political system to more participation as well. In South Korea an important event was the launching of the *Saemaul Undong* (New Community Nurturance) movement by President Park Chung-hee in 1970. This was a government-sponsored rural mobilization movement, which, however, provided a focus for participatory politics for large numbers of people in the countryside.[37] In recent years, much more far-reaching concessions to democratic opposition have been made by the regime. In Taiwan there was also the early development of participatory institutions in the countryside, followed later by progressive modifications of the Kuomintang monopoly on formal politics.[38] In recent years, here too, there has been a gradual but noticeable tendency of democratization, including the appearance of oppositional groupings (even though these are not yet allowed the status of parties), an expansion in the powers of elected local government, and increasing freedom of expression. Very similar developments are observable in Singapore. Hong Kong has been characterized by a very high degree of political passivity, but even here there appears to have occurred a growth of participatory attitudes.[39] As the time for the Chinese take-over of the colony approaches, these demands for participation and representation seem to be strengthening (perhaps tragically so).

Any proposition on this matter will have to be worded very cautiously. The following will have to do: *The East Asian evidence provides weak support for the thesis that successful capitalist development generates pressures toward democracy.*

Two additional considerations may, respectively, weaken further or make stronger this proposition. Each of the Four Little Dragons has been politically and culturally "dependent" on the West; thus it is difficult to assess to what extent the democratizing pressures would have been generated in the absence of Western influence (and, indeed, Western political manipulations). On the other hand, each of the four societies has found itself in a highly dangerous international environment and has been forced into a strongly defensive posture; thus it is possible that democratization would have gone further if the international milieu had been more benign.

To what extent can the economic performance of East Asian capitalism be explained in terms of cultural factors? More specifically, has East Asian culture provided a "functional equivalent" for the Protestant ethic that many, since Max Weber, have credited with a crucial role in the development of Western capitalism? These questions, as already remarked upon, are of practical as well as theoretical import because the answers (if they can ever be found) will largely determine whether one gives a chance to the export of the East Asian "model" to other parts of the world.[40]

Weber, as is well known, believed that all the cultures of Asia (though for different reasons, for instance, as between India and China) produced values and attitudes that were uncongenial to modernization (or, as he called it, to "rationalization"). The economic history of East Asia would appear to have falsified Weber's notions about the empirical consequences of what he called the "magic garden of Asian religiosity." Understandably, then, some analysts have tried, as it were, to stand Weber on his head—to find elements in the culture and especially the religious traditions of East Asia that could be interpreted as positive predispositions toward modern economic enterprise. There are serious methodological issues in such an undertaking.[41] There is always the danger of the fallacy *post hoc propter hoc*—after something happens, one tries to find causes in preceding events that may not have been causes at all (a fallacy that some critics have attributed to Weber in his own original work on Protestantism as a causal factor for capitalism); religion and ethics may be a *legitimation* rather than a *motive* for economic behavior; highly rational and highly "magical" attitudes may coexist in the same individual (especially in "pluralistic" Asia) so that it is perilous to assume *any* coherent value system underlying economic behavior.[42] Fortunately or unfortunately, the question is far too important to be put aside because of such methodological doubts.

For obvious reasons, the question about cultural factors in economic development has been most extensively debated in the case of Japan. Some time ago the American sociologist Robert Bellah argued for a quasi-Weberian thesis concerning religioethical tendencies in Japan prior to the Meiji Restoration.[43] More recently the Japanese economist Michio Morishima has argued forcefully (and, some would say, incautiously) that Japanese culture (especially religious culture) explains Japanese economic success.[44] These "culturalist" interpretations have been sharply contested by others who have explained Japan's success in terms of social and political institutions that are "willful" constructions relatively independent of culture. One of the best-known interpretations on such "institutionalist" lines is that of another American sociologist, Ezra Vogel.[45] The two avenues of interpretation, of course, are not necessarily contradictory, but they clearly differ in the *weight* given to culture as an explanation.

Weber distinguished between "this-worldly" and "other-worldly" religions, depending on whether secular activities were or were not religiously legitimated. One can make an argument that East Asian civilization has from very long ago produced a secularity of its own, distinct and differently rooted from that of the West, but nonetheless motivating values and attitudes that would eventually favor modern economic rationality.[46] Among these values and attitudes are a highly developed sense of practicality or pragmatism, an active rather than contemplative orientation to life, great interest in material things (emphatically including a positive valuation of wealth), and, last not least, a great capacity for delayed gratification and discipline (especially on behalf of one's family). These traits may then be deemed to be common to all the national cultures within the orbit of Sinitic civilization—certainly the Chinese, Japanese, and Korean, possibly also some of the cultures of Southeast Asia (notably that of the Vietnamese)—serving as a sort of substratum for all the "great traditions" that have emerged in the same region. In that case, the phenomena of folk religion would be more important to explore for the question at hand than any of the "great traditions."[47]

When it comes to these traditions, most attention has recently been given to Confucianism.[48] There is some irony in this, since in the 1950s a number of analysts pointed to Confucianism as one of the *obstacles* to the economic development of East Asia.[49] Not surprisingly, *other* elements of Confucian ethics were now stressed—not its (alleged) conservatism and antagonism to economic activity but rather its respect for superiors, its collective solidarity, and its emphasis on discipline. These are indeed common traits in all the national cultures of the region, and Confucianism did indeed play a very important role, not only in China, but in all the other countries under discussion as well.[50] The Confucianism that is relevant to this argument, of course, is not that of the mandarins of imperial China but Confucian-derived (or at least Confucian-legitimated) values motivating very ordinary and unlearned people—petty entrepreneurs in Taipei, say, or bank clerks in Manila (or, for that matter, in San Francisco). Robert Bellah has employed the apt term "bourgeois Confucianism" for this constellation of values.[51] It can also be argued that the same popular Confucianism serves the political stability of these countries, inculcating a sense of hierarchy and putting a very high premium on harmony in all social relations. This latter theory has recently received a very practical application in the efforts of the Singapore government to instill Confucian ethics into the curriculum of the public schools (an educational experiment slightly hampered by the fact that the classical texts had to be translated into English!).

If one turns to the "great traditions" of East Asia for a quasi-

Weberian argument, Confucianism is not the only candidate. Mahayana Buddhism would also have to be explored. Here an argument can be made that it was the genius of the Chinese mind which succeeded in changing a radically world-denying religion into an essentially world-affirming one—no mean accomplishment, if one looks at the Indian origins of the Buddhist faith. Taoism, with its peculiar attitudes to nature, would be another candidate. And certainly Shinto would have to be taken very seriously in the case of Japan.

As far as Meiji Japan is concerned, there is a widely held view among historians that there took place a conversion of the samurai ethic from military to economic applications.[52] The self-denial and discipline, traditionally applied to feats of armed valor, was now rechanneled into the unarmed combat of capitalist enterprise, resulting in "a happy mixture of militant patriotism and economically rationalized Confucian ethics."[53] This view was linked to the opinion that samurai did indeed play a predominant part in the formation of the new entrepreneurial class—an opinion that has not been unchallenged.[54] Be this as it may, there can be no doubt that individuals of samurai origin did play an important, if not predominant, part in the emergence of Meiji capitalism and that these individuals did accomplish a feat of ideological permutation that ingeniously combined traditional symbols with modern needs. One such individual was Fukuzawa Yukichi (1835–1905), founder of the first modern college set up to train businessmen. Yukichi was concerned to preach a business ethos to samurai students still imbued with an aristocratic contempt for commerce. By 1897 his books and pamphlets had sold about ten million copies. Another individual was Shibusawa Eiichi (1840–1931), a leading entrepreneur with a similar penchant for preaching the virtues of modern business, emphasizing diligence, honesty, and devotion to the common good. He discarded the old word for "merchant," *shonin,* and coined a new term for the new-style entrepreneur, *jitsugyoka* (literally, "a man who undertakes a real task"). This oriental Ben Franklin was so enamored of Confucius that his favorite slogan was "To manage business enterprise using the analects of Confucius," a copy of which he always carried in his pocket.[55] Perhaps the question whether this ad hoc business creed was sincerely believed in by its formulators or just a convenient legitimation for simple acquisitiveness is finally beside the point. The basic fact is that Meiji Japan managed to find a way of reconciling the new capitalist necessities with traditional values, and whatever the motives of those responsible for this feat, there did emerge a "spirit of Japanese capitalism" which was taken seriously by future generations and is still taken seriously today.

If one compares this ideological construction with Max Weber's rendition of the "spirit" of Western capitalism, both similarities and differences may be noted.[56] The most important similarity is precisely what Weber called "this-worldly asceticism"—a combination of secularity with a morality of self-denial and discipline. But in Japan this attitude had a much wider "time horizon" (that is, profit was sought in the context of an idea of national destiny), and it was combined with a nonindividualistic ethos of service to others—finally the nation, more proximately those associated with oneself in a particular business enterprise. This modification of the Western "spirit of capitalism" may help account for the willingness of Japanese businessmen to this day to tolerate low rates of profit for a long time with a future goal of success in mind.

If one turns now from Meiji Japan to the present, there is widespread agreement about two values continuing to dominate Japanese economic behavior—communalism (or "groupism") and hierarchy.[57] Thus the Japanese anthropologist Chie Nakane has argued that these values have been successfully transposed from the *ie,* or household, to modern institutions, including an ingenious modernization of the traditional system of permanent obligations *(giri)* between different social ranks to the hierarchy of modern business organization.[58] The "three treasures" of Japanese corporate life—"lifetime" employment, a wage system based on seniority, and company unionism—are the direct consequences of this transposition.[59]

The modernization involved here can be nicely described in the parlance of social science as a shift from *ascription* to *achievement*—that is, where traditionally obligations and loyalties were based on birth (social rank and family), they are now based on individual merit as determined by success or failure in the educational system.[60] One is confronted here with a possibly unique combination of castelike hierarchy and thoroughly rational meritocracy—a society with social mobility rates as high and as open as any in Western countries but with a few narrow "passes" which, early in the biography of the individual, decide pretty conclusively where he will be socially located for the rest of his life. It goes without saying that such a system is not without its human costs—as witnessed by the hysteria and, often, despair of young Japanese as they go through the well-named "examination hell." It is plausible to also see this system as a modernization of the traditional Confucian examination procedures, and indeed it can be found in very similar forms in the Four Little Dragons (being a secondary-school student in Seoul or Singapore is not much fun either, and the dominant role of the elite universities, including their networks of graduates, is similar in all five societies).

Again very cautiously, two propositions may now be formulated: *The East Asian experience supports the hypothesis that certain components of Western bourgeois culture—notably activism, rational innovativeness, and self-discipline—are necessary for successful capitalist development.*

*Specific elements of East Asian civilization, be it in the "great traditions" or in folk culture, have fostered these values and have consequently given the societies of the region a comparative advantage in the modernization process.*

The phrase "comparative advantage" in the latter hypothesis is deliberately chosen. It is derived, of course, from the vocabulary of economics. Its use points to a position, not only with regard to the phenomenon of East Asian capitalism but in the understanding of economic culture generally. It is a position somewhere in the middle between the "institutionalist" and the "culturalist" approaches. The idea that economic and other social institutions are simply the result of historical circumstances or can be freely constructed and reconstructed by a collective will contradicts what the social sciences have discovered about the power of human culture. Thus (to take the most "artificial" society of the region), it is inherently implausible to believe that Singapore would be what it is today if it were populated, not by a majority of ethnic Chinese, but by Brazilians or Bengalis—or, for that matter, by a majority of ethnic Malays. Specific elements of Chinese culture have contributed to the economic success of the city-state; they have given it a comparative advantage—no less, but also no more. Economic opportunities and policies, political structure, educational strategies have obviously played a decisive role as well, and without them the Chinese culture of these people might have remained as economically irrelevant as it was for many centuries in the country of origin. On the other hand, to say that culture is a variable is *not* to imply that it is the only, or even necessarily the principal, variable in the causal equation of economic success. Some historians and anthropologists tend to look at culture as if it were an ancient curse, delivered centuries ago and acting itself out as destiny for all subsequent generations. *That* view is as implausible as the one that ignores culture. Human beings are indeed determined by the past, but they are also capable of changing their cultural inheritance. Sometimes this change occurs spontaneously, in response to new challenges, crises, or opportunities (as, for an important example, in cases of migration). More rarely, culture is changed as a result of deliberate acts, as in the application of legal, political, or educational policies (Meiji Japan is a prime example of this). It follows that a cultural comparative advantage can be only temporary, that it can be positively or negatively tampered with by deliberate interventions, and that it could also be lost. Mutatis mutandis, similar statements can be made about comparative *dis*advantages rooted in culture. Come to think of it, Confucius may be aptly quoted here: "It is only the wisest and the stupidest who do not change."[61]

There is strong evidence to the effect that all over the world, at least in nonsocialist societies, modernization has an individuating effect—not, to be sure, in the full-fledged Western or American sense of "individualism" but in the sense of freeing the individual from the constraints of traditional groupings, such as those of kinship, village, caste, or ethnicity.[62] Put simply, modernization, at least under conditions of capitalism, increases individual autonomy. This, of course, has long been an assumption of sociological theory—from Ferdinand Toennies's theory of *Gemeinschaft* and *Gesellschaft* and Emile Durkheim's of "mechanical" and "organic" solidarity to Talcott Parsons's tables of "pattern variables." While the degree of this shift from communalism to individual autonomy may have been exaggerated in some of these theories (partly due to a certain myopia with regard to the importance of "mediating structures"), one can say that, by and large, empirical research has consistently supported the overall thesis. The interesting question here is whether East Asia offers another exception in this area. Has the cultural substance of Western modernity "infected" East Asia along with its external forms? To what extent has East Asia succeeded in modernizing itself under capitalist conditions without in the process becoming more "individualistic"?

Interestingly, these questions were already asked and hotly debated in the region in the nineteenth century. Thus Chinese intellectuals at that time were arguing as to whether it was possible to adopt the "function" *(yung)* of Western technological civilization without also having to adopt its "substance" *(t'i)*. There were two schools on this —those who thought that it was possible and those who thought that it was not. Needless to say, the latter school was more wary of all modernizing movements, though there were also some of that school who believed that accepting at least some of the "substance" of Western culture (notably its "individualism") would be a good thing for China.[63]

There is widespread agreement to the effect that East Asia in general and Japan in particular are characterized by strong communal solidarities and, consequently, by resistance to Western-style individuation. There are some dissenting voices, but the consensus on this issue remains strong.[64] At the same time it is quite clear that, from the beginning, Western individuating influences were felt in the East Asian societies. In Japan (possibly in imitation of similar neologisms in Chinese) a new term for "individualism" *(kojiushugi)* was coined in 1914, in a lecture by Natsume Soseki.[65] But there were earlier expressions of the concept if not the term. During the Meiji period a number of novels, by Futababei Shimei and others, dealt with the ideal of the individual struggling against traditional constraints. There were, of course, strong Western influences here, especially via Western literature; in some cases, there was a strong attraction to Christianity. In post-Meiji Japan there is further evidence of the spread of Western-style values of individual autonomy among intellectuals and in urban centers.[66]

In contemporary, postwar Japan the evidence is somewhat ambiguous. With high geographical and social mobility there has been a shift in identification from larger kinship groupings (say, "the house of Tanaka") to the more immediate family. There is also evidence of greater egalitarianism (a definite "democratization" of Japanese society). But this does not necessarily imply "individualism" in the Western sense.[67] Indeed, there are data showing that traditional communalism has increased rather than decreased. For example, in 1953, when asked to choose between the two questions, "Should one follow custom?" and "Should you do what you think right?" 35 percent chose the former; in 1978 this choice was made by 42 percent.[68] On the other hand, both the Japanese media and the sociological literature present evidence of young people rebelling against traditional communalism, asserting their individual rights, often with specific reference to Western ideas. At this time it is possible to interpret the evidence in two quite different ways. One interpretation is to the effect that Japanese society once again shows its remarkable powers of adaptability: Western-style individuation has now become institutionalized as a *biographical stage*—it is accepted, even expected, that young people will go through a phase of individualistic rebellion; after this is over, they will settle down and become loyal members of their respective groups. The other interpretation is that Japanese culture is indeed changing toward more individuated patterns.

Scattered data from other East Asian societies show a similar ambiguity. Thus data from Taiwan show both a persistence of some traditional communal values and a new "individualism." Survey respondents score highly in values like "family security" and "inner harmony," but there are also changes that can be called individuating: More respondents think that one should follow one's own views rather than be guided by what other people think; there is a stronger belief in controling events that affect one's life; "equality" and "individualism" *(expressis verbis)* are deemed more important than subordination in human relations.[69] In Hong Kong it was found that religious symbols shifted in symbolizing the aspirations of the nuclear family and its individuals rather than the community as a whole—a privatizing, as well as individuating change.[70] This shift has led one analyst to make the following statement: "The most formidable challenge facing Chinese traditional religion is the spirit of individualism fostered by the erosion of particularistic values."[71]

Max Weber already indicated that there was a progression from the Protestant ethic to its "laughing heir"—the Enlightenment, in which a disciplined individuation became an undisciplined one (or, if one prefers, in which "individualism" was transformed into "hyper-individualism"). Some would like to look on this progression as some sort of historical law. The more proximate question (one which, needless to add, is of immense import for the economic and political future of East Asia) is whether the societies of this region will be able to continue integrating individuals into groups with a strong sense of identity and common destiny. The empirical evidence does not permit a clear answer at this time.

It follows that any hypotheses on this issue will have to be formulated with particular cautiousness: *The societies of East Asia have succeeded for a long time in modernizing under capitalist conditions without undergoing individuation along Western lines.*

If this hypothesis could be strongly supported, one might eventually expand it in a broader formulation: A communal capitalism is possible. Or, put negatively: Individual autonomy is not an intrinsic quality of the economic culture of capitalism.

If one were only looking at data from East Asia itself, one would have to stop here and leave open the question of the future of this successful resistance to "individualism." However, the cross-national evidence on individuating modernity is strong enough to make one very skeptical about the ability of these societies to continue on their merry course of happy "groupism."

Thus, very tentatively indeed, the following hypothesis may also be formulated (it is, of course, very much open to falsification): *The values of individual autonomy are undermining East Asian communalism and are likely to continue doing so.*

If so, of course, it is likely that these societies will sooner or later face some of the current problems of Western societies, both in the areas of economic productivity and of political governability.

A final question must be addressed, if only briefly: Both in the area of political economy (particularly with regard to democracy) and in the area of economic culture (particularly with regard to individuation), what weight should be given to the fact that East Asian capitalism is part of a "world system" still dominated by the West? This fact, of course, means that these societies have been subjected to very strong political and cultural influences emanating from the West and in the postwar period especially from the United States. If there are indeed pressures toward democracy and individuation in these societies, how far can these be attributed to the intrinsic dynamics of industrial capitalism and how far to these Western influences? If, by some change in the international system, East Asia were no longer to be tied to the West, would these tendencies continue? Obviously, there is no empirical basis on which one could do more than speculate on this question —the future is not empirically available. East Asia presents us with clear cases of capitalism operating under nondemocratic regimes and in non-"individualistic" cultures. East Asia also provides evidence of democratizing and individuating pressures. Its future, in the long run (by which time, as John Maynard Keynes reminded us, we will all be dead), will provide some empirical answers as to whether democratization and individuation are intrinsic or extrinsic to the "capitalist engine" as such. In the meantime, all one can do is to propose a fairly obvious fact, which *may* cease to be a fact in the future:

*The movements toward democracy and individuation in East Asia have been greatly strengthened by the adherence of these societies to an international capitalist system centered in the West.*

This is less than satisfactory. By way of consolation, one may once more turn to Confucius: "Since doing is so difficult, can a man be otherwise than cautious in speaking?"[72]

# 8

# INDUSTRIAL SOCIALISM: A CONTROL CASE

WHY DEVOTE a chapter to socialism in a book on capitalism? In the preceding chapter the discussion of capitalism in East Asia was intended to bring into sharper relief those qualities of a capitalist economy that are intrinsic to this "mode of production," as against extrinsic elements due to the peculiar historical circumstances under which capitalism developed in the West. A discussion of those socialist societies that have attained the status of industrial economies is intended to serve a similar cognitive purpose. These societies, within the purview of the present argument, serve as a gigantic control case. Once again the image of three vast test tubes may be evoked—the large-scale "experiments" of Western industrial capitalism, East Asian industrial capitalism, and, now, the industrial socialist societies of the Soviet Union and its more advanced European allies. Needless to say, as should have been made clear by the discussion of developing societies in chapter 6, no positive value judgment is implied by this focus. Thus, as far as the future of socialism is concerned, it may well be that China will be far more important than the Soviet Union in the long run. The future, though, is not available for empirical analysis. In the present it makes little intellectual sense to compare the advanced capitalist societies with China; the comparison with the Soviet Union, on the other hand, is theoretically productive, not only for understanding the intrinsic workings of modern capitalism but also for constructing a general theory of economic culture under the conditions of modernity.

The basic "reaction" to be observed in those three huge test tubes is, precisely, that of modernization. Rooted in science and technology, it is the force that has been transforming human life everywhere, and regardless of any particular economic, political, or social system. It follows that there is the key theoretical issue of which aspects of the contemporary world are to be ascribed to modernization as such, and which aspects to this or that economic or sociopolitical system. In an earlier chapter Marxism has been criticized for its failure to make this distinction. Specifically, Marxism is typically prone to the fallacy of *pars pro toto,* by ascribing to the particular system of capitalism processes and traits that should be ascribed to the general phenomenon of modernity. A similar fallacy in the analysis of socialism should, obviously, be avoided. Thus, for example, one should not ascribe to socialism processes and traits that are common to all societies at a certain stage of modernization. There is also, however, the opposite fallacy— becoming fixated on those characteristics that socialist and capitalist societies at similar levels of modernization have in common and thereby tending to overlook the very important dissimilarities. *This* fallacy has always been dangerously close to the surface in so-called convergence theory, the approach (once quite popular, especially among authors comparing the Soviet Union with the West) that suggests that all modern societies, socialist as well as capitalist, are converging in their essential qualities.[1] Not surprisingly, those with intimate knowledge of socialist realities (or, as Marxists put it, with "real existing socialism") are much less prone to the fallacy than those contemplating the world from the safe, sanitized pinnacles of Western academia.

While it should then be clear why there must be some discussion of socialism in a theory of capitalism, it should also be stressed that what follows here is *not,* and cannot be, an attempt to draw an outline of a general theory of socialism. There is a great need for such a theory, and one of the many failures of Marxism has been its failure to supply one. Typically, Marxists have exercised enormous ingenuity in analyzing "real existing capitalism," but the comparisons then made have been *not* with empirically existent socialist societies but rather with this or that ideological conception of what socialism ought to be. There is indeed a large Marxist literature, from Trotsky to the New Left, seeking to explain why this or that socialist project failed to realize the ideological vision. Much of this literature, of course, deals with "what went wrong" with the Soviet Union.[2] Here too, however, the comparison is typically between socialist realities and a socialist utopia —again, not a very helpful modus operandi for an empirically oriented social science. In the latter context, of course, the only useful comparison is that between "real existing" phenomena—namely, between empirical data on the two dominant forms of modern industrial society.

Again in an earlier chapter, socialism was defined in terms of the dominance of political over market mechanisms in the organization of the economy. Hence the term "state capitalism," often applied by Marxist authors to the Soviet Union with pejorative intent, cannot be meaningfully employed here. There is no theoretical reason to deny the label "socialist" to the Soviet Union. On the contrary, the Soviet Union is indeed the world's "first socialist society," and for this reason it is of very great theoretical importance.[3] By the same token, the term "market socialism" is not meaningful theoretically—a society dominated by market mechanisms would not usefully be called socialist. The term "market socialism," however, does describe a number of important experiments in which socialist economies are modified by allowing greater latitude to market forces. Such experiments are indeed empirically available, and it will be important theoretically to look at them. If present trends continue, China will undoubtedly be the most important case. The focus here, though, will be on the two experiments that have had a run long enough for some empirical hypotheses— namely, the experiments with market mechanisms in Hungary and Yugoslavia.

Talcott Parsons, in his theory of modern society, called the United States the "lead society"—not in order to hold it up for admiration but to say that modernization had gone further here than anywhere else. In the same sense, with no admiration implied, the Soviet Union may be called the "lead society" in terms of modern socialism. It represents a run of well over half a century, a gigantic experiment of modernization under a socialist system and ipso facto the "ideal type" against which empirical deviations from it in other socialist societies can be usefully analyzed. In the same sense, one may speak of a "Soviet model," which, despite various modifications, continues to be the norm in the socialist societies in Eastern Europe. It should be emphasized that this by no means implies that these societies are monolithic; of course they are nothing of the sort. But precisely their differences from the Soviet case come into sharper focus as one compares them with the "lead" model.

How, then, can one describe the Soviet model of industrial (and, in an earlier stage, industrializing) socialism?

The model, of course, is centered in a highly centralized, planned economy from which market forces have (at least officially) been largely banned.[4] Apart from propagandists of the Soviet regime, most observers of this economy have been struck by its inefficiency and low productivity, especially in agriculture and in consumer industries, despite the enormous resources of the country and the coercive methods at the disposal of the regime. Yet there can be no doubt that, despite these shortcomings, there has been economic growth and modernization.[5] There can be no question but that the Soviet Union today is an advanced industrial society, that its economy has attained self-sustaining growth, and that the material standard of living of its population has been slowly but steadily improving. It is also clear that these facts, contrary to Soviet propaganda, do not constitute a "triumph of socialism" but rather are the consequence of applying modern technology to economic production—a consequence to be found everywhere in the world, regardless of sociopolitical system. These facts, in other words, are more relevant to a theory of modernity than a theory of socialism. The economic and social dynamism of modernization, once launched, is very difficult to stop, even in the most inefficiently organized system.

Most non-Marxist economists (and, increasingly, Marxist ones as well) agree that centralized planning on Soviet lines produces built-in and seemingly insuperable problems for the economy. It creates a vast bureaucracy, which, by its very nature, institutionalizes inefficiency. Max Weber was almost certainly right in his view that bureaucracy is the necessary form of administration for any modern polity. But the very characteristics of bureaucracy that he was the first to describe systematically guarantee that the bureaucratization of the economy guarantees inefficiency. It is intrinsically impossible to plan efficiently for the economy of a modern nation-state, especially if it is as vast as the Soviet Union (though the rate of success in the smaller socialist countries has not been much better). "The plan" rarely if ever works the way it is supposed to. Most economists agree that this problem is built-in precisely because the elimination of the market removes the information provided by the price system. Attempts to improve planning by introducing computers (the utopia of what some have called a "mathematical socialism") have also failed repeatedly. As one Hungarian economist put it, even a very rigid bureaucrat is more flexible than the most flexible computer.[6] To this built-in economic function of a bureaucratically ruled planned economy must be added social and political characteristics of bureaucracy that, in all likelihood, are intrinsic as well—empire building, vested interests, in-fighting and (last not least) corruption. As Trotsky once put it, "Whenever someone has something to distribute, he will not forget himself."

If the Soviet economy were what it is officially defined as being, it is doubtful whether it would work even on its present level of efficiency. It has modified its built-in problems by the development of the so-called second and third economies. The "second economy" is the largely illegal but officially tolerated system of free enterprise, an "underground" market economy that fills various gaps left by "the plan." This covers all the transactions that take place "under the table" —or, as the Russians put it, *"nalevo"* (on the left).[7] This second economy is by no means a small, unimportant phenomenon. Thus, in agriculture, private plots that contain less than 5 percent of the arable land produce more than 25 percent of the agricultural output. The "third economy" is free enterprise of a related but different sort—the informal dealings between various parts of the bureaucratic apparatus.[8] Here too accommodations are made to the built-in inefficiencies of the planned economy.

Now, in this as in all other characteristics of Soviet society, the question must be raised to what extent the present reality is due to the Soviet model of socialism and to what extent to the culture or the history of Russia. No answer is possible to this question if one looks at the Soviet Union only. Some tentative answers at least are suggested by comparing the Soviet Union with other societies in which the

Soviet model has been instituted. Thus it is clear that indigenous cultural and social traits, as well as political differences between communist regimes, do modify the working of the model. Thus the economies of Czechoslovakia and the German Democratic Republic, while operating with an essentially intact Soviet model, evince efficiencies that are superior to the Soviet Union and that are very probably to be ascribed to sociocultural causes. Even within the Soviet Union itself there is evidence of sociocultural factors affecting economic performance—for instance, in the Baltic republics, which apparently function much better economically than other parts of the Soviet Union. However, the aforementioned inefficiencies recur without exception in every society where the model has been instituted, be it by Soviet coercion or by indigenous forces. They appear to be endemic to "real existing socialism" under modern conditions.

These empirical facts permit the formulation of two hypothetical propositions: *There is an intrinsic linkage between socialism and the pervasive bureaucratization of the economy.*

*There is an intrinsic linkage between socialism and economic inefficiency.*

If one puts forth these propositions, one is ipso facto inviting falsifications. Socialist critics of the Soviet Union, especially if they are economists, are of course projecting the possibility of a future form of socialism in which bureaucracy would be less pervasive and in which the economy would work with much greater efficiency. If these projections were ever realized, the above hypotheses would be falsified and the conception of socialism indicated here would have to be revised. Somehow, looking at the history of socialist experiments to date, one is not inclined to worry too much about this possibility. Many of the notions of such an economically superior version of socialism are related to the idea of "market socialism," about which more will be said momentarily. But there is one additional observation to make in connection with the hypothesized inefficiency of socialism. The question here could be: "Inefficient *for whom?*" The Soviet model almost certainly inhibits the economic development of the societies that have adopted it, and its shortcomings impose great burdens on most of the population of those societies. There exists, however, an elite in all of those societies for whom the system works exceedingly well and who would almost certainly suffer if it became more efficient in the sense of abstract economics. In other words, economic inefficiency may well translate itself into political efficiency. For this if for no other reason, it is very important to look at the political features of this model of socialism.

The centralized command economy of the Soviet model coexists in great harmony with the centralized command polity euphemistically described as "democratic centralism" in Leninist parlance. It is, of course, a political system in which, both officially and to a large extent in practice, the party (whether it is called Communist or not) exercises a complete monopoly of power. This is not the place to go into the details of the Soviet political system.[9] There are only two questions to be asked in the context of the present argument: How is the political component of the Soviet model to be described in a comparative perspective? And to what extent is the political component of the model necessitated by its economic component?

There is hardly anyone today, no matter how sympathetic to the Soviet Union, who would deny that the latter is not a democracy in the Western meaning of the word. The Soviet Union is a dictatorial regime (precisely a "dictatorship of the proletariat"—or rather, in the ingenious Leninist interpretation of that Marxian phrase, a dictatorship of the putative "vanguard of the proletariat," the Communist party), and all other "real existing" socialist societies are governed by similarly dictatorial regimes. As observed previously in this book, there is not a single empirical case of socialist democracy. The debate as to how to describe the Soviet polity has been on other matters, notably the question of whether it is merely "authoritarian" or whether the category "totalitarian" can be applied to it. On that topic too there is a large literature, much of it irrelevant to the present argument.[10] To call a regime "authoritarian" means that it does not tolerate political opposition. In that sense the term is synonymous with "dictatorial," and self-evidently applies to the Soviet polity. The term "totalitarian," as originally conceptualized by Carl Friedrich and Hannah Arendt, pertains to a situation in which the polity seeks to absorb all other institutions of society within itself—an altogether different matter.[11] Indeed, the concepts of authoritarianism and totalitarianism should not even be placed on an empirical continuum; they refer to quite different constellations of traits. In principle, a highly authoritarian (meaning dictatorial) regime can allow considerable autonomy to nonpolitical institutions, as has often been the case with despotic governments (for example, in tsarist Russia); conversely, even a democratic regime can develop totalitarian tendencies.[12] Empirically, at least under modern conditions, the second possibility is unlikely: Democratic governance has typically generated limits on the power of the polity to absorb all other institutions into itself. But there are many authoritarian regimes that permit a pluralistic social life and that lack the totalitarian ambition.

Be this as it may, the category "totalitarian" has been criticized in its applicability to the Soviet regime on the grounds that it exaggerates the degree of political control and that it leads to a static view of Soviet society.[13] There is some merit to these criticisms. Not even in the heyday of Stalinism was political control total and monolithic, and there certainly has been a political development away from the Stalinist version of the Soviet state since 1954 (the abatement of mass terror in and of itself constitutes such a development). However, the essential totalitarian features of the regime have not been abrogated, in that the political structure not only proscribes all opposition but continually seeks to control every institutional expression within the society, from the economy to the family, including any and all activities that in Western democracies are subsumed under the rights of private individuals and private associations (some analysts have even claimed that the abatement of Stalinist-type terror has increased the efficiency of totalitarian control). Perhaps the issue can be clarified by speaking of a "totalitarian project." The project is total integration of all societal institutions within the political structure. The project never succeeds completely (there may even be anthropological reasons for this—both the spontaneity and the stupidity of human beings militate against total control). Yet it has succeeded sufficiently in some cases to justify calling these "totalitarian societies." In that perspective, the Soviet Union constitutes the most spectacular and durable success story. What is more, its model of totalitarian politics (monopolistic party, "democratic centralism," repressive apparatus, and all) has been successfully exported to other countries (and not only through imposition by Soviet military power).

It was none other than Lenin who summarized the question of all politics as "who whom?"—meaning "who is in a position to do what to whom?" This perspective illuminates the relation between economic inefficiency and political efficiency in the Soviet model of socialism.

The model is marvelously efficient, not only in terms of maintaining the material privilege of the political elite but more importantly in securing its monopoly of power. The way of life of this elite (the *nomenklatura,* as it is known in the Soviet Union) has been described in great detail—a small stratum of privileged and powerful people, far removed from the grubbiness of the masses, provided with exclusive stores, apartments, and vacation resorts, and associating mainly with each other.[14] The Soviet model is perfectly suited to the vested interests of this elite—and of any other group seeking to become such an elite. This fact goes a long way toward explaining why the Soviet model of socialism, despite its glaring weaknesses in terms of economic development, continues to be very attractive to actual and would-be elites in countries far beyond the reach of Soviet armies.

Needless to add, one must again confront the question of whether the political features of this model are intrinsic to socialism or whether, alternatively, they are to be ascribed to particular "accidents" of Russian history and culture.[15] The latter course is naturally favored by socialist and Marxist critics of the Soviet case, while antisocialist ideologists have an interest in the former interpretation. These ideological interests should be kept in mind, but they should not be allowed to obscure the empirical evidence. It is obvious that there are continuities in Russian history and that the Bolshevik Revolution, whatever else it was, was *also* an event in Russian history, with all that this implies. It is very unlikely that the first socialist regime in history would have taken on the same features, political and other, if it had been established in, say, France rather than Russia. Yet it is highly significant that both the dictatorial polity and what has just been called the totalitarian project of the Soviet Union have surfaced with almost monotonous regularity in other countries, including countries where Soviet power was not available to impose these patterns (such as China, Vietnam, Cuba, and, last not least, Yugoslavia). Minimally, one would want to apply the Weberian concept of "affinity" (*Wahlverwandschaft*) here: The Soviet political model appears to have a singular affinity with all efforts to establish socialism under modern conditions.

Nor is there any great mystery about the reasons for this affinity. What is more, one reason for this was very well understood by all the classics of Marxism: It is not possible to impose a socialist system without force, since those who are to be dispossessed in this imposition will not graciously assent to their fate. Hence, as Marx and all the other mainline Marxists argued, there must be a dictatorship. What neither Marx nor most of his epigones understood is that this need for dictatorship increases rather than decreases with the successful establishment of socialism: Central planning of the economy and despotic politics are intrinsically linked phenomena. The degree of power required by "the plan" requires dictatorial powers; conversely, there is a natural tendency for a despotic elite to seek control over the economy on which its power rests. Of course one can imagine different developments— all those included in the vision of a democratic socialism—and no social scientist can confidently assert that such developments are impossible. Yet enough is known now about the empirical workings of "real existing socialism" to make one highly skeptical of the chances for such a future possibility.

The following propositions, then, are strongly suggested by the empirical evidence to date: *There is an intrinsic affinity between socialism and authoritarian governance.*

*There is an intrinsic affinity between socialism and the totalitarian project for modern society.*

Arguably, the former affinity is more marked than the second. Authoritarian governance appears to be given by the very nature of socialist economics. The totalitarian tendency of Soviet-style regimes, on the other hand, may be rooted also in the messianic or soteriological ambitions of Marxist ideology, which is a doctrine of redemption far more than it is a social theory. It is possible that a socialist regime that gives up the all-embracing collectivism of the Marxian vision might permit greater institutional pluralism while retaining authoritarian control over the "commanding heights" of the society. Thus some analysts have claimed to see signs in the socialist world of a slow movement from totalitarianism to authoritarianism. It is significant for the argument of this book that such movement appears to be invariably accompanied by measures of economic liberalization (again, Hungary and Yugoslavia are important cases in point).

Finally, the question of stratification in the Soviet model of socialism must be addressed.[16] In the official Soviet ideology the classless society of Marx's vision is yet in the future, when communism will be attained. In the meantime, in the (merely) socialist present, there are still classes in the Soviet Union, but they are "nonantagonistic." Specifically, there are the two (putatively harmonious) classes of workers and peasants, to which is added an "intermediate stratum," the intelligentsia. Clearly, this ideological definition of the situation bears little resemblance to the empirical reality. Different sociologists have suggested a number of schemes to understand that reality. For the Soviet Union, Zev Katz enumerates six strata—*nachalniks* (rulers, or *nomenklatura*); intelligentsia; white-collar workers; blue-collar workers; *kolkhozniks* (those in agricultural collectives); the privately employed.[17] For Poland, Jan Szczepanski differentiates four strata—intelligentsia, manual workers, peasantry, private entrepreneurs.[18] Walter Connor (author of what to date may be called the definitive work on stratification in Eastern Europe) distinguishes four strata—elite or intelligentsia, routine nonmanual workers, manual workers, peasants.[19] Two Hungarian sociologists have argued that, in fact, it is the intelligentsia (or, more precisely, a segment of the intelligentsia) which constitutes the ruling class of the socialist society. György Konrád and Iván Szelényi interpret the empirical reality of Hungarian socialism in a (rather ironic) modification of the Marxian dual scheme: The two antagonistic classes are intellectuals and workers, with a middle stratum of people who are neither; the first class is subdivided into the ruling class, the technocracy, and "marginal intellectuals."[20]

As in the analysis of Western societies, stratification schemes are always disputed, there are long debates on concepts and methodology (aggravated here because any approach to stratification in Soviet-type societies is ideologically charged), and data are sparse and conflicting.[21] Yet a few fairly reliable statements can be made. Stratification in these societies, and especially in the Soviet Union, must be seen against the background of sluggish growth and economic inefficiency, which, of course, depress general living standards. In a society where there are chronic shortages in consumer goods and personal amenities (such as adequate housing), differences between strata become especially important and visible—the social world is sharply divided between "us" and "them." Thus the elite in the socialist societies is more visibly privileged than the upper classes in most Western societies (indeed, there are pronounced similarities in this respect between the Soviet elite and the upper crust of Third World societies, down to the exclusive availability to the elite of domestic servants). All the same, as was pointed out in an earlier chapter, the dynamics of income distribution appear to be similar in Western and socialist societies at comparable stages of economic development.[22] Both the Soviet Union and the other socialist societies in Europe seem to confirm the Kuznets thesis. Thus, in the Soviet Union, there was increasing income inequality after 1930, with the onset of massive industrialization; it peaked around the beginning of World War II; since 1956 there has been a trend toward less inequality. Income distribution data from the rest of socialist Europe appear to vary mainly in terms of the degree of industrialization, with the one possible difference from the West being a smaller income difference between lower white-collar and upper manual workers (a difference, however, that may be due to the "feminization" of the former category—meaning that socialist societies do not pay their industrial workers more but rather pay their women workers less). As far as redistribution via the welfare state is concerned, the social expenditures of the socialist countries compare unfavorably to the West.[23]

When it comes to the elite, straight income data are highly deceptive. The privileges enjoyed by this elite are, primarily, not in terms of official salaries but of "perks" attached to elite jobs—access to marked-down goods, special coupons of one sort or another, low-cost housing of superior quality, free transportation and holidays, and the like. Thus, if these "perks" are translated into monetary terms (always an exercise in approximation, of course), the income inequalities in these societies become much more glaring. Here, once again, there are similarities to a number of Third World societies. To this must be added the fact that, compared to the West, income is taxed at relatively low rates (meaning that a larger portion of even the official salary is taken home). In sum, whatever else may be said about stratification in "real existing socialism," it has not brought anything like the egalitarian income distribution desired by most socialists. Probably income distribution does not differ much from that in the societies of Western industrial capitalism; it may be somewhat more unequal.

As was also pointed out earlier in this book, there are also strong West/East similarities in the rates of social mobility.[24] The decisive variable, once again, appears to be the degree of modernization of any given economy. Thus, in Eastern Europe, Czechoslovakia appears to be most egalitarian in terms of social mobility, Poland least so. Following each revolution, there do appear to be changes in intragenerational mobility—middle-class people move down, working-class people move up. This, needless to say, is the obvious sociological consequence of the dispossession of the bourgeoisie. As the socialist society is consolidated, though, mobility patterns appear to approximate those in the West, varying by degree of economic development. The political elite does appear to differ from Western elites in the number of people of working-class origins, but this difference does not seem to carry over into the technocratic and intellectual elites. The prestige scales for different occupations are very similar to those in the West: Despite all the official propaganda about the dignity of manual labor, workers continue to want their children to enter nonmanual occupations, and most people regard these as more prestigious. As in the West, education is a crucial vehicle of mobility, the line between manual and nonmanual work is hard to cross, and farm workers are least likely to succeed in terms of upward mobility. Also, in the higher reaches of the system, there is an increasing "hereditization": Parents manage to pass their privileged positions on to their children—not directly (which is impossible) but through *"nalevo"* contacts and (probably most important) by support given to the educational efforts of the children.

One can only repeat here what was said earlier: In a modern society, income distribution and social mobility are largely the functions of the labor market. They can only be modified moderately by public policy, even in a postrevolutionary socialist society. Critics of socialism are, of course, happy to point out the inequalities in the Soviet Union and Eastern Europe (not to mention the even more glaring inequalities in the less developed socialist countries). But, ideological interests aside, the data merely confirm what one would predict sociologically—that industrial socialism, like industrial capitalism, must come to terms with the functional imperatives of a modern economy. As far as social mobility is concerned, though, one must stress that, while the mobility rates and *some* of the mobility vehicles (notably education) are the same as in the West, there is the additional important vehicle of (so to speak) *political mobility* in the socialist societies—that is, mobility via the apparatus of the party. There is no analogy to this in the West. Since it is *this* vehicle that leads to the highest elite positions, it is of great importance, even if only a small group can take full advantage of it.[25]

Should the societies of industrial socialism be called "class societies"? Critics of these societies, of course, have liked to do so, throwing the Marxist category, as it were, in the face of the Soviet ideologists.[26] Of course, ideological interests aside, there are different concepts of class in non-Marxist sociology as well, and the choice between them will determine how one ends up on this question. Even within Eastern Europe (wherever this was allowed) there have been different interpretations. Thus the Polish sociologist Zygmunt Bauman distinguished between two "hierarchies," one of "officialdom" and one of "class"; the social system of these societies must be understood in terms of the interaction between the two.[27] On the other hand, the Hungarian sociologist András Hegedüs avoids the term "class" but still differentiates between strata and group interests in terms of the division of labor.[28]

As class was defined earlier in this book, an approach similar to Bauman's would seem most satisfactory. That is, the societies of "real existing socialism" are not only clearly stratified, but they contain two different and interacting types of stratification. To the extent that these societies have modern industrial economies, they generate class systems that show remarkable similarities to those existing under industrial capitalism (including their degree of equality/inequality). But superimposed on this class system is a quite different system of stratification, in which privilege as well as power and prestige are linked to political office. Following Max Weber, one may call this a "patrimonial" system.[29] Privilege (the "patrimony," or in Weber's language, the *"Pfrund")* goes with the political job, is bestowed by the ruling elite. Furthermore, as these jobs are "hereditized," a patrimonial stratum (or, if one prefers, a *political* class) reproduces itself, in continuous interaction with the economically functional classes. This is, indeed, a situation very different from anything existing under industrial capitalism. To use this language, of course, represents a conceptual decision, but it is liable to empirical testing for its adequacy.

It may, therefore, be formulated in another hypothetical proposition: *Industrial socialism is characterized by the ongoing interaction of two distinct forms of stratification, a class system and a system of political patrimonialism.*

The Soviet model of socialism was imposed on most of the countries of Eastern Europe by direct Soviet force, but it was also imitated by socialist regimes that attained power on their own (Yugoslavia and Albania in Europe, and of course a by-now sizable number of countries in Asia, Africa, and Latin America). Its economic, political, and stratification features have been reproduced, with varying modifications, wherever socialism has been instituted. This is not the place to analyze all the modifications. In terms of the present argument, though, there is one modification that is of very great theoretical importance—namely, the attempt to modify Soviet-type industrial socialism through the introduction of market mechanisms.[30] There have been experiments along these lines since the Bolshevik Revolution—first during the so-called New Economic Policy (NEP) in the early 1920s. Since World War II, all the socialist economies in Europe have made experiments designed to make them more efficient—some by trying to make central control more effective ("mathematical socialism"), some by providing more incentives to managers and/or workers, some by *diminishing* central control ("market socialism"). The cases of Hungary and Yugoslavia are the most interesting in terms of the last of these strategies.

In Hungary the New Economic Mechanism (NEM) was inaugurated in 1968 and kept going (with some back-and-forth modifications) ever since.[31] Its features have been less centralized planning and control, partial price deregulation and consequent greater reliance on a freer price system, incentive pay, greater decision-making power for enterprise managers, and the legalization of small-scale private enterprise (later extended to include small private businesses operating within state enterprises, after hours). The results of all this have been clearly positive in terms of increased productivity and less shortages, especially in consumer goods. But there has been continuing central control, now exercised more indirectly through financial rather than operational controls. Familiar Soviet-style inefficiencies have continued, albeit in a less virulent form. There have also been political difficulties—internally, from conservative party elements and from occupational groups not benefiting from the reforms (such as unskilled workers); externally, from Moscow and Hungary's partners in the East European Council for Mutual Economic Assistance (CMEA). It should be noted that none of the Hungarian reforms affected the basically socialist character of the economy (as the Budapest regime, protesting its orthodoxy, correctly claims). Thus there is no private ownership in large-scale industry and no freely moving investment capital of any size; both the ownership of the basic means of production and of basic investment capital has remained in the hands of the state. What *has* happened is that managers have been asked to "play at capitalism" (to use Milton Friedman's eloquent phrase), with clear limits set to this "playing." At the same time, the Hungarian case supports the view that even this degree of market forces has beneficent effects on a socialist economy. The managers have indeed become more entrepreneurial, but they have continued to be controlled by the elephantine presence of the socialist economic bureaucracy. Not surprisingly, they have acted very conservatively. (One is reminded here of the old joke of how to get into bed with an elephant—"very carefully"!)

The Yugoslav experiment with "market socialism" is somewhat older than the Hungarian one, though it did not get into full gear until 1965.[32] Many of its features are similar to the NEM, but there are added features not found in Hungary—namely, the institutions of both "self-management" (meaning, far-reaching autonomy of individual enterprises) and "workers' management" (far-reaching participation of the work force in managerial decisions). The economic results have been less positive than those observed in Hungary, though the peculiar circumstances of Yugoslavia make it difficult to assess to what extent this is due to the economic reforms (among these circumstances are the sharp disparities in development between the north and the south and also the federal structure of the country). Nevertheless, there are some effects that can be ascribed with some confidence to the "syndicalist" character of the Yugoslav experiment.

Workers have no interest in the long-range economic fate of their enterprise, since they lose their "share" in it if they change jobs. Consequently, they have the inclination to avoid risky investments, and through the participatory mechanisms of the system, exert pressure on management to avoid risks. Again, this has a strongly conservative effect. Also, since the income share of each worker is diminished if the labor force of the enterprise expands, there has been pressure toward labor-saving/capital-intensive operations—a dubious strategy in any developing economy, resulting (predictably) in high unemployment (the social results of which have been mitigated by large-scale emigration of workers to Western Europe). As in Hungary, there is no private ownership of large-scale industry and no freely moving capital of any magnitude. The "commanding heights" of the economy remain under state control (though, in Yugoslavia, this has meant the several republic governments rather than the national government in Belgrade).

"Market socialism" has been an idea congenial to Marxist "revisionists" for a long time.[33] The empirical evidence furnished by the Hungarian and Yugoslav experiments in "market socialism" strongly suggests that there are definite limits to this strategy. It is not clear that either economy has been more efficient if compared with Soviet-style economies, with the exception of consumer goods. Yugoslavia is hardly an economic success story, though this may not necessarily be the result of its policies of "syndicalist socialism." In several economic areas, Hungary has been less successful than the German Democratic Republic (which has barely deviated from the Soviet economic model). It is plausible to argue that there are both political and economic reasons for the meager performance of "market socialism." The political factor of Soviet hegemony is irrelevant to the present argument and in any case does not pertain to Yugoslavia. But there are internal and probably intrinsic political limits to this type of experiment. In Marxist parlance one might say that there is a built-in "contradiction" between the market and bureaucracy as sociopolitical forces, and no socialist society appears capable of resolving this contradiction. Put more conventionally, the socialist bureaucracy, once established, will necessarily resist the diminishment of its power and privilege following upon any expansion of market forces within the economy. There are also economic limits. As long as the basically socialist character of the economy is maintained, Soviet-style inefficiencies can only be mitigated to a limited degree.

What happens in these cases is that an "artificial market" is instituted —artificial, that is, if compared with the manner in which the market operates in a capitalist economy. Put simply, this just isn't good enough. The limits of "market socialism" were predicted with remarkable accuracy by Ludwig von Mises as early as the 1930s.[34] Here is a key proposition of von Mises: "The market is . . . the focal point of the capitalist order of society; it is the essence of capitalism. Only under capitalism, therefore, is it possible; it cannot be 'artificially' imitated under socialism."[35] Why? Because the "artificial market" assumes that the only production factors are producers buying and selling commodities, omitting the supply of capital by capitalists and the demand for capital by entrepreneurs. Capital, of course, continues to be controlled by the state. This means that, under socialism, no one risks his own capital. The result is that basic investment decisions are made by bureaucrats with little if any personal stake in the matter—the dynamism of a modern market economy is thus arrested *in statu nascendi*. This fairly accurately predicts the Hungarian experience. But von Mises also predicted the Yugoslav experience in his discussion of "syndicalism."[36] Given such a system, von Mises argued, there are two possibilities. Either the workers lose their "shares" in the enterprise upon leaving it, or they are allowed to keep them. In the former case workers will have a vested interest in making no changes in production, a stultifying effect; in the latter case, to all intents and purposes, there will have been a reversal to a capitalist order. Yugoslavia, of course, has followed the former route. One may sum up von Mises's judgment on the two types of "market socialism" by saying that just as managers cannot be made to play at being capitalists, workers cannot play at being shareholders—or, rather, both "artifacts" are not possible as long as a system remains socialist.[37]

These insights may now be summed up in two propositions: *A modification of industrial socialism through the introduction of market mechanisms will encounter political limits, which are caused by the resistance of the patrimonial elite defending its vested interests.*

*A modification of industrial socialism through the introduction of market mechanisms will encounter economic limits, which are caused by the inability of the artificial market to replicate the efficiency of the capitalist market.*

The foregoing discussion of "market socialism," however, leads to an even wider proposition. Early on in this book the decision was made to define capitalism (and, conversely, socialism) in terms of the dominance of market forces rather than of the private ownership of the means of production. Such definitional decisions, of course, are arbitrary, and the empirical arguments in the book could be made just as well, after due rewording, if capitalism and socialism had been defined differently. The definition used here, though, has the advantage of allowing the relationship between the market and private ownership to be the subject matter of an empirical hypothesis rather than being posited by definition.

This hypothesis is simple but far-reaching; it follows logically from the foregoing discussion: *There can be no effective market economy without private ownership of the means of production.*

One must be open to the possibility that future experiments of "market socialism" will falsify this hypothesis. After all, it may be argued that the situation in Hungary and Yugoslavia has very distinctive features that need not be replicated elsewhere, such as the constraints imposed on the Hungarians by Moscow and the ethnic problems of Yugoslavia. The future course of the immense Chinese experiment, if it continues along present lines, will certainly help to clarify these issues. However, enough is known now about the intrinsic dynamics, economic as well as political, of *any* socialist society to make one very skeptical about the possibility of such experiments succeeding. Also, the hypothesis leaves open the question of so-called mixed economies. More specifically, it leaves open the question at what point the reduction or limitation of the private ownership of the means of production tilts over into the economic and political stagnation of the socialist societies as one knows them today. For example, if the more radical elements of the socialist party in Sweden have their way in squeezing out the private sector, how long will it take before the Swedish economy comes to resemble the economies of the Soviet bloc? Or, for an opposite example, how far must the quasi-socialist regulation of the economy of India be dismantled before an East-Asian type of economic vitality asserts itself? The present state of knowledge simply does not permit definitive answers to these questions. What *is* known, with a fair degree of reliability by now, is that market forces almost always invigorate an economy and that socialism almost always stultifies it. The Soviet Union is so important for a theory of socialism, not only because it constitutes the most long-lasting socialist case in history but because for the greater part of its duration it has consistently refused to allow any free play of market forces (except for the economic "underground").

Some additional observations on industrial socialism are in order now. They are related to the coexistence of industrial socialism with the international capitalist system in the contemporary world.

Socialism, no less than capitalism, is beset with "cultural contradictions" (to use Daniel Bell's apt phrase). One "contradiction" is between socialist collectivism and modern individualism. As has been pointed out earlier, modernization brings about a weakening of traditional solidarities, and this process facilitates the emergence of modern "individualism." And as was argued in a previous chapter, there exists a particular affinity between capitalism and modern individuation. All or nearly all socialist ideologies, and Marxism above all, have criticized this allegedly nefarious linkage of capitalism and "individualism"; socialism, by contrast, is an ideal of collective solidarity and unselfish morality. The empirical evidence from the socialist societies of Europe indicates that this collectivism meets with stubborn resistance—not so much politically (by and large this would be futile, and only the rare dissident attempts it), but as a withdrawal into a private sphere of family, friendships, and personal consumption that is at least relatively protected from the totalitarian grasp of the collective. This phenomenon of individuals resisting collectivization wherever they can is impressive, but it is unclear to what extent it may indeed be what the official ideology claims it to be—namely, "survivals of bourgeois consciousness"—fated to weaken or disappear as the totalitarian state continues in the future. Nor is it certain that the same "contradiction" must appear in cases of socialist modernization outside the orbit of Western civilization (developments in China will be very instructive on this). Finally, despite all totalitarian controls, there is the ever-present counterexample of the West, with its triumphantly exported "individualistic" culture. All socialist regimes have tried to control the inroads of this culture—from jeans and rock music to ideas of individual rights—but most have had to make some concessions to it, especially with the young. It is not possible to say how these individuating cultural forces would fare in the absence of the Western example.

There is also the cultural "contradiction" between Marxist ideology and socialist realities. The evidence from the Soviet Union and Eastern Europe is quite clear: There is widespread cynicism about the official Marxist rhetoric, extending into the very elite itself. Ironically, Marxism, still so attractive to intellectuals outside the socialist world, is taken seriously by very few people who live in that world. This certainly constitutes a problem of legitimacy for these societies. Once again, though, it is unclear to what extent this "contradiction" is brought into consciousness by comparison with the known realities of the nonsocialist world. Would it persist if the latter ceased to exist or if realistic knowledge of it were successfully barred? Could it be, in other words, that the totalitarian project is yet to be perfected, at which point this "contradiction" would disappear?

A case can be made that the persistence of religion, despite all Marxist expectations of its demise in socialist society, is at least one of the great obstacles to the achievement of a perfect totalitarianism. Religious faith, by its very nature, always transcends the givenness of any social order and ipso facto relativizes the latter: Even the most majestic social experiments are trivialized in the perspective of the religious attitude—all the empires of this world melt away in the presence of the biblical God, and, mutatis mutandis, they also lose their impressiveness when confronted with the transcendent insights of other world religions. A totalitarian society cannot tolerate such trivialization. If so, Marxists are probably quite correct in their view that religion, in any shape or form, is a crucial obstacle to their core intentions. It would then also follow that those who propagate a synthesis of Marxism and religion are operating under an illusion: They fail to perceive the totalitarian thrust of Marxist utopianism and, conversely, the inherently antitotalitarian tendency of the religious attitude. Since even the most repressive Marxist regimes have failed to eradicate religion, this is a cheering reflection for those who abhor totalitarianism. However, it is also possible to make a contrary argument. It is a very chilling argument. Perhaps, quite contrary to what has just been said, the totalitarian project suffers from not being legitimated in religious terms. Suppose that a Soviet-style totalitarian apparatus were left in place, but that it were now legitimated in solemnly religious terms. Would this perhaps greatly strengthen its plausibility? The final irony here might be that those who would marry Marxism and religion, along the lines of "liberation theology," might yet produce the sort of ultimate legitimation of the totalitarian project that will make the latter perdure for centuries.

There exist today not one but two "world systems." They are, of course, engaged in an ongoing political, economic, and military struggle, which is the major fact of international relations since World War II. But the two systems are also engaged in what one may call a process of mutual "contamination." Socialist ideas of one kind or another have penetrated, "infected," the consciousness of significant strata in the capitalist societies, creating problems of legitimacy as well as policy. But Western ideas, including values directly linked to the culture of capitalism, continue to "infect" the socialist societies, creating comparable problems of legitimacy and control. This global game of reciprocal subversion is likely to continue for a long time, barring the sort of military conflict that would eliminate one or both of the two contestants. Consequently, it is very difficult to untangle which of the aforementioned "contradictions" are endemic to socialism and which have to do with this great competition. This is one instance in which theoretical inconclusiveness may be a cause for thankfulness.

# 9

# CAPITALISM AND
# THE DYNAMICS
# OF MYTH

THE INSIGHT that an enduring human community requires a belief
in its essential rightness long antedates modern social science. It is
implied in the biblical statement (Deuteronomy 8:3, quoted approvingly by Jesus) that man does not live by bread alone, in the statement
of Confucius (Analects 12:7) to the effect that government requires
food, weapons, and the confidence of the people—and that it could,
if necessary, do without the first two but never without the last. This
age-old insight is, more or less, what modern social scientists mean by
the concept of "legitimation."[1] This concept has a longish history and
(hardly surprisingly) has gone through various permutations. What it
refers to, though, is a central and rarely disputed fact of human social
life—that a society is not held together simply by practical needs and
interests but by beliefs that explain and justify its particular institutional arrangements. Thus, a legitimation is any answer, on whatever
level of sophistication, to the question as to whether this or that
institutional arrangement is morally just or proper. If no one else asks
this question, two groups of people will, sooner or later: inquisitive
children, and those who perceive themselves to be at a disadvantage
under the particular arrangement. If an institution is to survive from

one generation to another and if it is to stave off the ever-present possibility of disruption, there better be some answers at hand, not just any old answers that someone might think up but answers that will indeed command the confidence of the people.

There are many levels of legitimating ideas—from the structure of ordinary language (which gives a name to an existing institution but may have no words for possible alternatives) through proverbs, maxims, and the clichés of folk wisdom to elaborate theories and systems of thought grounded in whatever people think of as valid knowledge about the world (be it in religious, philosophical, or scientific terms).[2] There is, however, one distinction that should be briefly developed here, because it is important for the present topic. This is the distinction between legitimations that sustain an institution (or an institutional order) in ordinary, everyday life, and legitimations that command a high degree of commitment and sacrifice on the part of those who believe in them. It is the distinction between ordinary legitimations and those that Georges Sorel called "myths."[3] As Sorel uses the term, it does not necessarily imply that the second type of legitimation is based on some error or illusion (as in the conventional use of the word "myth"). An outside observer (say, a scientific analyst) may or may not make this judgment; sociologically speaking, the judgment is irrelevant. What *is* relevant is that the ideas and images making up the "myth" are believed by people in the empirical situation and that these ideas and images inspire people to acts of commitment and sacrifice— in the extreme case, even the sacrifice of life itself.

The reason why this distinction is important in the present context is very simple: Capitalism, as an institutional arrangement, has been singularly devoid of plausible myths; by contrast, socialism, its major alternative under modern conditions, has been singularly blessed with myth-generating potency. No theory of capitalism (and, just so, no theory of socialism) can bypass this, so to speak, mythological inequality between these two modern systems of socioeconomic organization.

The mythic deprivation of capitalism is well caught in a joke originating in the milieu of New York's garment district. Abie and Nat's dressmaking business faces bankruptcy. The two partners draw straws to see which of them should commit suicide so that the other can collect the insurance and keep the business going. Nat loses. After bidding a tearful farewell to everyone, he takes the elevator up to the top floor and jumps off. As he falls, he looks into the windows of the other businesses in the building, competitors all. Abie is leaning out of his window, watching his partner fall. And as Nat goes by, he calls out urgently: "Abie, cut velvet!"

To explain a joke is to kill it. Since this is a book of social theory, not of humor, an explanation may be risked: The joke lies precisely in the absurdity of committing suicide in order to save a dressmaking business. By amplification, *any* kind of business and the sum-total of business activity called "capitalism" is not plausible as a motive for self-sacrificing heroism. The market tip to cut velvet is not plausible as the last words of a human being on earth. By contrast, any of the heart-stirring slogans by which the socialist vision has been propagated will do very nicely for such a moment. This discrepancy, in brief, is the topic of the present chapter.

It was, once again, Sorel who early in this century proposed that Marxism could only be understood as a myth (in his meaning of the term) and not as a scientific theory.[4] He probably overstated the case. Marxism is certainly a myth, one of the most important of the contemporary age, but it *also* can be understood as a scientific theory. As will be argued momentarily, it is precisely this double character that goes far in explaining its hold over many minds. Now, it should be stressed again that the appellation "myth" here carries no pejorative implication; it clearly did not in Sorel's case; he was indeed convinced that Marxism fell short of his mythological requirements, but he counterproposed what he believed to be a superior myth—that of the "general strike." And within the Marxist tradition itself, even if the term "myth" is not commonly used, there have been many authors who have proposed that Marxism should be understood as a moral or even "spiritual" faith rather than as merely a scientific doctrine. Ferdinand Lasalle, Antonio Gramsci, and Ernst Bloch may be mentioned here; Gramsci actually coined the term "fideistic" to denote this dimension of Marxism. Maoism should probably be given first place among Marxist movements stressing "spirituality," moral and quasi-religious inspiration. Even those more orthodox Marxists, who have been insisting that Marxism is, first and foremost, a matter of science, have been forced to make use of its mythic qualities as soon as they have engaged in revolutionary actions: Men are not prepared to risk their lives for a scientific theory.

The socialist myth, of course, is much broader than its various Marxist versions. Its roots are undoubtedly in the communitarian tradition of Western Christianity. It is an ideal of justice, equality, and redemptive community that goes back to the earliest times of the Christian Church and very likely to even earlier strands of secretarian Judaism. The genius of Marx managed to combine this emotionally and indeed religiously charged vision with a sober ideal of scientific inquiry, derived not from the Judeo-Christian tradition but from the thought of the Enlightenment. Marx himself, in his early work, made the distinction between "utopian socialism" and "scientific socialism." Not to put too fine a point to it, essentially every variety of socialism preceding him was relegated to the former category, while his own work, mirabile dictu, was supposed to embody "scientific socialism" in its pure form. There is heavy irony in all of this, since it is difficult to believe that, of the millions of people who have embraced Marxism since *Das Kapital* saw the light of day, more than a handful could have been converted to the revolutionary faith by the pretty much unreadable prose of those ponderous tomes. Needless to say, these considerations need not impede anyone from taking Marxist thought as one set of theories among others and applying to it the usual criteria of empirical evidence (as has been done several times in this book). But anyone who believes that such a procedure will either convince or disabuse large numbers of people of the scientific merits of Marxism would be laboring under a far-reaching illusion (there are always exceptions, of course, but these are few and far between).

As Nicholas Berdyaev and other critics of Marxism have argued (and some advocates of Marxism as well, notably Ernst Bloch), there is a more specifically biblical theme that has played an important role in the popular appeal of Marxism—the theme of eschatology. That is, Marxism can also be understood as a peculiar secularized version of the classical biblical view of history as consisting of a fall from grace, a set of redemptive events embodied in a human community, and as leading up to a great climax that will bring ordinary history to an end. Marxism has substituted private property and its "alienations" for original sin, the revolutionary process for the *kairoi* of God's redemptive activity, the proletariat (and later, with Lenin, the party as the "vanguard of the proletariat") for the church, and the attainment of true communism for the advent of the Kingdom of God. Critics of Marxism (such as Berdyaev) have, of course, taken these parallels as grounds for dismissing it as a sort of Christian aberration. It is important to stress, however, that some Marxists have taken the same parallels as grounds for claiming that this revolutionary creed rightfully embodies the deepest human aspirations of Western history.[5]

There is yet another synthetic aspect of the Marxist vision of socialism that is particularly appealing in non-Western countries. This is the synthesis between modernizing and countermodernizing themes.[6] Marxism is modern, and modernizing, in all the features that are subsumed under the label "scientific socialism"—not only the pretension to be scientific in its insights but in its ethos of rational control and planning, its explicit espousal of the great ideals of the Enlightenment (including the revolutionary values of liberty, equality, and fraternity), and, last not least, in its claim to embody the idea of "progress" in the contemporary world. It is no accident that Marxists, and indeed most other socialists as well, like the adjective "progressive" to denote themselves and their political or ideological allies. In the non-Western world, these themes feed perfectly into the modernization process. It is, therefore, quite logical that neotraditionalist opponents of modernity (for example, Muslim fundamentalists in Iran and elsewhere) perceive Marxist socialism as being a sort of twin of Western capitalism—*both* are modernizing movements, *both* are antagonistic to traditional forms of life, thus *both* must be equally opposed in the name of tradition. This perception is correct as far as it goes; it fails, though, to include the other, the countermodernizing themes in Marxism. For the Marxist vision *also* promises redemption from the specific discontents of modernity commonly labeled "alienation"—the severance of the individual from communal ties, "excessive individualism" and "egotism" (commonly identified with the capitalist "profit motive"—"one against all"), the decline in moral and religious certitudes, the condition called *anomie* by sociologists. In the Marxist eschatology, all these maladies will be overcome (in Hegelian parlance, *aufgehoben*) when communism is attained. But even now, in the premillennial period of "building socialism," there is a foreshadowing of this redemptive community in the various collectives of Marxist political activity—party cells, "base communities," "affinity groups," or other revolutionary coteries. These themes, on their part, fit neatly with the countermodernizing sentiments of large numbers of people, not only in the Third World but in Western societies as well. Marxism thus promises *both* the fruits of modernity (including its material ones) *and* the restoration of the lost treasures of premodern ways of life. Put a little crudely, one reason for the perduring appeal of Marxism is that it seems to allow its adherents to eat their cake and have it too. It is an appeal that is hard to beat.

Both in the Third World and in the West, intellectuals have been prime candidates for this "fideistic" commitment. In an earlier chapter in this book the argument was made that, at least in part, the affinity of intellectuals for socialism can be explained in terms of vested class interests. Again to put it a little crudely, intellectuals tend to favor socialism because they believe that a socialist society will give them powers and privileges denied to them under capitalism. (The fact that this expectation has thus far proven to be mistaken in all "real existing" socialist societies is irrelevant to the extent that the belief continues despite these empirical disconfirmations.) But this crude (if one prefers, "vulgar Marxist") explanation is not sufficient. It should be amplified by an explanation in terms of precisely the mythic propensities of intellectuals. How is one to account for that? A plausible answer would be in terms of secularization: There are good grounds for saying that in most countries intellectuals have become more estranged from religion and religiously based morality than any other significant population group. Consequently, more than other groups, intellectuals suffer from the "alienation" and the *anomie* of modernity. They are ipso facto more susceptible to any secular messages of redemption from these ills. The socialist myth, especially in its Marxist version, is unusually well suited to meet these needs. Thus it is very probably an oversimplification to say that intellectuals have flocked to Marxism because they are "children of the Enlightenment."[7] There is a correct element in this: Modern intellectuals are indeed "children of the Enlightenment"—but not very happy children at that. They do aspire to Enlightenment ideals—progress, reason, scientific truth, humanistic values. But they also desire at least some of the traditional virtues that modernity has undermined—collective solidarity, transcendence of individualism, and, last not least, moral certainty and ultimate meaning. Marxism has plausibly offered this curious mélange of modern and countermodern appeals from its inception. It should not surprise that intellectuals have been particularly prone to go for it.

If one looks at the contemporary world in terms of the distribution of the socialist myth, the results are somewhat ironic. Socialism in general and the Marxist version of it in particular continue to have strong appeal among Western intellectuals, though there has been a shift to the right in a number of culturally important countries (France being the most intriguing example of this in recent years). Also in the West, socialism has manifested itself in various ideological combinations with other "progressive" and "liberationist" doctrines, such as environmentalism and feminism (doctrines that often have little in common except a general animus against "bourgeois capitalism"). Socialism, and especially Marxism, have *least* appeal in the countries within the Soviet orbit, that is, those countries in which there is not only "real existing" socialism but in which Marxism has been elevated to the status of a monopolistic state creed. It is very difficult to find intellectuals in Eastern Europe who, once they are candid with an outsider, take Marxism in any of its forms seriously. It appears from scattered accounts that a similar situation has come to prevail in China in the wake of the Cultural Revolution. It must remain somewhat open to what extent this dismissal of Marxism also includes ideas of a non-Marxist version of socialism yet to come; certainly no significant reform movement in Eastern Europe has called for a return to capitalism. It is at least possible that the one experience capable of shattering the socialist vision is living under the conditions of socialist reality; the latter experience clearly discredits Marxist modes of analysis in a fairly definitive manner for the majority of intellectuals who have undergone it. The synthesizing capacity of Marxism, however, can be seen most clearly in the Third World. There, in one country after another, one can observe how both the socialist myth in general and its Marxist edition coalesce the modernizing themes of progress, rationality, and human uplift with nostalgias for the (real or imagined) tribal solidarities of the past. This coalescing of modernizing and countermodernizing themes can be seen in "Indian socialism," "African socialism," and in the utopian imagery of the liberation theologies of Latin America, to mention but three important cases.

One should be careful here not to confuse the inner consistency of myth with the logic of scientific reasoning. Myths are never the products of dispassionate analysis, and the socialist myth is by no means in a special category in this respect; in the modern age, it is not even unique in its claim to be based on science (one look at the American religious scene, from Christian Science to the recent flowering of "creation science," suffices to make this point). Thus an uninvolved outsider may decide that the modernizing and countermodernizing themes in, say, African socialism are logically incompatible with each other. Be this as it may, it is not intrinsically implausible for people to desire both the advantages of modernity and the preservation of their cultural heritage. The question is which symbols best succeed in capturing and expressing this mix of aspirations; the symbols of socialism appear to have a marked edge in this regard.

To make the two statements offered thus far in this chapter—to wit, that socialism has strong mythic power and that capitalism has little if any—is not to ignore other myths operative in the contemporary world. Throughout most of human history, of course, religion was the source of all myths. The ideas that legitimated social order and that inspired human beings to sacrifice their own interests if not their lives to a social purpose were rooted in religious experience. Indeed, speaking sociologically, one can say that such legitimation has been the principal *social* function of religion from archaic times to the present.[8] One of the liveliest issues in the sociology of religion in recent years has been the debate over the extent to which modernity has changed this—that is, the extent as well as the nature of secularization.[9] This is emphatically not the place to go into this debate. Let it be stipulated that secularization is a real phenomenon, and that, especially in the West and in modern educated groups elsewhere, secularization has weakened the legitimating and myth-generating power of religion. But even if this stipulation is made, it is very clear indeed that religion continues both to legitimate society and to produce very powerful myths in many parts of the world. The most dramatic instance of this today is the rise of Muslim neotraditionalism in virtually all the countries of Islamic civilization, from the North African Maghreb to the southern Philippines. The Iranian Revolution, in and of itself, may serve as a falsification of the thesis that modernization precludes the social efficacy of religious myths. But the Muslim world is by no means unique when it comes to powerful relgious revivals. At least as widespread and significant as the Islamic renascence is the rapid spread of conservative Protestantism in the Third World, notably in East Asia (with the exception of Japan, South Korea being the most dramatic case), black Africa (often in syncretistic combinations with indigenous

African religion), and, perhaps most surprisingly, in Latin America. The upsurge of Evangelicalism in the United States, dramatic enough in itself, is thus part of a global religious movement of immense power. But other religious traditions, such as Buddhism, Hinduism, and Judaism, have also experienced strong revivalistic movements, frequently with important social and political side-effects.

However widespread secularizing influences may be, religion continues worldwide as a major source of legitimation both for the status quo and for various proposed alternatives (myths, needless to say, can be both conservative and revolutionary, and often the *same* religious symbols can be employed to legitimate either purpose). In a number of cases, the religious myths have been synthesized with socialist symbols—as with "Buddhist socialism" or "Islamic socialism." Thus far at least, Third World Protestantism, with the exception of denominations led by intellectuals, has proven infertile ground for this particular religio-socialist synthesis; as if determined to validate Max Weber's notions about capitalism and the "Protestant ethic," Evangelicals from Seoul to Guatemala City appear to hold favorable attitudes toward capitalist development. (One may add, though, that this may change if and when the leadership of these groups falls to intellectuals, especially such as may have been trained in accredited theological institutions in the West.)

There are other ideas of modern origins that, along with socialism, have shown themselves to be myth generating. The Enlightenment ideas of progress and liberty continue to have an appeal that, in some places, may plausibly be called mythic. The idea of liberty in particular, linked to the aspiration toward political democracy, is particularly potent (not surprisingly) in countries ruled by dictatorial regimes—including those under Marxist hegemony (Poland may serve by way of example). But, next to socialism, the most potent secular myth of modern times would appear to be nationalism.[10] The question of how and why the symbol of the nation came to play such an important part in the modern mind is an intriguing one, and clearly beyond the scope of this book.[11] Once again, the myth of nationalism has been frequently linked to the socialist myth. It is unfortunate for this particular ideological alliance that the most famous/infamous instance is that of German National Socialism, but it would be obviously distortive to associate every other instance with Hitler's Nazism.[12] Thus, for example, the democratic movement led by Tomas Masaryk, which came to fruition in the establishment of an independent Czechoslovakia after World War I, also called itself "National Socialist"—and was emphatically a different kettle of ideological fish from the movement that arose in Germany under that name a few years later. More contemporaneously, a number of political movements and regimes in the Third World, with no affinity of any sort with German Nazism, have claimed to embody both nationalist and socialist ideals.[13] Frequently, both the nationalist and the socialist components of these ideologies are claimed to be rooted in indigenous, traditional notions of collective solidarity, as, for example, in the idea of *ujamaa* (Swahili for "familyhood") that was proclaimed by Julius Nyerere as the centerpiece of the Tanzanian ideology.[14] The socialist myth, one may say, has been happily polygamous in the ideological marriages it has entered into in different parts of the world.

Especially in the Third World, however, there is an additional element in virtually *all* Third World ideologies, socialist or not. This is the promise to effect a social transformation that will bring with it "development," that will bring to people the material benefits of modernity. In this sense, all third World ideologies are "cargo cults," to give a broader, generic meaning to the Melanesian religious movement, which had as its centerpiece the belief that the ancestors would return in ships (later, in planes) bringing with them a cornucopia of modern goods and appliances—a marvelous vision of ghostly vessels from the realm of the supernatural disgorging refrigerators, radios, television sets, pickup trucks, and electric hair driers and, not so incidentally, a marvelous synthesis between traditional and modern symbolisms.[15] Every credible Third World leader or movement must promise the relevant constituency that the "cargo" of modern benefits will be delivered quite soon and with a degree of certainty. To the extent that socialism fails to make such delivery with depressing regularity, the built-in "cargo" expectation serves as a principle of "reality control." Nonintellectuals, at any rate, may get tired of waiting after a while; nonintellectuals have a greater propensity to test myths by means of empirically verifiable expectations (though this point should not be exaggerated—all human beings, on whatever level of education, are capable of adhering to myths in the teeth of mountains of empirical counterevidence).

Be this as it may, Western intellectuals adhering to the socialist vision, be it in its Marxist or some other articulation, may serve as a very clear illustration of the meta-empirical nature of a true myth. The manner in which one generation after another of Western socialists have held onto the vision despite repeated empirical disappointments is one of the more intriguing aspects of recent intellectual history. In one of the classics of French sociology, Maurice Halbwachs analyzed the way in which the Western mind imagined the geography of the Holy Land.[16] This "legendary topography," as he called it, had of course very little to do with the actual geography of Palestine. The accounts of Western socialists of the countries of "real existing" socialism furnish similar materials for a social psychology of imaginary promised lands.[17] There have been, indeed, some shifts in this "topography" as the tensions between the myth and the empirical evidence have become too great. And some individuals have, indeed, turned away from the socialist vision or from Marxism as a result of these tensions. What is remarkable, though, is the ingenuity with which many have succeeded in explaining (or explaining away) the empirical discrepancies. And, in many cases, what has also happened is that the location of the promised land was simply shifted on the map of the world: If the Soviet Union could no longer be held up as the locale of realized socialist ideals, then it had to be China; if not China, then Cuba or Vietnam or Mozambique or Nicaragua, and so on, in principle ad infinitum. Nothing illustrates the impermeability of myth to empirical disconfirmation as powerfully as the propensity of intellectuals to locate "true socialism" in one place after another—an endlessly shifting topography of the mind, propelled by a dialectic of hope, disappointment, and hope rekindled.[18]

Much more could be said about the mythic dynamics of socialism and its ideological allies. For the present purpose, though, it must suffice to propose a simple hypothesis: *Socialism, in addition to being a set of political programs and the source of social-scientific interpretations, is also one of the most powerful myths of the contemporary era; to the extent that socialism retains this mythic quality, it cannot be disconfirmed by empirical evidence in the minds of its adherents.*

Minimally, giving credence to this proposition sobers the expectations one may have about the weight of evidence concerning "real existing" socialism. It is possible to falsify this or that Marxist interpretation of the world; perhaps it is even possible to falsify Marxism as a body of theory; it is *not* possible to falsify Marxism (or socialism in general) as a mythic vision of human hope. This, of course, by no means implies that there are no ex-Marxists or ex-socialists. But only very rarely is the career that leads to such a status comparable to the process by which a scientist formulates, tests, and discards hypotheses. Rather, it is a career comparable to that of a religious believer. One makes an act of faith; one can also lose one's faith. One undergoes conversion; one may also be de-converted. Just as it is unlikely that the former movement of the mind is brought about by reading the works of Marx or any other socialist theorist, so it is unlikely that the latter movement will be triggered by reading a book such as this one.

By contrast with the mythopoetic productivity of socialism, capitalism is and always has been mythically deprived. What is more, some of the most important protagonists of capitalism would not have been in the least bothered by this observation. Surely, if capitalism has a theoretical father, it would be Adam Smith. Yet Smith believed that the economic system he was describing (of course he did not use the later term "capitalism") was, quite simply, the natural ordering of society; that which is natural, almost by definition, does not require legitimation, mythic or otherwise (who would think of legitimating the law of gravity, or of concocting myths so that people will be inspired to act in accordance with it?). F.A. Hayek, probably the most prominent advocate of capitalism in the present period, would not quite agree with Smith's notions of what is natural, but his defense of capitalism is indirect by reference to its linkage with liberty, and he explicitly rejected the idea that a legitimating concept of justice is relevant to the operations of a market system.[19] A roughly similar line is taken by Milton Friedman.[20] Now, this does not mean that various authors have not thought of more direct or more exciting ways to legitimate capitalism or even to put together something that one might call a capitalist myth.[21] What is at issue here, though, is not the quality of certain ideas in themselves, but their potential for gaining acceptance and enthusiastic support among significant social groups. Legitimation is as legitimation does. Any number of people can propose myths; these will remain sociologically irrelevant unless they acquire plausibility among groups of living human beings. To paraphrase the famous dictum of W. I. Thomas, a legitimation will be real to the extent that people consider it so; the same applies to the category of legitimations called myths.

The mythic deprivation of capitalism is, very likely, grounded in the fact that capitalism is an economic system and nothing else (by contrast, socialism is a comprehensive view of human society). All economic realities are essentially *prosaic,* as against the poetry that inspires, moves, and converts human minds. Max Weber, in his well-known analysis of charisma as a force in history, describes charisma as *wirtschaftsfremd*—as inimical to economic concerns.[22] Without doing violence to Weber's thinking, one may reverse the proposition: Economic reality is inimical to charisma, or, put in Sorelian language, economics is averse to myth. Economic rationality and the mythopoetic impetus occupy very different compartments of human consciousness. Efforts to combine the two are unlikely to be successful, in the sense of success as plausibility to significant numbers of people.

This is not a new problem in the history of capitalism. From its inception, capitalism legitimated itself indirectly—by being linked up with other legitimations, *not* of the economic system as such but rather of other, more myth-prone realities of human life. Max Weber's classical argument about the relation between Protestantism and the "spirit of capitalism" can be understood as a brilliant illustration of this point. The last thing in the world that the great Calvinist moralists wanted to explain and justify was capitalist economics. They were concerned with glorifying their awesome deity and, more immediately, with the salvation of souls. The Protestant legitimation of capitalism was indirect, unintended, and, at least in the earlier period, unperceived. Probably at no time would it make sense to speak of a Protestant myth of capitalism. As the drama of modern capitalism unfolded, the latter came to be associated with other, secular myths, notably the myth of progress.[23] In other words, capitalism was linked with the overall "progressivism" of bourgeois culture. Once again, the legitimation here was indirect. The indirect legitimation by means of Protestantism came to be weakened by secularization as well as by changes in Protestant morality, while the indirect legitimation via bourgeois "progressivism" came to be weakened by the very success of the bourgeois revolution. Even the Calvinist churches, let alone other wings of Protestantism, developed moralities that were less functional in terms of capitalist enterprise than the old Protestant ethic, and bourgeois culture (as discussed in an earlier chapter) developed hedonistic and "hyper-individualistic" traits that also diminished its affinity with the "spirit of capitalism."

Joseph Schumpeter believed that the very success of capitalism as an economic system undermines the cultural foundations on which it rests.[24] Here too, although the phrase is not used by Schumpeter, there is an assumption of indirect legitimation: Capitalism does not legitimate itself; it depends for its legitimation upon traditional values, such as those furnished by religious morality; but the very dynamics of capitalism, its "creative destruction" (Schumpeter's eloquent phrase), increasingly weakens all traditions and thus pulls away the rug from under its own cultural credibility. These and similar reflections have led to the notion that contemporary capitalism is undergoing a crisis of legitimacy.[25] The notion is then translated into a prediction that, divested of its legitimacy, capitalism is headed for its demise (depending on the individual author, the prediction may be made gleefully or morosely).

This interpretation should be taken with a grain of salt, mainly for two reasons. First, as was pointed out before, there is nothing new about the incapacity of capitalism to legitimate itself directly (let alone to generate inspiring myths about itself). It was characterized by such an incapacity from the beginning. If specific religious or social-ethical myths that used to legitimate capitalism in the past have indeed lost plausibility, this is not to say that other myths may not take over that function, for example, the myth of liberty (including the aspiration toward political democracy) or the myth of personal liberation. In any case, problems of legitimation are not limited to "late capitalism" and if such problems indicate an imminent demise, then capitalism has been on its last legs for a very long time. Second, legitimations are most needed when a society or a social institution is in trouble and when, in consequence, there is a need for inspirational symbols. When a society is more or less in a state of tranquillity, or when a social institution is functioning reasonably efficiently, these very facts provide tacit legitimation for the status quo. Put differently (back to Adam Smith, though in a sense not intended by him), what is "natural" need not be legitimated; "nature" legitimates itself; when a society is working reasonably well, most people will look upon it as "natural." This is what Hans Kelsen had in mind when he spoke of the "normative power of facticity." As was shown in various chapters of this book, at least in Western societies capitalism has created a wealth of "facticities"—economic and social facts that, to a large extent, have come to be taken for granted and thus legitimate themselves.

It has been argued that changes in the Western class system since World War II have created a new situation in this regard (as in the previously discussed notion of the new knowledge class and its anticapitalist animus). Be this as it may, it is remarkable to what extent capitalist economics continues to be taken for granted by the majority of people in Western societies, even working-class people, some of whom belong to labor unions and political parties with an ostensibly anticapitalist ideology. England (arguably the most class-conscious country in the Western world) may serve here for an argument a fortiori. The British sociologist Frank Parkin has discussed data showing the basic acceptance of capitalism by working-class people in England.[26] He distinguishes acceptance from commitment: To say that these people accept capitalism does not imply that they would be willing to defend it at any high cost to themselves or that they imbue it with the kind of symbolic dignity that would inspire self-sacrifice in times of trouble. Consequently, this acceptance of capitalism cannot predict what people would do if such times broke upon them in the future. Nevertheless, as Western societies are "working" today, Parkin sees no empirical basis for the idea of a legitimacy crisis.

The final proposition of this book follows from the foregoing considerations: *Capitalism has a built-in incapacity to generate legitimations of itself, and it is particularly deprived of mythic potency; consequently, it depends upon the legitimating effects of its sheer facticity or upon association with other, noneconomic legitimating symbols.*

This hypothesis would be falsified on the day when poets sing the praises of the Dow Jones and when large numbers of people are ready to risk their lives in defense of the Fortune 500. This does not seem like a probable eventuality.

George Bernard Shaw once observed that the worst thing that can happen to a man is that all his wishes come true. It is possible that the root cause for the mythic superiority of socialism is the fact that, or so it appears, its realization never takes place. It is a fugitive vision, tantalizing those who adhere to it from one near-miss to another. But Tantalus goes on trying—and believing. Thus there is the unending quest for the first case of "true socialism," always just out of reach, the quest taken up again after each disappointment. There is no capitalist equivalent of this (profoundly mythological, indeed religious) quest. The benefits of capitalism *are* attainable. In the successful capitalist societies of the West and in Eastern Asia they abound on all sides, part and parcel of ordinary, everyday experience. The ordinary breeds contempt and the attainable, once attained, looks cheap. A special kind of perception is required to link these prosaic facticities with the values and aspirations for which people are prepared to sacrifice. Such perception is not easy to come by and it lacks popular appeal.

# 10

# THE SHAPE AND USES
# OF A THEORY
# OF CAPITALISM

Social theorists frequently use the language of architecture. They speak of theoretical "edifices" or "constructions," and they describe their activity as "theory building." This is useful language. It suggests the laborious, step-by-step character of such an enterprise. This book makes no pretense at delivering the completed house to all who would buy. However, as the argument has proceeded in the preceding pages, first in the author's mind and then (one hopes) in the reader's, the design for this particular house has increasingly come into view. There are missing pieces. Here and there something will have to be removed, something else sketched in. One statement can be made with great assurance: These are the major issues for any comprehensive theory of capitalism, even if it will eventually work with a greatly changed design. Put simply, the house is not yet there, but its shape is becoming increasingly visible.

Specifically, the argument of this book has produced a set of hypothetical propositions. Their sum constitutes a large agenda for empirical research and for further theoretical reflection. The purpose of this final chapter is twofold: to take a look at these propositions as a whole and then to ask what practical uses the emergent theory may have. To facilitate this, it is appropriate to restate the propositions as they are scattered throughout the preceding text. They are these:

## A BODY OF PROPOSITIONS

### CONCERNING CAPITALISM AND MATERIAL LIFE

1. Industrial capitalism has generated the greatest productive power in human history.
2. To date, no other socioeconomic system has been able to generate comparable productive power.
3. An economy oriented toward production for market exchange provides the optimal conditions for long-lasting and ever-expanding productive capacity based on modern technology.
4. The early period of industrial capitalism in England (where it began) and probably in other Western countries exacted considerable human costs, if not in an actual decline in material living standards then in social and cultural dislocations.
5. Advanced industrial capitalism has generated, and continues to generate, the highest material standard of living for large masses of people in human history.
6. In Western societies and in most societies elsewhere technological modernization and economic growth, if they persist over time, first cause a sharp increase in income and wealth inequalities, then a sharp decline in these inequalities, and then a relatively stable plateau.
7. These changes in income and wealth inequalities are caused by the interplay of technological and demographic forces and are relatively independent of the forms of socioeconomic organization (such as, most importantly, capitalist and socialist forms of organization).
8. The leveling phase of this process can be strengthened and accelerated by political interventions (notably redistributionist policies), but if these interventions exceed a certain degree (which at this time cannot be precisely specified), there will be

negative consequences for economic growth and eventually for the standard of living.

## CONCERNING CAPITALISM AND CLASS

9. Under industrial capitalism there has been the progressive displacement of all other forms of stratification by class.
10. Ongoing industrialization, regardless of its socioeconomic organization (be it capitalist or socialist), is the basic determinant of social mobility.
11. In all advanced industrial societies there have been moderate increases, but no dramatic changes, in the overall rates of upward mobility.
12. In all advanced industrial societies education has become the single most important vehicle of upward mobility.
13. Industrial capitalism, especially when combined with political democracy, is most likely to maintain openness in the stratification system of a society.
14. Contemporary Western societies are characterized by a protracted conflict between two classes, the old middle class (occupied in the production and distribution of material goods and services) and a new middle class (occupied in the production and distribution of symbolic knowledge).
15. The new knowledge class in Western societies is a major antagonist of capitalism.

## CONCERNING CAPITALISM AND DEMOCRACY

16. Capitalism is a necessary but not sufficient condition of democracy under modern conditions.
17. If a capitalist economy is subjected to increasing degrees of state control, a point (not precisely specifiable at this time) will be reached at which democratic governance becomes impossible.
18. If a socialist economy is opened up to increasing degrees of market forces, a point (not precisely specifiable at this time) will be reached at which democratic governance becomes a possibility.
19. If capitalist development is successful in generating economic

growth from which a sizable proportion of the population benefits, pressures toward democracy are likely to appear.

## CONCERNING CAPITALISM AND THE CULTURE OF INDIVIDUAL AUTONOMY

20. The origins of individual autonomy in Western culture long antedate modern capitalism and it is this premodern "individualism" of Western culture which engendered the particular "individualism" associated with capitalism.
21. Bourgeois culture in the West, especially in Protestant societies, produced a type of person strongly marked by both the value and the psychic reality of individual autonomy.
22. At least in Western societies, if not elsewhere as well, capitalism is the necessary but not sufficient condition of the continuing reality of individual autonomy.
23. Certain components of Western bourgeois culture (notably those of activism, rational innovativeness, and self-discipline) are prerequisites of successful capitalist development anywhere.
24. Capitalism requires institutions (notably the family and religion) that balance the anonymous aspects of individual autonomy with communal solidarities.

## CONCERNING CAPITALISM AND THIRD WORLD DEVELOPMENT

25. The inclusion of a Third World country within the international capitalist system tends to favor its economic development.
26. The superior productive power of capitalism, as manifested in the advanced industrial societies of the West, continues to manifest itself wherever the global capitalist system has intruded.
27. Capitalist development is more likely than socialist development to improve the material standard of life of people in the contemporary Third World, including the poorest groups.
28. Capitalist development in Third World societies leading to rapid and labor-intensive economic growth is more likely to equalize income distribution than strategies of deliberate policies of income redistribution.

## CONCERNING CAPITALISM IN EAST ASIA (A "SECOND CASE")

29. East Asia confirms the superior productive power of industrial capitalism.

30. East Asia confirms the superior capacity of industrial capitalism in raising the material standard of living of large masses of people.

31. East Asia confirms the positive relation between industrial capitalism and the emergence of a class system characterized by relatively open social mobility.

32. East Asia disconfirms the thesis that early economic growth under modern capitalism must *necessarily* increase income inequality, though it confirms the thesis that income distribution stabilizes as this economic growth continues.

33. The East Asian evidence falsifies the thesis that successful development cannot occur in a condition of dependency upon the international capitalist system.

34. The East Asian evidence falsifies the thesis that a high degree of state intervention in the economy is incompatible with successful capitalist development.

35. The East Asian evidence provides weak support for the proposition that successful capitalist development generates pressures toward democracy.

36. The East Asian evidence supports the proposition that certain components of Western bourgeois culture (notably activism, rational innovativeness, and self-discipline) are necessary for successful capitalist development.

37. Specific elements of East Asian societies, be it in the "great traditions" or in folk culture, have fostered values conducive to successful development and have consequently given these societies a comparative advantage in the modernization process.

38. The societies of East Asia have succeeded for a considerable time in modernizing under capitalist conditions without undergoing individuation along Western lines.

39. The values of individual autonomy are undermining East Asian communalism and are likely to continue doing so.

40. The movements toward democracy and individuation in East Asia have been greatly strengthened by the adherence of these

societies to an international capitalist system centered in the West.

## CONCERNING INDUSTRIAL SOCIALISM (A "CONTROL CASE")

41. There is an intrinsic linkage between socialism and the pervasive bureaucratization of the economy.
42. There is an intrinsic linkage between socialism and economic inefficiency.
43. There is an intrinsic linkage between socialism and authoritarian governance.
44. There is an affinity between socialism and the totalitarian project for modern society.
45. Industrial socialism is characterized by the ongoing interaction of two distinct forms of stratification, a class system and a system of political patrimonialism.
46. A modification of industrial socialism through the introduction of market mechanisms will encounter political limits, which are caused by the resistance of the patrimonial elite defending its vested interests.
47. A modification of industrial socialism through the introduction of market mechanisms will encounter economic limits, which are caused by the inability of the artificial market to replicate the efficiency of the capitalist market.
48. There can be no effective market economy without private ownership of the means of production.

## CONCERNING THE LEGITIMATION OF CAPITALISM

49. Socialism is one of the most powerful myths of the modern era; to the extent that socialism retains this mythic quality, it cannot be disconfirmed by empirical evidence in the minds of its adherents.
50. Capitalism has an intrinsic incapacity to generate legitimations, and it is particularly deprived of mythic potency; consequently, it depends upon the legitimating effects of its sheer facticity or upon association with other legitimating symbols.

Is the theory that emerges from these propositions "procapitalist"? And what are its practical uses?

Simply taken as a body of empirical hypotheses, this emergent theory is neither pro- nor anticapitalist. Whether it is either will be determined *not* by the empirical support or falsification that it will eventually acquire but rather by the values to which it will be related. Again, simply taken as a social-scientific exercise, the emergent theory has no uses at all, except for the use of reducing the intellectual perplexities of the theorist. As soon as one is interested in uses in the realm of social praxis, the values by which one wishes to orient the latter will once again be decisive.

There is always a disjunction between theory and praxis. This is true even of the theoretical insights generated by the physical sciences. Thus one may have an intellectually satisfying theory of the etiology of a particular disease, but (depending on the values of, say, a physician as against a practitioner of biological warfare), this theory will be equally useful for the purposes of curing or spreading the disease. Similarly, the proposition that capitalism is a necessary condition for democracy is "procapitalist" (and ipso facto useful for the propagandists of capitalism) only if one values democracy, or the proposition that capitalism is unlikely to lead to a much greater degree of income equality than now exists in Western societies is "anticapitalist" (and thus useful to socialists) only if one attaches values to ever-greater equality. No praxis is possible without value judgments. This is even true of the praxis of individual life; it is very much true of the social and political praxis commonly called "policy." (This implies, incidentally, that the phrase "policy sciences" contains a *contradictio in adjecto*.)

Contrary to assumptions that have acquired widespread credence in recent years, it is not, cannot, be the task of the social scientist qua social scientist to make moral judgments. (He may, of course, make such judgments, so to speak, from under a "different hat"—qua concerned citizen, committed religious believer, lover of humanity, or what-have-you—but as soon as he does so, he cannot claim the authority of social science for these judgments.) There are very fundamental methodological reasons for making this assertion, reasons that touch upon the essential character of the scientific enterprise. But it may be observed in passing that there are also moral and political implications to this assertion of the disjuncture of theory and praxis. The theorist who claims to know what uses his insights should be put to arrogates to himself the right of others (most of whom, of course, are neither theorists nor intellectuals of any kind) to live their lives in accordance with their own values. Such arrogance is not morally neutral. Perhaps more importantly, the idea that theoretical insights provide a warrant for moral judgments and practical guidance is intrinsically antagonistic to democracy. It is an idea that implies an intellectual and moral elite, which has the right to rule because of its superior theoretical insights. One of the key moral and political problems of the modern intelligentsia is that it has repeatedly seen itself as such an elite, a new priesthood based on education as the ordaining sacrament. Democracy, like Protestantism, is based on a rejection of this priestly prerogative by ordinary lay men and women.

There is, however, one further step of analysis that is possible within the framework of social-scientific theorizing. This is an attempt to clarify the relation between theoretical insights (all of them subject to empirical testing and therefore never final) and praxis based on this or that value. Put differently, the social scientist can make statements of an "if/then" type: "*If* your values are X, *then* situation Y will accord with your values more than situation Z." Or: "*If* you hold value A, then, given the empirical state of the world as I have reason to believe it to be, practical option B will probably be more useful to you than practical option C." This is not the stuff of which myths are made or by which heroic actors will be inspired. But it is precisely in such dry, pedantic, and invariably probabilistic statements that the social scientist can make a distinctive contribution to public discourse.

One can, of course, introduce *any* values into *any* set of empirical data. For example, if one's principal political value is the restoration of absolute monarchy based on a doctrine of the divine right of kings, most of the propositions put forth in this book are of no moral significance and, very probably, are practically useless. Very few people would take the position that the most important moral and practical choice of the age is that between absolute monarchy and all other types of regime, so that the introduction of the aforementioned value has little bearing on any actual empirical situation. In actuality, the most significant choice of the age, for most people, is that between capitalism and socialism (or, admittedly, various versions of either), and the values relevant to this choice are fairly limited in number (and emphatically do not include the divine right of kings). Therefore, in the framework of the social sciences, the most reasonable clarifying exercise lies in the juxtaposition of this limited (and empirically operative) set of values and the capitalist/socialist alternative. More precisely, what can still be done here, however briefly, is to look at the import of the foregoing propositions in terms of seven commonly held values:

*The material well-being of people, especially of the poor.* This value can be stated positively by saying that, given the standard of living possible under conditions of modern technology, people should have a materially decent life. Obviously, there is a high degree of relativity and, indeed, subjectivity to the notion of "decency" here. What was an undreamed-of luxury yesterday may turn into a basic need and a moral entitlement today. The practical use of this value becomes much clearer if it is stated in negative terms: Certain types of material misery, rather easily spelled out, should be progressively diminished if not eliminated outright. At issue here are all the circumstances that were common to most of humanity in premodern times and that are still the lot of millions of people in the Third World today—massive infant mortality, hunger, disease, fragile housing, vulnerability to the ravages of nature, low life expectancy—to which (since they greatly affect material well-being) one may add such sociocultural circumstances as illiteracy and physical immobility. Since in every human society, even the most advanced, liberation from these debilitating conditions is not uniform or total, it makes further sense (empirically as well as morally) to focus attention on the poorest segments of the population: To what extent, and with how much consistency over time, are the poor freed from such circumstances and moved into a decent (or, to put it cautiously, a *more* decent) material life? This, of course, is the principle of the "preferential option for the poor," which recent Catholic social thought has introduced into the discussion of development. If the foregoing propositions hold up, there can be no question that capitalism, as against any empirically available alternatives, is the indicated choice.

*Equality.* This, needless to say, is a shadowy notion, since no reasonable person expects a society, under whatever institutional arrangements, to provide perfect equality in all things for all people. A more cautious formulation of this value would either use a term like "equity" or speak of "equalities," in the plural (allowing a semantic distinction between equalities that may reasonably be attained, such as equality before the law, and those that no society can guarantee, such as equal attractiveness to the opposite sex). Still, in current controversies the value of equality primarily refers to something that can be empirically located, namely, a relatively low and preferably ongoing diminishing ratio in the income and wealth of the richest and poorest segments of the population. As these matters were dealt with in the present arguments, inequalities in wealth are harder to measure, but the data on income inequalities in most of the world (the East Asian exceptions are puzzling and remain to be fully explained) point to a tentative conclusion: Income distribution is a function of modern economic growth and is affected to only a limited degree by the institutional arrangements and policies of a society. Capitalism, then, does not come out very well in the perspective of this value. But neither does socialism, or any presently existent or plausibly imagined form of societal organization. Those for whom equality is a paramount value would then be well advised to cease blaming *or* defending either of the two major contemporary systems for the existing state of affairs. Their concern would logically lead to an overall critique of modernity and to the practical question as to how modernization could be reversed or at least modified. This question, interesting though it is, does not fall into the purview of a theory of capitalism or of moral reflection about such a theory.

*Political liberties and democracy.* The two can be theoretically differentiated; empirically, in the contemporary world, they tend to be closely linked. The value here is what in ordinary parlance is meant by "freedom." If the propositions of the emergent theory hold up, this value clearly dictates a choice in favor of capitalism.

*Protection of human rights.* Even leaving aside the category of political rights (roughly equivalent to political liberties), anyone who has delved into the contemporary literature on human rights knows the complexities of definition and delineation in this area (such as those brought on by the discussion of different "generations" of rights, with economic and cultural rights being added by some to the older "generation" of civil and political rights). In ordinary parlance it is fairly clear what most people mean by human rights. Most importantly, they mean protection of individuals and groups against the most common acts of tyranny—massive terror, arbitrary executions, torture, mass deportations, the forced separation of families. To this may then be added such rights as protection against economic misfortune (this protection, of course, being the principal purpose of the modern welfare state) and cultural rights, such as protection of a language or other aspects of ethnic life-style. The very important area of religious rights spans the categories of civil and cultural rights as conventionally defined. Now, it is difficult to argue that capitalism per se favors the protection of human rights as against alternative systems of socioeconomic organization. There is, however, the simple but exceedingly significant fact that, empirically, democratic regimes have by far the best record on the protection of human rights in *all* the categories (including the category of economic rights) employed by human-rights theorists. And capitalism has the aforementioned empirical linkage with democracy. Once again, this value prompts a choice in favor of capitalism.

*Individual autonomy.* This, of course, is the value commonly termed (approvingly or pejoratively) "individualism" in ordinary language. Once more, the empirical evidence strongly suggests that capitalism offers the most plausible context for a realization of this value, as indeed both its critics and its advocates agree.

*Preservation of tradition.* This is a value that, while present everywhere among different groups of people, is of special importance in many Third World countries today. It is the core motivating force of all neotraditionalist movements, most dramatically (but by no means exclusively) expressed in the contemporary Islamic resurgence. Seen in the perspective of traditionalists, capitalism is an enemy in that its dynamics (precisely the one called "creative destruction" by Joseph Schumpeter) undermines traditional institutions and ways of life. In the same perspective, however, socialism (at least in any of its empirically existent forms and especially in the form of Western-derived Marxism) is *also* perceived as a threat. Typically, traditionalists will call for a "third way," somehow equidistant from Western-type capitalism or socialism. The very notion of the "Third World," as first proclaimed at the Bandung Conference of 1955, intended such an option. The ideology of the Iranian Revolution has stated the same notion very forcefully. To date, no such "third way" has been effectively institutionalized, and it is possible to argue that, whatever its ideology, every modern or modernizing society will essentially have to choose between capitalist or socialist forms of socioeconomic organization. Be this as it may, the following can be said with some assurance: Modernization as such, no matter whether it takes capitalist or socialist forms, threatens tradition. Socialism, too, as long as it is coupled with modernization, releases forces of "creative destruction." The consistent traditionalist must (and, let it be said, usually does) engage in a more fundamental critique of modernity. If, however, the inevitability (if not necessarily the desirability) of modernization is posited, then neither capitalism nor any empirically available alternative appears conducive to the preservation of tradition. A good argument can be made, though, that traditional institutions and life-styles fare better under democratic regimes, for reasons that are not difficult to spell out. This value, then, will also tend (at least mildly) toward the capitalist choice, because of the aforementioned linkage between capitalism and democracy.

*Community.* To some extent, of course, this value overlaps with the value of preserving tradition. There are, however, new forms of community in the world, both existent and aspired-to communities created deliberately and de novo, communities that are *not* grounded in traditional ways of life. There can be no question but that socialist *movements* have been very fertile in the generating of such communities, while capitalism has not been able to generate the myths upon which such communities are based. Socialist *regimes* once established, on the other hand, do not have a good record of either preserving or creating anew the sorts of community to which this value refers. For those people whose value of community is attached to existing (frequently traditional) institutions, the question of capitalism must be answered in the terms just outlined in connection with the preservation of tradition. For those, however, who aspire toward some new, all-embracing community, transcending anything to be found in the world today, socialism will very probably continue to be the preferred choice.

Let there be no doubt about the outcome of the foregoing value-oriented reflections: In terms of the values held by the majority of people in the world today, a choice in favor of capitalism is more plausible in the light of the empirical evidence as presently available.

The commonly raised issues of "mixed systems" and "third ways" generally obfuscate the empirically available options. Of course all sorts of "mixed systems" exist and additional "mixes" can be plausibly imagined; indeed, every existing system is "mixed" to a certain degree; nevertheless, at the end of the day, the question will be whether any particular economy is *primarily* organized along capitalist or socialist lines—and *that,* precisely, is what the crucial choice is all about. The same consideration applies to any putative "third way" (including the projections of neo-Islamic ideology), as long as the modernization process is deemed to be essentially irreversible. Now, it can certainly be maintained (as it is maintained by many) that the future is always open, that institutional arrangement unthought-of today may come into being, and that one should not allow the realities of the present to dictate the limits of one's social imagination. These ideas are at the very core of all utopian thought. Following Karl Mannheim, it should be emphatically stressed here that the category of utopian thought by no means implies a pejorative judgment: Very likely the utopian element in the human imagination is one of the driving forces of history, and humanity would be immeasurably impoverished if that element ever disappeared. Who would like to imagine a world in which there are no Quixotes tilting their lances against the windmills of the future and in which the only acceptable rationale is that of Sancho Panza?

One must ask further, though, whether the utopian imagination transcends or simply ignores the empirical contours of human existence. It would not be utopian (in the very best sense of the word) if it did not transcend the limits of the empirically given; it will ignore empirical reality at great peril. The peril is not that of failure. There can be grandeur in failure (precisely the grandeur of Don Quixote). The peril is rather that immense human costs may result from the experiments of the utopian imagination, costs that are typically borne by those who neither conceived nor requested the utopian project. A moral principle is suggested by these thoughts: that the utopian is responsible for the human costs of his projections. It probably follows that the only morally acceptable utopians are very careful ones.

The present book, an exercise in social-science theory, has produced an assemblage of hypotheses. Social science can never do more. It is, by its very nature, tentative, ever in need of revision, probabilistic even in its most well-supported findings. If one looks with any degree of detachment at the empirical evidence concerning the relation between capitalism and society (and indeed all phenomena subsumed under the present category of economic culture), one is impressed by the vast remaining areas of ignorance. The scientist, qua scientist, will be undaunted by this. Every area of ignorance is a challenge for further inquiry. By its very nature, science is infinitely patient and open ended. The man of action cannot afford such patience and open-endedness. Every act (political or other) is an act of closure. And when the urgencies of the situation are pressing, especially in terms of human suffering and human passions, patience is rarely a political option. The man of action, then, must always operate under a postulate of ignorance—he must act despite the fact that there are many things he does not and cannot know about the situation in which he is acting. Put simply, to act means to gamble. All the empirical evidence that the social sciences can accumulate for the use of an actor in the end does no more than indicate which bets are likely to be safer. The social sciences can do no more—but also no less. That is both their intrinsic limitation and the measure of their useful contribution.

It is in this sense, and in this sense only, that the empirical evidence discussed in this book is useful for the choice for or against capitalism as a form of socioeconomic organization. It is probable that, in the end, this choice will be decided on meta-empirical grounds. At issue is the status accorded to history and to human nature. The socialist myth of the modern era is grounded in a redemptive expectation both with regard to history and to human nature—history moving toward an eschatological fulfillment and human nature being transformed in the process. Those to whom this mythic vision is implausible are likely to have much more modest expectations regarding the collective future of mankind and, ipso facto, they will tend to accept much narrower limits to the human condition. This modesty may have religious or secular roots. *Homo religiosus* does not expect redemption in history because he has found it elsewhere. Insofar as *homo religiosus* has been informed by the Judeo-Christian tradition, he does indeed harbor an eschatological hope, but it looks to God and not to the political acts of men for its fulfillment. The aforementioned modesty, however, may also take a secular form. It is a modesty classically expressed in the Stoic maxim that the most fundamental wisdom is knowing the difference between what one can and what one cannot do. The modern social scientist, probabilistic to the end, will modify this maxim only slightly: Wisdom is to know the difference between what one can *probably* do and what one can *probably* not do. Stoic secularity learns to accept this uncertainty; the religious attitude looks to its resolution when God's purposes with men will become ultimately manifest.

# NOTES

## Chapter 1

1. See Werner Sombart, *Der moderne Kapitalismus* (Munich, 1928 [1902]); Max Weber, *Wirtschaftsgeschichte* (Berlin, 1958 [1923]); Henri Sée, *Les origines du capitalisme moderne* (Paris, 1926); Henri Pirenne, *Economic and Social History of Medieval Europe* (New York, n.d. [French 1933]); Lance Davis and Douglass North, *Institutional Change and American Economic Growth* (Cambridge, 1971); Douglass North and Robert Thomas, *The Rise of the Western World* (Cambridge, 1973); Immanuel Wallerstein, *The Modern World System* (New York, 1974); idem, *The Capitalist World-Economy* (Cambridge, 1979); Fernand Braudel, *Civilization and Capitalism* (New York, 1982 [French 1979]).

2. See Braudel, p. 232 ff.

3. Braudel, p. 233.

4. Weber, p. 238 ff.

5. Again, I'm generally following Weber here.

6. One question that has been much discussed, especially recently, is whether private property (in Marxist terms, private ownership of the means of production) should be included as a defining criterion of capitalism. It certainly has been a crucial element in the historical development of capitalism. But, as James Burnham and others have pointed out, the twentieth-century corporation (certainly a key institution of capitalism today) largely separates legal ownership and functional control. Capitalism, by definition, requires entrepreneurs. As to the question of whether the latter require property rights or only effective control to carry out their economic activity, I prefer to leave this for empirical exploration rather than include it in the definition of capitalism. It should be stressed that this in no way prejudges the empirical issue. As will be argued in a later chapter, I'm strongly inclined to the hypothesis that capitalist entrepreneurship without private property rights (as in the various conceptions and experiments of "market socialism") is unlikely to succeed economically; as Milton Friedman has suggested, these experiments are like playing at being capitalists, not the real thing (of all places, incidentally, he made the suggestion in an address in Peking). Also, freedom of the market has been affected by the powerful interventions of government, monopoly-seeking conglomerates and labor unions; thus one should properly speak of a *relative* freedom of the market.

7. See George Dalton, *Economic Anthropology and Development* (New York, 1971).

8. Joseph Schumpeter, "Die Krise des Steuerstaates," *Aufsaetze zur Soziologie* (Tübingen, 1953 [1918]), p. 1 ff.

9. Methodologically, these poles are "ideal types" in Weber's sense. Indeed, this way of looking at these phenomena is Weberian in inspiration.

10. My attempt at definition excludes two terms used often by socialist theorists with democratic commitments—"market socialism" and "state capitalism." I have sympathies for the aspirations of democratic socialists, and though I think that these aspirations are based on empirical illusions (as will become clear later in this argument), I believe that the basic moral divide today is between democrats of any economic philosophy and the apologists for totalitarianism. All the same, these two terms impress me as ideological devices that only serve to confuse the theoretical and empirical issues. The question of whether socialism is compatible with democracy is, in principle, open to empirical exploration, as is the question of the effects of various degrees of state intervention on a capitalist economy. These two terms, however, in no way facilitate such explorations. Rather, they are concepts analogous to, say, "circular square" or "macho femininity." Their ideological motivation is clear. The term "market socialism" expresses the hope that, now or sometime in the future, a planned economy could allow the free play of market forces without accepting private ownership or private capital formation. This hope may be attractive to some, but this does not change the intrinsic contradiction of the term. Those sharing this hope might be better advised to drop the term and simply explore empirically how far a planned economy can allow the introduction of market mechanisms without coming to resemble the capitalist economies on the other side of the fence. For a critique of this term as applied to Yugoslavia, thus far the case par excellence of "market socialism," see Wilhelm Roepke, *A Humane Economy* (Chicago, 1960), p. 93 ff.

As to the term "state capitalism," its ideological function is also clear. Not to put too fine a point on it, this allows people to say that the Soviet Union is bad news and still to go on calling themselves socialists; the Soviet Union, of course, is the principal candidate for the label "state capitalism." Thus, for instance, Immanuel Wallerstein takes the position that all the societies calling themselves "socialist" today are in fact "state capitalist," because they all still undertake production for profit instead of production for use, with the state replacing private capitalists in the role of profiteer. But this is simply saying that "true" socialism (presumably some sort of cooperative syndicalism) does not yet exist but will appear in the future. This is an eschatological proposition that cannot be empirically explored. It seems to me that people with socialist commitments who do not like the Soviet Union or China or Cuba have little to gain from denying that these are indeed socialist societies. Instead of pronouncing excommunication by means of definition, they should explore why these socialist societies have "gone wrong" and then try to conceive of a possible socialist society without these putative defects. My own view is that the defects are intrinsic to the socialist model, but that is an empirically falsifiable proposition, *not* an a priori definition of socialism.

11. This concept is very close to that of "package," which I used in an earlier work. See Peter Berger, Brigitte Berger, and Hansfried Kellner, *The Homeless Mind: Modernization and Consciousness* (New York, 1973). Looking back on this work now, I find it rather remarkable that capitalism is not discussed in it as an item in the "package" of modern consciousness—undeniable proof that I too have not been immune to certain blind spots of modernization theory. (Marxists have been obsessed by capitalism; "bourgeois sociologists" have at times failed to notice it.)

12. See, for example, Marc Bloch, *Feudal Society* (Chicago, 1961).

13. This insight was central to Weber's vast program of comparative historical

analysis. On the relation of capitalism and race, cf. Thomas Sowell, *The Economics and Politics of Race* (New York, 1983).

14. The best source to date for an overview of this vast intellectual effort, almost a century and a half in duration by now, is Leszek Kolakowski, *Main Currents of Marxism* (Oxford, 1978).

15. For a useful overview, see Myron Weiner, ed. *Modernization* (New York, 1966).

16. Properly speaking, this note should contain a concise history of the development of sociological theory during and since the classical age of the discipline. In lieu of such a masterpiece of pedagogical conciseness, I will only refer to one work (in its area as magisterial as Kolakowski's on Marxist theory) that offers the best summary I know: Raymond Aron, *Les étapes de la pensée sociologique* (Paris, 1967).

17. See, for example, Marion Levy, *Modernization: Latecomers and Survivors* (New York, 1972).

## Chapter 2

1. Fernand Braudel has given the phrase "material life" a somewhat technical meaning, which is not intended here. In this chapter the phrase is simply used to denote material standards of life.

2. Marion Levy, *Modernization: Latecomers and Survivors* (New York, 1972), p. 3.

3. See Arnold Toynbee, *The Industrial Revolution* (Boston, 1956 [1884]); T. S. Ashton, *The Industrial Revolution* (London, 1948); David Landes, *The Unbound Prometheus* (Cambridge, 1969); Douglass North and Robert Thomas, *The Rise of the Western World* (Cambridge, 1973); Fernand Braudel, *Civilization and Capitalism* (New York, 1982 [French 1979]); Nathan Rosenberg and L. E. Birdzell, *How the West Grew Rich* (New York, 1985).

4. See Milton and Rose Friedman, *Free to Choose* (New York, 1980); George Gilder, *Wealth and Poverty* (New York, 1981); Michael Novak, *The Spirit of Democratic Capitalism* (New York, 1982). The core belief in the beneficent effects of market forces goes back, of course, all the way to the classical formulation of a "system of liberty" by Adam Smith. It is safe to say that a positive view of the market is shared by the great majority of non-Marxist economists, and even by some Marxist ones (vide the previously mentioned notions about "market socialism"). A full-blown theory of capitalism will have to spell out, in sociological and social-psychological detail, just how market forces stimulate the ingenuity and inventiveness of individuals. I am inclined to agree with the classical view that the much-maligned "profit motive" will have to play an important part in any such explanation.

5. This view is diametrically opposed to that of Thorstein Veblen, who saw the entrepreneur and the engineer as intrinsically antagonist human types. I think that Veblen was wrong.

6. In social-psychological terms, this question is very similar to the questions raised by the disappointment of religious expectations, following the failure of a predicted eschatological event to occur. Thus, in the history of early Christianity, the expectation was that Jesus would return in glory (the so-called *Parousia*) in the lifetimes of the disciples. When he failed to do so, Christianity was not abandoned but

reinterpreted. Church historians have coined the term *Parousieverzoegerung* for this nonevent—freely translated, a slight delay in Jesus's return. Mutatis mutandis, similar hermeneutic contortions may be observed in other eschatological movements, especially in Christianity, Judaism, and Islam (the three eschatological faiths par excellence). Marxists thus stand in a long Western tradition of frustrated apocalyptics.

7. Essentially, there have been three methods to cope with the falsified immiseration thesis. The first has been to shift attention from absolute to relative deprivation —to focus on inequality rather than misery. This is popular today among Marxist economists and left-leaning analysts generally. The second method has been to admit the material gains of capitalism but then to argue that they are meaningless because capitalism is "alienating," "dehumanizing," or otherwise reprehensible. The New Left has favored this approach. The third method, probably the most interesting intellectually, has been to retain the whole thesis but, as it were, to relocate it. This has been at the core of the Leninist theory of imperialism (though it was Rosa Luxemburg rather than Lenin who first stated it most persuasively). This is the theory that the advanced capitalist societies *as a whole* constitute a sort of transnational "bourgeoisie," exploiting an "external proletariat" (Luxemburg) consisting of the colonial peoples—or, as we would say today, the peoples of the Third World. Not surprisingly, this particular offshoot of the Marxian theory of immiseration has attained the status of a quasi-official ideology in many Third World regimes and within the United Nations system. It will have to be taken up again later in this book.

8. See Gertrude Himmelfarb, *The Idea of Poverty* (New York, 1984).

9. Himmelfarb, p. 270 ff.

10. For the "pessimists," see Karl Polanyi, *The Great Transformation* (New York, 1944); J. L. and Barbara Hammond, *The Bleak Age* (London, 1947); E. P. Thompson, *The Making of the English Working Class* (New York, 1963). For the "optimists," see Ashton, *Industrial Revolution;* F. A. Hayek, ed. *Capitalism and the Historians* (Chicago, 1954); N. J. Smelser, *Social Change in the Industrial Revolution* (Chicago, 1959).

11. For overviews of the recent debate, see R. M. Hartwell et al., *The Long Debate on Poverty* (London, 1972); A. J. Taylor, ed. *The Standard of Living in Britain in the Industrial Revolution* (London, 1975); Peter Lindert and Jeffrey Williamson, "English Workers' Living Standards During the Industrial Revolution," *Economic History* (Univ. of Wisc. Discussion Paper Series, 1980). I have been strongly influenced by Jeffrey Williamson's views in this area.

12. See David Potter, *People of Plenty* (Chicago, 1954), esp. p. 78 ff.; John Kenneth Galbraith, *The Affluent Society* (Boston, 1958)—in fairness, it should be stated that Galbraith subsequently took a less sanguine view of the course of capitalism; François Hetman, *L'Europe de l'abondance* (Paris, 1967); Sidney Pollard and David Crossley, *The Wealth of Britain* (London, 1968), p. 223 ff. I am indebted to Samuel McCracken for "Democratic Capitalism and the Standard of Living" (paper for the Seminar on Modern Capitalism, 1982).

13. Since gender and race today constitute the major foci of most discussions of inequality in the United States, the data on life expectancy are interesting: The gender gap in 1900 was 2 years, favoring women; in 1979 it was 7.9 years, favoring women. The racial gap (between whites and blacks) in 1920 was 14.6 years, favoring whites; in 1979 it was 4.5 years, favoring whites. Speaking biologically, one might say that

American society in this century has progressively liberated blacks, while increasingly oppressing males!

14. McCracken, "Democratic Capitalism."

15. Joseph Schumpeter, *Capitalism, Socialism and Democracy* (New York, 1947), p. 67.

16. During this walk most of the points already noted could be covered: The stroller may observe what people are wearing and what they eat. He can make a nose count (many sunburned noses, to be sure) by gender and race. The same exercise, by the way, will help him to understand why the common people of the Philippines almost all want to move to the United States, why many in the elite of the same country hate the United States (nothing enrages like invidious comparison), and indeed why many in the *American* elite dislike their own country (did one fly all this way from Harvard Square in order to be surrounded by Boston taxi drivers?).

17. Simon Kuznets, "Economic Growth and Income Inequality," *American Economic Review*, XLV (1955), 1. Cf. idem, *Modern Economic Growth* (New Haven, 1966).

18. See Martin Bronfenbrenner, *Income Distribution Theory* (Chicago, 1971); Jan Tinbergen, *Income Distribution* (Amsterdam, 1975); J. R. Moroney, ed. *Income Inequality: Trends and International Comparisons* (Lexington, Mass., 1978); Jeffrey Williamson and Peter Lindert, *American Inequality* (New York, 1980). Again, I am much indebted to Jeffrey Williamson here, especially to "The Great Egalitarian Levelling Under Twentieth Century Capitalism" (paper for the Seminar on Modern Capitalism, 1984).

19. See Harold Lydall, "Some Problems in Making International Comparisons of Inequality," in Moroney, p. 21 ff.; and Janet Chapman, "Are Earnings More Equal Under Socialism?" in Moroney, p. 43 ff. In view of current controversies, it is interesting to note that there are no significant differences in the gender income gap between capitalist and socialist countries, though there are considerable differences *within* each group of countries. See J. R. Moroney, "Do Women Earn Less Under Capitalism?" idem, p. 141 ff.

20. See Williamson and Lindert, *American Inequality*, passim and p. 290 ff.

21. See Robert Jackman, *Politics and Social Equality* (New York, 1975); Edgar Browning, *Redistribution and the Welfare System* (Washington, D.C., 1975); idem, "Income Distribution and Redistribution" (paper for Seminar on Modern Capitalism, 1982). For a skeptical view of fisc effects on income distribution, see Morgan Reynolds and Eugene Smolensky, *Public Expenditures, Taxes and the Distribution of Income* (New York, 1977).

22. See Arthur Okun, *Equality and Efficiency* (Washington, D.C., 1975). It should be pointed out that Okun is not ideologically opposed to liberal redistributionism; he seeks to identify the costs as well as possible measures to reduce these costs.

23. See Irving Kristol, "Thoughts on Equality and Egalitarianism," in Colin Campbell, ed. *Income Redistribution* (Washington, D.C., 1977). Okun also has a contribution to this symposium, and the exchange between him and Kristol is an interesting one.

24. Tinbergen, passim.

25. Irving Kristol has pointed to several factors that, if taken into account, would present a much more egalitarian picture of the distribution of income and wealth in Western societies. In terms of income distribution, there is the factor of age. The

increase in longevity means that there are constantly larger numbers of people over the age of sixty-five whose income, in most cases, has declined sharply. And the increase in education means that large numbers of young people (say, under the age of twenty-five), many of them married, live on what, to the statistical eye, look like poverty-level incomes—even if they are the partially family-supported children of upper-income professionals. These two age factors will, obviously, make income distribution appear to be considerably more unequal. Yet both are the result, not exactly of the inequities of capitalism but of two developments that almost everyone would consider to be social progress—the fact that people live longer and the fact that many more people have extensive education. If those two (quite sizable) groups were taken out of the population statistically, Kristol suggests, income distribution might turn out to have become *more* equal, rather than being held in a more or less steady state (as I have hypothesized here). At least in the United States one might add a further factor, that of female-headed households (especially among blacks), which tends to give an excessively unequal picture. This, of course, does not mean that there are no real social problems involved here—the frustrations of old age, the difficulties of broken families, and so on—but none of these can be plausibly ascribed to the alleged inequities of a capitalist system. As far as wealth distribution is concerned, there is the remarkable role of pension funds in the holding of market shares—to the point where Peter Drucker, for example, has spoken of an economic revolution. Kristol suggests that this can be interpreted as meaning that lower-income people hold wealth collectively rather than individually; obviously, if this interpretation were acknowledged statistically, the distribution of wealth would appear less unequal. For all this, see Irving Kristol, *Two Cheers for Capitalism* (New York, 1978), p. 194 ff. I find these arguments quite persuasive, and certainly in line with my own overall inclinations. However, I have chosen to formulate the propositions in this chapter in a very cautious manner, which here has meant the eschewing of the more radical revision of the conventional view among economists. If Kristol and others are right in this matter, of course, one might arrive at the view that the Kuznets curve is continuing in its leveling phase (though probably at a more modest rate than at the outset of this phase).

## Chapter 3

1. The treatment of stratification by sociologists since World War II can be usefully divided into two periods—before and after the ascendancy of neo-Marxism in the late 1960s. For the earlier period, see Reinhard Bendix and Seymour Martin Lipset, eds. *Class, Status and Power* (New York, 1953); Bernard Barber, *Social Stratification* (New York, 1957); Ralf Dahrendorf, *Class and Class Conflict in Industrial Society* (Stanford, 1959); Gerhard Lenski, *Power and Privilege* (New York, 1966). The most ambitious neo-Marxist theory of class can be found in Nicos Poulantzas, *Classes in Contemporary Capitalism* (London, 1975); also see Rosemary Crompton and Jon Gubbay, *Economy and Class Structure* (New York, 1978). There have been some interesting attempts to transcend the class theories of both conventional ("bourgeois") sociology and neo-Marxism, notably those of Anthony Giddens and Frank Parkin; see Giddens, *The Class Structure of the Advanced Societies* (London, 1973) and idem, *A Contemporary Critique of Historical Materialism,* vol. 1 (Berkeley, 1981); see

Parkin, *Class Inequality and Political Order* (London, 1971), and idem, *Marxism and Class Theory* (New York, 1979); also see John Scott, *Corporations, Classes and Capitalism* (New York, 1979).

2. That is, all stratification categories are "ideal types" (Weber).

3. It is quite conventional, in terms of contemporary sociology. It straddles the Marxian and Weberian traditions, which have, respectively, stressed the "mode of production" and the distribution of benefits in conceptualizing class. It also seeks to avoid the forbidding language of some of the recent efforts at conceptualization.

4. In this, it is Weberian rather than Marxian in inspiration.

5. In *this,* the conceptualization is Marxian-derived or (as sociologists have liked to put it) is an expression of "conflict theory." But there is no implication here that these conflicts of interest must be "class struggles" in a Marxist sense.

6. The cultural dimension of class (as expressed in "life-styles") was one of the chief interests of American sociologists before the recent Marxist revival, as, for instance, in the work of Lloyd Warner and his associates.

7. Max Weber, especially in his major treatise *Wirtschaft und Gesellschaft,* placed the contrast between estates and classes at the core of his theory of stratification.

8. For an understanding of this social transformation, one will still profit greatly from Alexis de Tocqueville's *L'ancien régime et la revolution* (1856). Also see Elinor Barber, *The Bourgeoisie in XVIIIth Century France* (Princeton, 1955); Dieter and Karin Claessens, *Kapitalismus als Kultur* (Duesseldorf, 1973).

9. For example, Christopher Jencks et al., *Inequality* (New York, 1972). In Marxist parlance, the family is an important vehicle by which a class "reproduces" itself. Quite so.

10. Of course, there are factors *besides* family background that ensure this—all those traits built into an individual's physical and mental makeup.

11. A classical study of this is John Dollard, *Caste and Class in a Southern Town* (New York, 1937). For a good overview of these crisscrossing variables, see Lenski, *Power and Privilege,* p. 389 ff. (though, in my opinion, Lenski confuses the issue by subsuming all these subsystems of stratification under the category of "class").

12. See Dahrendorf, *Class and Class Conflict,* p. 36 ff.; Giddens, *Class Structure,* p. 177 ff.

13. The advent of what some have called the "new middle classes" is frequently used to criticize the dualistic ("capital versus labor") class model of Marxism. This criticism is probably misguided. Marx himself was aware of the more complex nature of the class system and many contemporary Marxists, especially in the West, have made due allowance for it (see Crompton and Gubbay, *Economy and Class Structure,* p. 202 ff.). Where Marx was probably correct was in his view that, at any given moment of history, the *conflict* (or, as he would have said, the "class struggle") is primarily between two contesting groups. For such a "limited" defense of the Marxian view, see Theodor Geiger, *Die Klassengesellschaft im Schmelztiegel* (Cologne, 1949).

14. For discussions of this in American terms, see two very influential works: C. Wright Mills, *White Collar* (New York, 1951) and William Whyte, *The Organization Man* (New York, 1957).

15. See A. A. Berle and G. C. Means, *The Modern Corporation and Private Property* (New York, 1932); Peter Drucker, *The New Society* (New York, 1950); Scott, *Corporations.*

16. See Crompton and Gubbay, p. 50 ff. It is curious that Marx believed that the

emergence of "joint-stock companies" (the British term for corporations) meant a progressive transition from private to collective ownership, a sort of herald of socialism, while the corporation today is the bête noire of most Marxist analyses of "monopoly capitalism."

17. A very influential statement of this view (in the event, by an *ex*-Marxist) was James Burnham, *The Managerial Revolution* (New York, 1941). For a good discussion of the ensuing debate, see Dahrendorf, p. 87 ff.

18. I have also left it aside in the definition of capitalism (see ch. 1). This in no way prejudges the question of whether legal ownership (in Marxist language, "private ownership of the means of production") is empirically significant for an effective capitalist economy. In my opinion, it is.

19. On the question of social mobility during the earlier period of industrial capitalism, see Hartmut Kaelble, *Historical Research on Social Mobility* (New York, 1981). Still the most comprehensive treatment of the subject is Seymour Martin Lipset and Reinhard Bendix, *Social Mobility in Industrial Society* (Berkeley, 1959). Unfortunately, to my knowledge, there has been no comparably comprehensive work since. Important empirical studies are the following: Natalie Rogoff, *Recent Trends in Occupational Mobility* (Glencoe, Ill., 1953); Peter Blau and Otis Duncan, *American Occupational Structure* (New York, 1967); David Featherman and Robert Hauser, *Opportunity and Change* (New York, 1978). On the more recent "state of the art" (to use a phrase that, for some mysterious reason, is greatly favored by sociologists), see the articles on the subject by James Davis and Seymour Martin Lipset in *Public Opinion*, V (1982), 3, p. 11 ff. and p. 41 ff. respectively.

20. See Kaelble, *Historical Research*.

21. The question of ethnic and racial differences in social mobility is left aside here, not because it is unimportant but because it has little bearing on a theory of capitalism: Ethnic or racial conflict and discrimination are, alas, cross-culturally universal, with no respect for the differences in socioeconomic organization.

22. This is one of the most important conclusions in Lipset and Bendix.

23. The old Marxian distinction between "class-in-itself" *(an sich)* and "class-for-itself" *(fuer sich)* is relevant here. Thus the objective mobility chances of working-class sons in England and America are quite similar, but the subjective views of these chances and of the class system in general vary greatly between the two countries. Working-class people in England continue to be obsessed with the notion of hard lines between classes, while most Americans tend to view the system as "soft," permeable, open to individual initiative. Given the empirical data on social mobility, one could argue that *either* group is in "false consciousness"—as is so often the case, it is a question of whether one perceives the glass as half empty or half full.

24. See Richard Coleman and Lee Rainwater, *Social Standing in America* (New York, 1978); also Daniel Yankelovich, *New Rules* (New York, 1981), p. 134 ff.

25. Christopher Jencks, for instance, was very disturbed by the role of apparent randomness (the statistical equivalent of "luck") in his mobility data.

26. The place of luck in all this (if you will, the relation of the wheel of fortune to the ladder of success) merits more theoretical attention than can be given to it here. One avenue of exploration would be to look at Las Vegas as a rival to Wall Street in the popular image of American capitalism—perhaps a symbol of its playful aspect. This also has an egalitarian dimension—anyone can throw *some* dice, and Las Vegas is a very democratic place.

27. The example is not without data. See William Medlin et al., *Education and Development in Central Asia* (Leiden, 1971).

28. *Public Opinion*, VII (1984), 3, p. 58.

29. Michael Novak, *The Spirit of Democratic Capitalism* (New York, 1982).

30. On the institutionalization of class conflict, see particularly Dahrendorf, *Class and Class Conflict*.

31. Again, see Geiger, *Klassengesellschaft*.

32. The term "New Class," originally coined by Milovan Djilas to denote the party elite of Eastern Europe, came to be applied to American society in the 1970s. There seems to be some uncertainty as to who first did this (Daniel Patrick Moynihan and David Bazelon are likely candidates for the honor). Irving Kristol was probably most responsible for injecting the term into political discourse; see his *Two Cheers for Capitalism* (New York, 1978), p. 25 ff. (the article first appeared in *The Wall Street Journal* some years before). For general discussions of the phenomenon, see Barry Bruce-Briggs, ed. *The New Class?* (New Brunswick, N. J., 1979), and Alvin Gouldner, *The Future of Intellectuals and the Rise of the New Class* (New York, 1979). It is interesting that most of the contributors to the former volume are right-of-center politically, while Gouldner was emphatically a "man of the left." There is little disagreement between Gouldner and these neoconservatives on the empirical facts of the matter; the difference is that Gouldner sees hope in what they perceive as bad news. I don't like the term "New Class," both because it evokes Djilas's critique (which dealt with a very different situation) and because it is unwise to make "new" into a social-scientific category, especially when the phenomenon in question is likely to be around for a long time. Hence my choice of the term "knowledge class."

33. This fact has led some to speak of a "postindustrial society." See especially Daniel Bell, *The Coming of Post-Industrial Society* (New York, 1973). I am not much enamored of this term either, because it tends to draw attention away from the continuing necessity of an effective industrial base, without which the social and cultural efflorescence discussed by Bell would collapse overnight. It is somewhat ironic that Bell's book was published on the eve of the energy crisis, which made all too visible the vulnerability of industrial civilization.

34. To my knowledge, the scope of this was first analyzed by Fritz Machlup; see his *The Production and Distribution of Knowledge in the United States* (Princeton, 1962).

35. Helmut Schelsky, *Die Arbeit tun die anderen* (Opladen, 1975). This is an important book, though, in my opinion, much of what Schelsky says about intellectuals should be applied to the broader stratum of the knowledge class.

36. The sociology of intellectuals is a fascinating area of investigation. See, for examples, Florian Znaniecki, *The Social Role of the Man of Knowledge* (New York, 1940); Theodor Geiger, *Aufgaben und Stellung der Intelligenz in der Gesellschaft* (Stuttgart, 1949); George de Huszar, ed. *The Intellectuals* (Glencoe, Ill., 1960).

37. Some analysts, while conceding the empirical phenomena subsumed under what (somewhat prematurely) has been called "New Class theory," would prefer not to use the category of class here. Daniel Bell has taken this position. It seems to me that, on the contrary, class analysis serves to clarify these phenomena.

38. For an analysis of some aspects of this, see Brigitte Berger and Peter Berger, *The War Over the Family* (Garden City, N.Y., 1983).

39. The role of organized teachers in the two cases would be an excellent topic for comparative analysis—the ideological changes in the National Education Associ-

ation in the United States, as compared with the ideological climate in Mitterand's first socialist-dominated National Assembly (aptly called *le parlement des instituteurs* by some commentators, it had the highest percentage of teachers in French parliamentary history).

40. Joseph Schumpeter, *Capitalism, Socialism and Democracy* (New York, 1947 [1942]); Daniel Bell, *The Cultural Contradictions of Capitalism* (New York, 1976). For a (soi-disant) "critical" approach to the same topic, see Juergen Habermas, *Legitimationsprobleme im Spaetkapitalismus* (Frankfurt, 1973).

41. One possible scenario would be a political realignment, pitting those interested in production against those with a primary interest in the redistributive state. Recent political events in the United States, Britain, and West Germany (notably the elections of Ronald Reagan, Margaret Thatcher, and Helmut Kohl) give some credence to this scenario. But, of course, these political realignments may turn out to be transitory. One may add that people do not vote their class interests only.

## Chapter 4

1. My overall perspective on this phenomenon has been basically shaped by Max Weber, augmented (or, one might say, "hardened") by the Italian school of political sociology (Vilfredo Pareto, Gaetano Mosca, and Roberto Michels). In this connection, I may also mention the influence of Friedrich Meinecke, *Die Idee der Staatsraeson* (Munich, 1963 [1924]).

2. See James Bryce, *Modern Democracies* (New York, 1921); Bertrand de Jouvenel, *Power* (London, 1952); Robert Dahl, *A Preface to Democratic Theory* (Chicago, 1963); Giovanni Sartori, *Democratic Theory* (New York, 1965); Charles Cnudde and Deane Neubauer, eds. *Empirical Democratic Theory* (Chicago, 1969); Jack Lively, *Democracy* (New York, 1975).

3. I am indebted to Myron Weiner for clarification of the issues raised by various empirically oriented definitions of democracy.

4. Was Switzerland a democracy when women were not allowed to vote? Is South Africa a democracy today? Rather than *define* democracy in terms of some standard of universal adult suffrage, I think it is more useful to omit this matter from the definition and *then* to explore the range of democratic participation and its consequences as an empirical issue.

5. Again, Max Weber may be cited here, but so may a long tradition of modern political thought going back all the way to Machiavelli. By contrast, Marxist thought has consistently maintained that this differentiation is an illusion and that the modern state exists in order to guarantee the dominance of the capitalist class (in Marx's own parlance, that the state is merely the "executive committee" of this class). Recent Marxist authors have somewhat modified this position, conceding a greater measure of autonomy to the state (thus Antonio Gramsci, Nicos Poulantzas, and Ralph Milliband). Clearly, the position taken here presupposes a different view of the empirical relationships. For useful recent discussions, see Nicos Poulantzas, *Pouvoir politique et classes sociales* (Paris, 1968); Gianfranco Poggi, *The Development of the Modern State* (Stanford, 1978); Frank Parkin, *Marxism and Class Theory* (New York, 1979).

6. It may be observed that a confusion between the two issues—that of the capitalist/socialist alternative and that of the modern welfare state—can be found both on the "right" and the "left." On the "right," the growth of the welfare state is often perceived as identical with "creeping socialism." On the "left" it is commonly posited, as if self-evident, that socialism must mean more welfare. Both assumptions are questionable. I argue later in this chapter that the growth of the welfare state is indeed related to what one may call "creeping socialism," but this does not mean that the two are identical processes. A further empirical point that *can* be made is that capitalist societies, with their superior wealth-generating capacity, can *afford* a more lavish welfare state and that the pressures of democratic politics tend in that direction. Economically ineffective and nondemocratic socialist regimes are in a quite different situation.

7. Joseph Schumpeter, *Capitalism, Socialism and Democracy* (New York, 1947 [1942]). Cf. a recent reassessment of Schumpeter's views, Arnold Heertje, ed. *Schumpeter's Vision* (New York, 1981).

8. For example, Charles Lindblom, *Politics and Markets* (New York, 1977).

9. Milton and Rose Friedman, *Free to Choose* (New York, 1980), p. 69 (italics added). Also see, by the same authors, *Capitalism and Freedom* (Chicago, 1962). A similar position is taken by Michael Novak, *The Spirit of Democratic Capitalism* (New York, 1982), esp. p. 171 ff.

10. A very similar argument (albeit with the use of a rather idiosyncratic vocabulary) is made by Dan Usher, *The Economic Prerequisite of Democracy* (New York, 1981). Usher argues that democracy is impossible unless there are basic economic rights (which he calls a "system of equity") that are separate from the state. Usher's argument is essentially a "deductive" one (as Lively, *Democracy,* calls it), but it can readily be tested by empirical data. For a similarly "deductive" argument, cf. Anthony Downs, *An Economic Theory of Democracy* (New York, 1957).

11. The sociological theory of bureaucracy, as pioneered by Max Weber and Roberto Michels, buttresses this argument.

12. See especially F. A. Hayek, *The Road to Serfdom* (Chicago, 1944); *The Constitution of Liberty* (Chicago, 1960); and *The Political Order of a Free People* (Chicago, 1979). I do not share many of Hayek's theoretical presuppositions, let alone his philosophical ones, but I give credence to his central argument.

13. These considerations suggest that orthodox Marxists were quite right in their insistence on the "dictatorship of the proletariat" as against the democratic factions within the socialist movement. And Lenin was correct in his view that, since "the proletariat" as such is in no position to exercise political power, the dictatorship must be vicariously exercised by a much more cohesive elite (the party in the role of self-defined "vanguard of the proletariat"). Interestingly, Max Weber, writing shortly after the Bolshevik Revolution, came to the same conclusion "from the other side of the fence," as it were. See his essay "Der Sozialismus," written in 1918, in his *Gesammelte Aufsaetze zur Soziologie und Sozialpolitik* (Tübingen, 1924), p. 492 ff. Weber opined that Trotsky was right in thinking that socialism required *Standrecht* (summary justice).

14. The same formulation was made by Dan Usher, *Economic Prerequisite,* p. 6 ff.

15. When Jeane Kirkpatrick, soon after her appointment as ambassador to the United Nations by President Reagan, made use of this distinction in some of her

speeches, the liberal press depicted this as a disingenuous invention of the administration designed to justify support for sundry right-wing dictatorships. In fact, the distinction was elaborated in the works of Carl Friedrich and Hannah Arendt, who wrote about this in the 1950s and who can hardly be described as ideological forerunners of Ronald Reagan. It should also be pointed out that the distinction is *descriptive,* quite apart from any moral judgments. Liberal critics said that if you are being tortured, you don't care whether your torturers are serving an authoritarian or a totalitarian government. Of course. For that matter, the police forces of democratic governments have been known to torture people, who will also not be consoled by the thought that their torturers are servants of a democracy. The point of the distinction is *not* that authoritarian regimes are morally superior but that they are different. Thus, at the time of writing, I would probably prefer to be arrested by the police in Hungary (with a totalitarian regime that, as far as I know, rarely tortures people nowadays) than in Iran (whose authoritarian regime reportedly engages in torture as a standard operating procedure). None of this negates the distinction—or, not so incidentally, Kirkpatrick's assertion—that authoritarian regimes are more likely to be removed or modified than totalitarian ones (a point forcefully made by Arendt).

16. It is perhaps worth recalling that the word "totalitarian" was coined by Mussolini, not at all pejoratively but to denote the positive purpose of the Fascist Revolution—"nothing against the state, nothing without the state, nothing outside the state."

17. Indeed, the only case thus far of a totalitarian state with a capitalist economy was Nazi Germany (Fascist Italy, despite Mussolini's pious intentions, was authoritarian rather than totalitarian). The question of how seriously one should take the Nazis' self-definition as a new form of socialism is beyond the present scope. Certainly the totalitarian design of Nazism (in their own terminology, the *Gleichschaltung* of every institution within German society) included the progressive imposition of state control over the economy.

18. See Peter Berger and Richard Neuhaus, *To Empower People: The Role of Mediating Structures in Public Policy* (Washington, D.C., 1977). We coined the phrase "mediating structures," but its substance, of course, is an old idea in political thought.

19. This position has been vigorously argued by Grace Goodell, inter alia, in "The Importance of Political Participation for Sustained Capitalist Development" (paper for Seminar on Modern Capitalism, 1983).

20. The second correlation is readily visible in the annual Freedom House reports.

21. See Peter Berger, *The Heretical Imperative* (Garden City, N.Y., 1979), p. 11 ff.

22. See Schumpeter, *Capitalism,* passim. Also, see John Scott, *Corporations, Classes and Capitalism* (New York, 1979).

23. See Usher, *Economic Prerequisite,* p. 105 ff.

24. *The Rise and Decline of Nations* (New Haven, 1982). It is interesting that Schumpeter also foresaw this in his early conceptualization of the "tax state." See his "Die Krise des Steuerstaates," *Aufsaetze zur Soziologie* (Tübingen, 1953), p. 1 ff.; the article was first published in 1918. Schumpeter described the "tax state" as parasitical vis-à-vis private enterprise and as tending to undermine the latter's productivity.

## Chapter 5

1. See Steven Lukes, *Individualism* (New York, 1973). Lukes enumerates no less than eleven uses of the term (p. 43 ff.).

2. See Thomas Luckmann, *The Invisible Religion* (New York, 1967). Once again, this term need not imply a positive evaluation. Luckmann presents it in a value-free manner; others have either celebrated or deplored it.

3. These statements presuppose, on my part, a theory of the relation of individuals and society that cannot possibly be reiterated here. The groundwork of the theory was developed in Peter Berger and Thomas Luckmann, *The Social Construction of Reality* (Garden City, N.Y., 1966). Also see my articles, "Identity as a Problem in the Sociology of Knowledge," *European Journal of Sociology* (Spring 1965); "Sincerity and Authenticity in Modern Society," *The Public Interest* (Spring 1973); and "Modern Identity," in Wilton Dillon, ed. *The Cultural Drama* (Washington, D.C., 1974). The most important influences on this theory, insofar as it deals with the interaction of identities and institutions, have been the works of George Herbert Mead, Alfred Schutz, and Arnold Gehlen.

4. This sentence does *not* imply a rigid sociological determinism. There are always individuals who undergo liberations in thought, self-experience, and even conduct in the most constraining circumstances. But such individuals are very rare. Most of us, well socialized and well behaved, require a social context that permits and encourages our projects of personal liberation. I stipulate that Socrates would have become a liberated individual if he had been born, instead of in Athens, in a primitive Neolithic tribe; I do not flatter myself by thinking that this would be true of me.

5. For Marx, of course, man is a collective being ("species-being"), so that his freedom can only be realized in collectivity. Thus his concept of freedom is quite different from Smith's. However, I would contend that, despite these differences, both correctly perceived the empirical reality of capitalism as individuating.

6. See Lukes, p. 4 ff. The most interesting part of Lukes's book is in the beginning, where he traces the "semantic history" of the term "individualism."

7. Karl Polanyi, *The Great Transformation* (New York, 1944), p. 163. Polanyi, a man of the left, viewed the change as profoundly dehumanizing. But so did Toennies, a conservative. Durkheim, on the other hand, believed that the change spelled good news—precisely because it freed the individual.

8. Alan Macfarlane, *The Origins of English Individualism* (New York, 1979).

9. Macfarlane, p. 196.

10. I am greatly indebted to Brigitte Berger on this point. Cf. Peter Laslett, ed. *Household and Family in Past Time* (New York, 1972); Jean-Louis Flandrin, *Families in Former Times* (New York, 1979); Emmanuel Ladurie, *Montaillou* (New York, 1979).

11. To forestall predictable objections, this is *not* to argue that David or Socrates should be understood as modern individualists. Of course not. Both were embedded in profoundly nonmodern communalisms, respectively those of the *brith* and of the polis. What is at issue here are roots, origins, seeds of developments that came to fruition many centuries later. The important point is that other ancient civilizations, especially those of India and China, lacked these particular seeds. This, however, does not preclude the possibility that other civilizations developed *different* notions of individual autonomy, such as the autonomy of an individual who has attained

enlightenment in either its Hindu or Buddhist forms, or the autonomy of the Confucian cultivated man. But these different notions of "individualism" led to greatly different historical developments compared to those stemming from the Hebrew and the Hellenic "moments of truth"; they are, if you will, other truths.

12. The literature on the history of bourgeois culture is, of course, vast. I do not pretend to have mastered it. I have found the following works useful: Elinor Barber, *The Bourgeoisie in XVIIIth Century France* (Princeton, 1955); Walter Houghton, *The Victorian Frame of Mind* (New Haven, 1957); James Laver, *Manners and Morals in the Age of Optimism* (New York, 1966); Dieter and Karin Claessens, *Kapitalismus als Kultur* (Duesseldorf, 1973); Raymond Williams, *Culture and Society* (New York, 1983).

13. Norbert Elias has written the epic account of the march through history of this bourgeois fastidiousness, in his *Der Prozess der Zivilisation* (Bern, 1969). On the fastidiousness of bourgeois as against aristocratic language one may profitably read Nancy Mitford, ed. *Noblesse Oblige* (New York, 1956), even though this delightful little volume can hardly be regarded as a model of scholarly research.

14. I am again indebted to Brigitte Berger for this suggestion.

15. This is not the place to criticize the feminist writers, *femmes de la gauche,* who have portrayed bourgeois culture and by extension capitalism as agencies of the oppression of women. I am inclined to the opinion that pretty much the opposite occurred: To a large extent, bourgeois culture was shaped and transmitted by women.

16. See Bernard Groethuysen, *The Bourgeois* (New York, 1968 [French, 1927]).

17. Philip Greven, *The Protestant Temperament* (New York, 1977).

18. Greven, p. 31.

19. Greven, p. 38 ff.

20. To *that* extent the approach here is compatible with the Marxist one. This compatibility, though, is merely formal. The Marxists are quite right when they single out class as an important influence on intellectual life; they are wrong on many if not most of the specifics of this influence. Also, of course, the present concept of class culture does not view the influence as one of mechanical or inexorable determination. Rather than operating within the classical Marxist paradigm of infra- and super-structure *(Unterbau/Ueberbau),* one will be better advised to think of these relationships along the lines of Max Weber's concept of "elective affinity" *(Wahlverwandschaft).* This means that intellectual processes come to "fit" a particular class constellation, but this does not mean that the latter determines the former in a one-way causal nexus. For the theoretical underpinnings of this approach, see Berger and Luckmann, *Social Construction.*

21. Arnold Gehlen, *Urmensch und Spaetkultur* (Bonn, 1956), and *Die Seele im technischen Zeitalter* (Hamburg, 1957). If one combines Gehlen's ideas with the American school of social psychology deriving from George Herbert Mead, one begins to see the possibility of what I have elsewhere called a "sociological psychology." This should not be confused with so-called psychohistory. Much of what has gone under the latter name, in my opinion, has entailed an inadmissible retrojection into the past of modern psychic elements (as, for example, in Erik Erikson's treatment of Martin Luther). A "sociological psychology," by contrast, would take seriously the historicity of specific psychic configurations and relate them to the social context in which they arose. Thus one might conclude that Freudian psychoanalysis is indeed a useful method for understanding *modern* psyches, but quite useless in trying to grasp

the workings of a sixteenth-century mind (not to mention minds in archaic or non-Western cultures). On this, see my article "Toward a Sociological Understanding of Psychoanalysis," *Social Research* (Spring 1965).

22. Again, the relevant material is nearly endless. I have found the following works useful: Eugene Goodheart, *The Cult of the Ego* (Chicago, 1968); Joan Webber, *The Eloquent "I"* (Madison, Wisc., 1968); Paul Zweig, *The Heresy of Self-Love* (New York, 1968); Quentin Anderson, *The Imperial Self* (New York, 1971); Calvin Bedient, *Architects of the Self* (New York, 1972). For an attempt to develop this idea with reference to one modern novelist, see my article "Robert Musil and the Salvage of the Self," *Partisan Review* (1984), 4. It should be noted that an interpretation of modern Western literature in terms of "subjectivization" has a much wider scope than the specific development *within* that literary history known as "Modernism."

23. See Peter Berger, Brigitte Berger, and Hansfried Kellner, *The Homeless Mind* (New York, 1973).

24. The term is Brigitte Berger's. See Brigitte Berger and Peter Berger, *The War over the Family* (Garden City, N.Y., 1983), p. 118 ff.

25. See César Graña, *Bohemian versus Bourgeois* (New York, 1964); Helmut Kreuzer, *Die Boheme* (Stuttgart, 1968).

26. Graña, p. 88.

27. Anderson, *Imperial Self*, p. 58.

28. In *The Homeless Mind* we coined the terms "carryover" and "stoppage" to denote the way in which attitudes and actions relevant to one sector of life may or may not spill over into other sectors. The terms apply here. Thus the anticapitalist stereotype does have empirical realizations in the case of individuals for whom *all* of life is one single business enterprise. Here structures of conduct and consciousness appropriate to capitalist enterprise carry over into other zones of life. As a generalization about life in capitalist societies, though, this stereotype is a caricature. There is a multitude of institutional stoppages operating within capitalist societies to prevent such carryover—those of family, religion, and law, to name but the three most powerful ones. Most people, even very successful entrepreneurs, do *not* treat their families in the same way as their business associates.

29. David McClelland placed the "need to achieve" at the top of the list of personality traits conducive to economic development. See his *The Achieving Society* (Princeton, 1961). That was probably one-sided, but McClelland was right in emphasizing this trait within the overall personality of the successful entrepreneur.

30. For example, both Talcott Parsons and Marion Levy were of this opinion. For a more recent empirical exploration, see Alex Inkeles et al., *Exploring Individual Modernity* (New York, 1983).

31. This, of course, was Joseph Schumpeter's view (given his values, a pessimistic one).

32. Georg Simmel, *Philosophie des Geldes* (Berlin, 1958 [1900]).

33. On this, cf. Benjamin Nelson, *The Idea of Usury* (Chicago, 1969). The subtitle of the book summarizes Nelson's thesis: *From Tribal Brotherhood to Universal Otherhood*. Among other things, a contribution of this idiosyncratic and perceptive work is that it sheds light on the role of the Jews in the development of Western "universal otherhood": Usury was an economic activity into which Jews were forced in Christian Europe. And, lo and behold, Jews have figured prominently in some of the most important movements of universalistic liberation (intellectual as well as

practical) in modern Western history. Anti-Semites of the left as well as the right have regularly blamed the Jews for their "corrosive individualism"—the "corrosion," of course, pertaining to this or that "tribal brotherhood."

34. Daniel Bell, *The Cultural Contradictions of Capitalism* (New York, 1976).

35. This example should not be construed as implying a moral judgment on any specific entitlement cited. What is good for enterprise is not necessarily the supreme good for society. The point is simply that the expansion of contractually codified entitlements is in tension with, "contradicts," important features of the entrepreneurial "spirit of capitalism."

36. See Peter Berger and Richard Neuhaus, *To Empower People* (Washington, D.C., 1977). We coined that term, but the idea, of course, was not new at all.

37. The importance of this particular set of institutions was seen very clearly by Alexis de Tocqueville and has been frequently commented upon ever since.

38. See Michael Novak, *The Spirit of Democratic Capitalism* (New York, 1982), p. 128 ff. Cf. Robert Benne, *The Ethic of Democratic Capitalism* (Philadelphia, 1981), p. 247 ff.


## Chapter 6

1. The question should be asked without parody. A positive answer need *not* imply that development is a deterministic, inexorable process, with each developing country mechanically repeating the stages passed through by England and the other "metropolitan" economies. One can conceptualize an overall process of developmental stages while also accepting that this course of events can be modified or even derailed by cultural conditions, government policies, or international relationships.

2. W.W. Rostow, *The Stages of Economic Growth* (Cambridge, 1960). Significantly, the book was subtitled *A Non-Communist Manifesto*.

3. Cf. Talcott Parsons, *Structure and Process in Modern Societies* (Glencoe, Ill., 1960); Everett Hagen, *On the Theory of Social Change* (Homewood, Ill., 1962); Gino Germani, *Política y sociedad en una época de transición* (Buenos Aires, 1963); Myron Weiner, ed. *Modernization* (New York, 1966); Marion Levy, *Modernization and the Structure of Societies* (Princeton, 1966); Talcott Parsons, *The System of Modern Societies* (Englewood Cliffs, N.J., 1971). Within sociology the "stages" notion of the development economists was readily combined with the equally "systemic" bias of structural-functional theory (though Parsons replaced England with America as the "lead society"). Germani was important in transmitting this generally upbeat approach to a generation of Latin American social scientists.

4. Cf. Robert Heilbroner, *The Great Ascent* (New York, 1963); Jacques Austruy, *Le scandale du développement* (Paris, 1968); Gunnar Myrdal, *The Challenge of World Poverty* (New York, 1970), which summarized earlier work of his. Also, cf. Robert Packenham, *Liberal America and the Third World* (Princeton, 1973).

5. V. I. Lenin, *Imperialism: The Highest Stage of Capitalism* (Peking, 1965). The Russian original was published in 1916.

6. The first was proposed by Rosa Luxemburg, the second (which influenced Lenin more) by Rudolf Hilferding. For a discussion of this intellectual history, see Benjamin Cohen, *The Question of Imperialism* (New York, 1973).

7. All of this is highly instructive in sociology-of-knowledge terms. The Leninist interpretation of imperialism can serve as a textbook example of how to save a theory that has been empirically falsified or, if one prefers, of how to snatch political victory from intellectual defeat.

8. Cf. Paul Baran and Paul Sweezy, *Monopoly Capitalism* (New York, 1966); Harry Magdoff, *The Age of Imperialism* (New York, 1969).

9. One of the best summaries of these criticisms may be found in Cohen, *Question*.

10. This criticism was first made by Joseph Schumpeter in his 1919 essay on imperialism. See his *Social Classes and Imperialism* (Cleveland, 1968).

11. The term "comprador class" is derived from the Portuguese *comprador* meaning "buyer." It was used to describe native representatives of Portuguese enterprises in places like Goa or Macao. In contemporary Marxist parlance (and invective) it is often coterminous with "national bourgeoisie," though at least segments of the latter are viewed as possible allies of the revolutionary movement—inescapably so, since Third World Marxist theoreticians almost always come from this class (as, for that matter, do most Third World revolutionaries).

12. It was first used in an influential article with that title in the American Marxist journal *Monthly Review*, XVIII (September 1966), 4. Also cf. Frank's *Capitalism and Underdevelopment in Latin America* (New York, 1969).

13. Again, this position should be examined without caricaturing it. Frank and other dependency theorists are cognizant of the fact that these countries were poor before Western capitalism arrived there, if compared to the standards of modern affluent societies. The point, though, is that this poverty was supposedly frozen or even aggravated in consequence of capitalist penetration.

14. I have discussed this coincidence in "The Third World as a Religious Idea," *Partisan Review* (1983), 2.

15. For a good introduction to the genesis of dependency theory, see Joseph Kahl, *Modernization, Exploitation and Dependency in Latin America* (New Brunswick, N.J., 1976).

16. Fernando Henrique Cardoso and Enzo Faletto, *Dependencia y desarrollo en América Latina* (Mexico City, 1969); Cardoso, *Estado y sociedad en América Latina* (Buenós Aires, 1973); Pablo Gonzalez Casanova, *Sociología de la explotación* (Mexico City, 1970).

17. He has in recent years moderated his position even further. At the time of writing he is a federal senator from the state of São Paulo and an important leader in one of the two major political parties.

18. For example Frank, *Capitalism and Underdevelopment*.

19. For example Samir Amin, *L'Afrique de l'Ouest bloquée* (Paris, 1971).

20. For example Richard Barnet and Ronald Muller, *Global Reach* (New York, 1975).

21. See Jyoti Shankar Singh, *A New International Economic Order* (New York, 1977).

22. For an important alternative interpretation, see Claudio Véliz, *The Centralist Tradition in Latin America* (Princeton, 1980).

23. Cf. Cohen, *Question*.

24. Cf. P. T. Bauer, *Dissent on Development* (Cambridge, Mass., 1972), esp. p. 147 ff. and 307 ff.; idem, *Equality, the Third World, and Economic Delusion* (Cambridge, Mass., 1981), esp. p. 42 ff.; Robert Tucker, *The Inequality of Nations* (New York,

1977), esp. p. 115 ff. and 161 ff. Bauer, a British economist and a prolific writer, has been a major figure in the criticism of dependency theory and other "left" interpretations of the Third World. Having recently been elevated to the peerage by Prime Minister Margaret Thatcher, he now has no less a pulpit than the House of Lords for his ongoing barrage against *gauchismes* of every variety.

25. For a Marxist analysis of this case, see Paul Baran, *The Political Economy of Growth* (New York, 1957), p. 144 ff.

26. For a balanced view of the role of multinationals, see Raymond Vernon, *Storm over the Multinationals* (Cambridge, Mass., 1977).

27. Cf. Ronald Nairn, *Wealth of Nations in Crisis* (Houston, 1979), esp. p. 161 ff.; Melvyn Krauss, *Development Without Aid* (New York, 1983).

28. This has far-reaching implications for two important current controversies—the one over aid and the one over the "New International Economic Order" (NIEO). Those who advocate more aid and the proponents of NIEO share a common statist bias. This assumes that actions favoring Third World *states* will also benefit Third World *populations*. This is a very wild assumption. In many instances aid is absorbed by groups far removed from the poor who are intended as beneficiaries. Even more regrettably, there are a good many cases where one cannot even assume that the elites in charge of government have any interest whatever in the development of their respective societies. A good many elites have discovered that poor peasants tend to be less troublesome politically than people in the throes of successful development: Peasants with refrigerators have a disconcerting propensity to becoming "uppity."

29. See Carlos Rangel, *El tercermundismo* (Caracas, 1982).

30. See my article "Third World" in *Partisan Review*. A peculiarly interesting excrescence of "Third Worldism" is the idea that something called the "right to development" should be codified as a human right in international law—a very clear case of the belief that development can be brought about by the action of states. Cf. Alain Pellet, *Le droit international du développement* (Paris, 1978); International Commission of Jurists, *Development, Human Rights and the Rule of Law* (Oxford, 1981).

31. Some dependency theorists have noticed the problem. It bothers them. One response has been to argue that East Asia has special circumstances not prevailing elsewhere. This is a weak argument. Every case has special circumstances, but a general theory must be able to deal at least with those cases that cannot plausibly be called marginal. Another response has been to coin a new concept, "dependent development." *That,* to put it bluntly, is double-talk, a verbal maneuver by dogmatists whose dogmas have been shot out of the water by empirical evidence. Cf. Helmut Asche, *Industrialisierte Dritte Welt?* (Hamburg, 1984). Asche is an honest analyst and he tries to do justice to the empirical evidence, but his efforts to salvage the essentials of a *dependencia* perspective out of the East Asian material are of more interest to social psychology than to a theory of development.

32. It should be stated that this hypothesis constitutes a substantial change of mind on my part. In an earlier book on the problems of development, *Pyramids of Sacrifice* (New York, 1974), I rejected this hypothesis in favor of a position that was even-handed as between capitalist and noncapitalist development strategies. I argued then that each country must consider its course in terms of its concrete circumstances and without any a priori preferences for this or that development model. The reasons why I changed my mind are very simple and directly relevant to the present

argument. When I wrote that book, the only part of the Third World with which I had significant acquaintance was Latin America; in the latter part of the 1970s I "discovered" East Asia. Rio de Janeiro looks different once one has seen Singapore.

33. The best source for the relevant data is the *World Development Report,* issued annually by the World Bank.

34. Exceptions to this generalization would be countries devastated by natural disaster. The countries of the African Sahel would be the most important cases. It is frequently argued, though, that this disaster, while primarily caused by draught, has also been aggravated by policy factors.

35. Cf. Myrdal, *Challenge of World Poverty;* Paul Bairoch, *The Economic Development of the Third World since 1900* (Berkeley, 1975); and Sylvia Hewlett, *The Cruel Dilemmas of Development* (New York, 1980), a study of Brazil.

36. I have relied heavily here on Nick Eberstadt, "Progress Against Poverty" (paper for the Seminar on Modern Capitalism, 1983).

37. Richard Critchfield, *Villages* (Garden City, New York, 1981), p. 336.

38. Eberstadt, "Progress Against Poverty."

39. Bauer, *Equality,* p. 47. This observation is also relevant to the conventional view that population growth is always a negative factor in development. Cf. Mahmood Mamdani, *The Myth of Population Growth* (New York, 1972). Mamdani, another field researcher, studied birth control programs in Indian villages. He was able to show that, even if an argument can be made that India as a whole suffers from population growth, the economic well-being of individual peasants increased with each child.

40. There has been a long debate over the effects on the poor of India's "Green Revolution." Myron Weiner has shown that, by the available evidence, the poor have generally gained as a result of this agricultural transformation. (See his "Capitalist Agriculture, Peasant Farming and Well-Being in India" paper for the Seminar on Modern Capitalism, 1983.)

41. This does not mean that the process has been without some darker sides. For a rare field account, see Steven Mosher, *Broken Earth* (New York, 1983).

42. See Arthur Okun, *Equality and Efficiency* (Washington, D.C., 1975). The subtitle of the book is, appropriately, *The Big Trade-Off.*

43. Simon Kuznets, *Modern Economic Growth* (New York, 1966). For a more skeptical view, cf. David Morawetz, *Twenty-Five Years of Economic Development* (Washington, D.C., 1977).

44. Gustav Papanek, "Capitalist Development and Income Distribution" (paper for the Seminar on Modern Capitalism, 1983). Papanek, incidentally, is one of those who feel that the universality of the Kuznets effect has been exaggerated.

45. This argument is similar to the view of Mancur Olson, who argued that what he calls "distributional coalitions" tend to inhibit economic development. Cf. his *The Rise and Decline of Nations* (New Haven, 1982), esp. p. 146 ff.

46. This should *not* be imputed to Papanek in those terms. The formulation is mine, not his. Papanek recommends a strategy he calls "capitalist production, socialist consumption"—leaving the market free to operate but subsidizing unskilled labor (which, he believes, is best done by providing *services* to the poor, such as food, housing, health, transport and, of course, education). I, for one, see no reason why the adjective "socialist" should be attached to such a strategy.

## Chapter 7

1. Taking this position is making a heuristic choice, *not* proposing a hypothesis. It follows that the position as such is not falsifiable, any more than one can falsify a statement that a glass is half full or half empty. The purpose of the heuristic choice (or, if one prefers the Weberian phrase, of the ideal-typical construct) is to facilitate useful comparisons. As these comparisons are made, though, falsifiable hypotheses are generated—as will presently be done.

2. Needless to say, this does not imply that the East Asian societies are not fascinating objects of study for their own sakes. What is at issue here is the wider theoretical relevance of these societies.

3. See Edward Chen, *The Hyper-Growth Economics of Asia* (New York, 1979); Roy Hofheinz and Kent Calder, *The Eastasia Edge* (New York, 1982); and Chalmers Johnson, "The Taiwan Model," in James Hsiung, ed. *The Taiwan Experience* (New York, 1981), p. 9 ff.

4. Chalmers Johnson, *loc. cit.,* suggests further political similarities: a differentiation between "reigning" and "ruling" functions, the former performed by politicians (who are by no means powerless), the latter by bureaucrats; single-party rule, whether achieved by democratic means (in Japan) or not; a "soft" authoritarianism (again, both under democratic and nondemocratic regimes). Hong Kong, in Johnson's view, shares these characteristics, despite its peculiar colonial status, with an economic elite performing the "reigning" function in collusion with the "ruling" British administrators.

5. See Kazushi Ohkawa and Henry Rosovsky, *Japanese Economic Growth* (Stanford, 1973); Edward Denison and William Chung, *How Japan's Economy Grew So Fast* (Washington, D.C., 1976).

6. As far as I have been able to find out, there has been no systematic assessment of the Meiji period in terms of what has come to be known as development theory since the 1950s. It would be a very instructive exercise.

7. See Kamekichi Takahashi, *The Rise and Development of Japan's Modern Economy* (Tokyo, 1969); Hugh Borton, *Japan's Modern Century* (New York, 1970), esp. p. 93 ff., p. 129 ff., and p. 304 ff.

8. See Takahashi, p. 148 ff.

9. See Takahashi, p. 10 ff. and p. 58 ff.; cf. Johannes Hirschmeier, *The Origins of Entrepreneurship in Meiji Japan* (Cambridge, Mass., 1964).

10. See Takahashi, passim.

11. Cf. Chen, *Hyper-Growth Economics;* Hofheinz and Calder, *Eastasia Edge.*

12. See Parvez Hasan, *Korea: Problems and Issues in a Rapidly Growing Economy* (Baltimore, 1976).

13. See Hsin-Huang Hsiao, *Government Agricultural Strategies in Taiwan and South Korea* (Taipei, 1981).

14. Cf. Shirley Kuo et al., *The Taiwan Success Story* (Boulder, Colo., 1981); Hsiung, *Taiwan Experience;* Bureau of Statistics, Executive Yuan, *National Conditions* (Taipei, 1984).

15. See Hsiao.

16. Cf. A. J. Youngson, *Hong Kong Economic Growth and Development* (Hong Kong, 1982); also, Michael Herrmann, *Hong Kong versus Singapore* (Stuttgart, 1970), an interesting comparative study. Herrmann argues that the plentiful supply of

refugee labor in Hong Kong made for more consistent free-trade policies in Hong Kong than in Singapore, where this factor was absent.

17. Cf. Chen, p. 10; Lee Soo Ann, *Industrialization in Singapore* (Melbourne, 1973); Riaz Hassan, ed. *Singapore Society in Transition* (Kuala Lumpur, 1976). For a dependency-theory interpretation, see Frederic Dego, *Dependent Development and Industrial Order* (New York, 1981).

18. See Alan Gleason, "Economic Growth and Consumption in Japan," in William Lockwood, ed. *The State and Economic Enterprise in Japan* (Princeton, 1965), p. 391 ff.

19. This is Gleason's position, *loc. cit.*

20. See Chen, p. 161 ff.

21. See Todashi Fukutake, *The Japanese Social Structure* (Tokyo, 1982).

22. Cf. Hasan, esp. p. 45 ff.; Chen, p. 164 ff.

23. Cf. Kuo et al., passim; Chen, p. 171 ff.

24. See Charlotte Wong, "Social Mobility in Taiwan," in Hsiung, p. 246 ff.

25. Cf. Chen, p. 157 ff.; Youngson, p. 42 ff.

26. Cf. Chen, p. 168 ff.

27. Kuo et al., p. 143.

28. See Helmut Asche, *Industrialisierte Dritte Welt?* (Hamburg, 1984).

29. Cf. Lockwood; Borton, *Japan's Modern Century;* Takahashi, *Rise and Development,* esp. p. 134 ff. In the Lockwood volume there is a very interesting essay by David Landes comparing nineteenth-century developments in Japan and Germany (p. 93 ff.).

30. See Kanji Haitani, *The Japanese Economic System* (Lexington, Mass., 1976), p. 39 ff.

31. Chalmers Johnson, *MITI and the Japanese Miracle* (Stanford, 1982). Critics have argued that Johnson exaggerates the importance of MITI, but few have challenged his overall picture of government-business cooperation.

32. For example on South Korea, see Kyong-Dong Kim, *Man and Society in Korea's Economic Growth* (Seoul, 1979), p. 65 ff. Kim uses the term "political capitalists" to describe the business component of this elite.

33. See Youngson, p. 119 ff.

34. See Johnson, *MITI.* He stresses that this is a modern, highly rational form of polity. Its rationality he calls "plan rationality," as against the "market rationality" and the "ideological rationality" of the other two (equally modern) forms.

35. Ambrose King, "Administrative Absorption of Politics in Hong Kong," in Ambrose King and Rance Lee, eds. *Social Life and Development in Hong Kong* (Hong Kong, 1981), p. 127 ff.

36. See Borton, *Japan's Modern Century,* passim.

37. Kim, p. 81 ff.

38. Cf. John Copper's two essays on Taiwan's political development in Hsiung, p. 359 ff. and p. 374 ff.

39. Ambrose King, "The Political Culture of Kwon Tong," in King and Lee, p. 147 ff.

40. I have ruminated (no more, I'm afraid) on these questions in three earlier articles: "Secularity, West and East," *This World* (Winter 1983); "Can the Caribbean Learn from East Asia?" *Caribbean Review,* XIII (1984), 2; and "An East Asian Development Model?" *Economic News* (Taiwan), September 17–23, 1984.

41. Cf. Winston Davis, "Religion and the Development of the Far East" (paper for the MIT-Harvard Joint Seminar on Political Development, March, 1984).

42. These three issues are discussed extensively, and pessimistically, in Davis's paper.

43. Robert Bellah, *Tokugawa Religion* (Boston, 1957).

44. Michio Morishima, *Why Has Japan Succeeded?* (Cambridge, 1982). Davis classifies Morishima's book as belonging to a more or less self-congratulatory genre known as "Japan theory," a sort of ideology of Japanese exceptionalism (Americans will readily recognize the genre).

45. Ezra Vogel, *Japan as Number One* (Cambridge, Mass., 1979). Cf. Chalmers Johnson, *MITI.*

46. I made that argument, with only moderate conviction, in my article "Secularity," cited in *This World* (see note 40).

47. I am indebted to Yih-Yuan Li for this idea.

48. There is some uncertainty as to who first argued that Confucian ethics serve to explain East Asian economic success. An important article in this discussion was Roderick MacFarquhar, "The Post-Confucian Challenge," *The Economist* (February 9, 1980).

49. This little item strengthens one's suspicion that, in all of this, the fallacy of *post hoc propter hoc* may be vigorously in play. If, say, Papua New Guinea should ever take off economically, for whatever reasons, will we be regaled with theories demonstrating the capitalist values of Melanesian mythology?

50. Morishima argues ingeniously in *Why Has Japan Succeeded?* that the stress on the virtue of *loyalty* by Japanese Confucians, as against the stress on *benevolence* in Chinese Confucianism, helps explain the (alleged) superior Japanese predisposition to modernize.

51. Robert Bellah, "Cultural Identity and Asian Modernization," in Institute of Japanese Culture and Classics, Kokugakuin University, *Cultural Identity and Modernization in Asian Countries* (Tokyo, 1983), p. 24.

52. See Takahashi, *Rise and Development,* p. 76 ff.

53. Hirschmeier, *Origins of Entrepeneurship,* p. 44.

54. See, for example, Koza Yamamura, *A Study of Samurai Income and Entrepeneurship* (Cambridge, Mass., 1974). Yamamura stresses the role of other groups in the genesis of this new class and argues that even *samurai* entrepreneurs were often inspired by a plain profit motive. One must reflect, however, that greed and more lofty motives have often dwelled together harmoniously in human hearts.

55. On both these individuals, see Hirschmeier, p. 164 ff.

56. Here I follow Hirschmeier, p. 196 ff.

57. Cf. Chie Nakane, *Japanese Society* (Berkeley, 1972); Haitani, *Japanese Economic System,* p. 9 ff.; Fukutake, *Japanese Social Structure,* p. 123 ff. It is interesting that Fukutake, a social critic, deplores the same "groupism" that others (such as Nakane) have cited favorably as a clue to Japan's economic success; Fukutake regards it as repressive.

58. See Nakane.

59. Chalmers Johnson, p. 11 ff. It must be said that these "treasures" are *not* enjoyed by the many Japanese working for smaller firms and generally do not apply to women even in the large corporations (though this latter discrimination may now be gradually changing).

60. Cf. Haitani, p. 29 ff.; Herbert Passin, *Society and Education in Japan* (New York, 1965).

61. Analects XVII: 3, cited in E. R. Hughes, ed. *Chinese Philosophy in Classical Times* (London, 1942), p. 19.

62. Cf. Joseph Kahl, *The Measurement of Modernism* (Austin, 1968); Alex Inkeles and David Smith, *Becoming Modern* (Cambridge, Mass., 1974); and Alex Inkeles et al., *Exploring Individual Modernity* (New York, 1983).

63. See Joseph Levenson, *Confucian China and Its Modern Fate* (Berkeley, 1965), p. 59 ff.

64. See, for example, Wm. Theodore deBary, *The Liberal Tradition in China* (Hong Kong, 1983), p. 43 ff., where deBary argues for "a kind of individualism" in neo-Confucianism. I do not read this argument as implying equivalence with Western-style ideas of individual autonomy.

65. Cf. Janet Walker, *The Japanese Novel of the Meiji Period and the Ideal of Individualism* (Princeton, 1979).

66. Cf. Masao Maruyama, "Patterns of Individuation and the Case of Japan," in Marius Jansen, ed. *Changing Japanese Attitudes Toward Modernization* (Princeton, 1965), p. 489 ff.

67. Cf. R. P. Dore, "Mobility, Equality and Individuation in Modern Japan," in *Aspects of Social Change in Modern Japan,* ed. R. P. Dore (Princeton, 1967), p. 113 ff.

68. See Fukutake, p. 144. On the continuing importance of groups in adult socialization, among middle-class and working-class youth, cf. Kazuko Tsurumi, *Social Change and the Individual* (Princeton, 1970).

69. Cf. Sheldon Appleton, "Sex, Values and Change on Taiwan," in Hsiung, p. 257 ff.; Kuo-shu Yang, "Transformation of the Chinese People," in Hsiung, p. 268 ff. The changes were registered in surveys made between 1969 and 1976.

70. Cf. John Myers, "Traditional Chinese Religious Practices in an Urban-Industrial Setting," in King and Lee, *Social Life,* p. 275 ff. Very similar observations have been made concerning the so-called New Religions in Japan.

71. Meyers, p. 287.

72. Analects XIV:2, cited in Hughes, p. 20.

## Chapter 8

1. A prominent example was Talcott Parsons, *The System of Modern Society* (Englewood Cliffs, N. J., 1971). Parsons was an erudite and sometimes brilliant theorist (and, incidentally, an American patriot with no great sympathy for socialist ideologies), and I would not want to ascribe this fallacy to him. All the same, Parsonian theory lent itself well to the misleading notion of inexorable convergence. For a discussion of "convergence theory" as applied to the industrial socialist societies, see David Lane, *The Socialist Industrial State* (Boulder, Colo., 1976), p. 54 ff.

2. Cf. Leszek Kolakowski, *Main Currents of Marxist Thought,* III (Oxford, 1978), passim; Lane, p. 28 ff.

3. Needless to say, this is a theoretical, not a moral, statement. To say that the Soviet Union is a socialist society is to *describe* it. The description neither condemns nor praises. David Lane (p. 13 ff.) calls the Soviet Union and other communist

societies "state socialism." In terms of our definition here, the phrase is redundant. Lane uses it to distinguish the communist societies from "democratic socialism" and "syndicalist socialism." He cites Sweden to exemplify the former category; this, in my opinion, confuses the organization of the economy with the scope of the welfare state. "Syndicalist socialism," properly speaking, exists nowhere. The Yugoslav experiment is a certain approximation of it and will be discussed later in this chapter.

4. On the Soviet economy, cf. E. H. Carr, *Foundations of a Planned Economy* (London, 1971); Alec Nove, *The Soviet Economic System* (London, 1971); idem, *The Economics of Feasible Socialism* (London, 1983), p. 68 ff.; and Constantin Krylov, *The Soviet Economy* (Lexington, Mass., 1979).

5. Official Soviet data on the economy are notoriously suspect (as, of course, are such data in other dictatorial regimes, especially Communist ones). Thus foreign analysts have to engage in complicated detective exercises to arrive at an approximation of the empirical realities (see Krylov, p. 89 ff.). The consensus is that they have been reasonably successful.

6. Cited by Nove, *Feasible Socialism,* p. 105.

7. For a vivid description of how this works in everyday life, see Hedrick Smith, *The Russians* (New York, 1977), p. 106 ff.

8. The phrase was coined by the Hungarian economist György Markus (cited by Nove, *Feasible Socialism,* p. 78).

9. Cf. Paul Cocks et al., eds. *The Dynamics of Soviet Politics* (Cambridge, Mass., 1976); Donald Barry and Carol Barner-Barry, *Contemporary Soviet Politics* (Englewood Cliffs, N.J., 1982); Timothy Colton, *The Dilemma of Reform in the Soviet Union* (New York, 1984).

10. The best-known formulations of the "totalitarian model" for understanding the Soviet polity are Carl Friedrich and Zbigniew Brzezinski, *Totalitarian Dictatorship and Autocracy* (New York, 1966), and Hannah Arendt, *The Origins of Totalitarianism* (New York, 1966). For a recent criticism of this approach, cf. Stephen Cohen, *Rethinking the Soviet Experience* (New York, 1985). For defenses of the approach, cf. Lane, p. 44 ff., and Barry and Barner-Barry, p. 352 ff.

11. In the early 1980s, when Jeane Kirkpatrick popularized the distinction to explain certain policies of the Reagan administration, it was attacked in the liberal press as spurious, designed merely to justify supporting right-wing dictatorships and attacking left-wing ones. The distinction is not spurious, as anyone knows who has experienced both types of regime. It is, essentially, the difference between having to be passive politically and being coerced into continuous political activity. (In this matter, any taxi driver in, say, Prague is way ahead of many American social theorists.) In itself, the distinction also has nothing to do with a regime being right-wing or left-wing, though the fact remains that since the demise of Nazi Germany all totalitarian regimes have been of the latter ideological stripe. Further, the distinction is not as such a criterion for moral judgments. It may well be that some authoritarian regimes are more reprehensible and humanly intolerable than some totalitarian ones (I may prefer to live in the Soviet Union than in Idi Amin's Uganda). But totalitarianism has its own very special features, which must be understood. Some of them do indeed have moral implications—at least if human freedom is accorded a moral status.

12. See J. L. Talmon, *The Origins of Totalitarian Democracy* (New York, 1960).

13. See Cohen, *Rethinking.*

14. See Michael Voslensky, *Nomenklatura* (Garden City, N.Y., 1984).

15. For an excellent discussion of this, see Alec Nove, *Political Economy and Soviet Socialism* (London, 1979), p. 219 ff.; also, idem, *Feasible Socialism,* passim.

16. See especially Walter Connor, *Socialism, Politics and Equality* (New York, 1979). Also, cf. Lane, p. 177 ff.; Paul Hollander, *Soviet and American Society* (New York, 1973), p. 202 ff.; Basile Kerblay, *Modern Soviet Society* (New York, 1983), p. 203 ff. On the Soviet elite, cf. Voslensky; also Nove, *Political Economy,* p. 195 ff.

17. Connor, p. 79.

18. Connor, p. 76.

19. Connor, p. 90.

20. György Konrád and Iván Szelényi, *Die Intelligenz auf dem Weg zur Klassenmacht* (Frankfurt, 1978).

21. Connor, after a careful discussion of these matters, concludes with the highly persuasive observation that bad data are better than no data.

22. Cf. J. R. Moroney, ed. *Income Inequality: Trends and International Comparisons* (Lexington, Mass., 1978); Connor, p. 215 ff.

23. This point is developed for the two Germanies (a natural comparison) by Norman Naimark, "East and West Germany: A Comparison" (paper for Seminar on Modern Capitalism, 1984).

24. See Connor, p. 106 ff.

25. For a good account of a *nomenklatura* "career in the making," see Voslensky, *Nomenklatura,* p. 75 ff. The career, of course, is a bureaucratic one and as such has some similarities with bureaucratic careers in nonsocialist societies. These similarities should not obscure the fundamental difference that no Western bureaucracy holds a monopoly of power.

26. The most influential example of this is Milovan Djilas, *The New Class* (New York, 1960).

27. Cited in Connor, p. 104 ff. Bauman has since moved to the West, but this interpretation dates from the period when he was still working in Poland.

28. András Hegedüs, *The Structure of Socialist Society* (New York, 1977). Hegedüs, who continues to live and work in Hungary, has walked a narrow line between independent analysis and observing the official ideological conventions, and it is consequently hard to know how to interpret his position. Be this as it may, it represents a very astute attempt to do justice to the empirical realities without jettisoning some favorite Marxist doctrines.

29. Max Weber, *Wirtschaft und Gesellschaft,* I (Tübingen, 1956), p. 133 ff. One might also apply here the concept, coined by Shmuel Eisenstadt to describe some Third World societies, of "neopatrimonialism." This type of stratification, looked at historically, represents a throw-back to feudal societies, in the sense that here, once again, political and economic hierarchies are merged—precisely the hierarchies which capitalism separated. Pierre Bourdieu, describing socialism in Algeria, has used the phrase "socialo-feudalism." "Neofeudalism" would be another possibility. There are analytic gains in comparing modern socialism with feudalism, but this terminology is so polemical that it is better avoided in social-scientific discourse.

30. On "market socialism" in general, cf. Lane, p. 73 ff. and p. 120 ff.; Nove, *Political Economy,* p. 112 ff. and p. 133 ff.; idem, *Feasible Socialism,* p. 118 ff.

31. Cf. David Granick, *Enterprise Guidance in Eastern Europe* (Princeton, 1975), p. 234 ff.; Paul Hare et al., eds. *Hungary: A Decade of Economic Reform* (London,

1981); Rudolf Tökés, "Hungarian Reform Imperatives," *Problems of Communism* (September–October, 1984), 1 ff.

32. Cf. Fred Singleton and Bernard Carter, *The Economy of Yugoslavia* (London, 1982); Lane, p. 143 ff.; Granick, *Enterprise Guidance,* p. 323 ff. (Granick deals only with Slovenia, the economically most advanced region.)

33. See Kolakowski, *Main Currents,* passim; Nove, *Feasible Socialism,* passim. An early protagonist was the Polish economist Oscar Lange; cf. his *Political Economy* (London, 1963). An important contemporary theorist is the Czech economist Ota Sik; cf. his *Plan and Market Under Socialism* (New York, 1967), and *The Third Way* (London, 1976). Sik played an important role in the reform movement in Czechoslovakia in the late 1960s; he now lives in the West. The latter movement was the most drastic attempt to modify the political system along with the economy. It ended, of course, with the Soviet invasion of 1968. The presumed motives for the Soviet intervention are instructive for an understanding of the political limits of "market socialism"—it was not so much the economic reforms as the perceived threat to the dominance of the party that alarmed the Soviet leadership. One reluctantly concludes that they were probably right (a conclusion, let it be stressed most emphatically, that in no way implies moral approval). For this tragically brief episode, see Lane, p. 163 ff.

34. Ludwig von Mises, *Socialism* (New York, n.d. [German 1932]), esp. p. 137 ff.

35. Von Mises, p. 138.

36. Von Mises, p. 270 ff.

37. Von Mises makes a useful distinction between ownership of consumption goods and of means of production (ownership being defined, not legally but in economic terms, as the "immediate power of disposal"). The former, of course, is possible under socialism, the latter not—and *that* is where the built-in problems are rooted. Idem, p. 37 ff.

## Chapter 9

1. See Peter Berger and Thomas Luckmann, *The Social Construction of Reality* (Garden City, N.Y., 1966), p. 85 ff. What we did here was to amplify Max Weber's concept of "legitimacy" (which had a narrower political focus) with ideas derived from Alfred Schutz about the meaningful ordering of all social life.

2. Ibid.

3. Georges Sorel, *Réflexions sur la violence* (Paris, 1908); cf. Hans Barth, *Masse und Mythos* (Hamburg, 1959), p. 66 ff.

4. Georges Sorel, *Décomposition du marxisme* (Paris, 1908).

5. See Ernst Bloch, *Das Prinzip Hoffnung* (Frankfurt, 1959).

6. For a fuller discussion of this, see my article "The Socialist Myth," *Public Interest* (Summer 1976).

7. Thus, David Caute, in his otherwise exemplary study *The Fellow-Travellers* (New York, 1973).

8. See Peter Berger, *The Sacred Canopy* (Garden City, N.Y., 1967).

9. See, for example, David Martin, *A General Theory of Secularization* (Oxford, 1978).

10. On nationalism as a modern ideology, cf. Hans Kohn, *The Idea of Nationalism* (New York, 1944); Karl Deutsch, *Nationalism and Social Communication* (Cambridge, Mass., 1956).

11. One of the more puzzling aspects of the question is how a nation comes to be defined as such in the first place. How did it happen, for example, that a subject of the Habsburgs looked at himself in the mirror one morning and said: "I am a Czechoslovak!" A nineteenth-century English wit once defined a nation as a language equipped with a navy. This may be as good a definition as any, but it fails to explain why some languages acquire such military-political accoutrements while others continue to survive as tranquil dialects without aspirations toward sovereignty as nation-states. The socialist movement, of course, has had a problem relating to nationalism for a long time. There have been repeated conflicts between "socialist internationalism" and various efforts to synthesize the two modern symbol systems in a "national socialism." World War I, when the working classes on both sides (including labor unions and working-class parties) succumbed to the nationalist frenzy, marked a particularly sharp conflict.

12. The word "Nazi," of course, was the (originally Bavarian) diminutive of *"Nationalsozialist."* The fact that it has become *the* term in English for Hitler's movement and regime has a curious side-effect: It serves as a semantic impediment for the recognition by English-speakers that one of Hitler's most powerful ideological assets was his claim to reconcile the ideals of nationalism and socialism. Thus the full title of the Nazi party, or NSDAP, was the National Socialist German Workers Party. Its ideology was fiercely anticapitalist and antibourgeois from the beginning, both antagonisms being couched in anti-Semitic terms.

13. See, for example, S. N. Eisenstadt and Yael Azmon, eds. *Socialism and Tradition* (Atlantic Highlands, N.J., 1975).

14. Julius Nyerere, *Ujamaa* (Dar es Salaam, 1968). For an analysis, cf. John Nellis, *A Theory of Ideology: The Tanzanian Example* (Nairobi, 1972). There is also the fact that Tanzanian socialism, in addition to creating havoc in the economy and requiring increasingly repressive state actions, has very little in common with traditional African kinship values. But that is another story.

15. For the original Melanesian phenomenon, see Peter Worsley, *The Trumpet Shall Sound* (London, 1957). For a broader analysis of cargo cults, see Bryan Wilson, *Magic and the Millennium* (New York, 1973). Wilson coined the rather delightful term "commodity millenarianism" to describe this type of utopianism.

16. Maurice Halbwachs, *La topographie légendaire des évangiles en terre sainte* (Paris, 1941).

17. Cf. Caute, *Fellow-Travellers;* Paul Hollander, *Political Pilgrims* (New York, 1981). Both books constitute records of credulity hard to match in the history of human folly.

18. I am conscious of the likelihood that I may be accused here of an argument ad hominem. This is one of the perils of any *Ideologiekritik* or any sociology of knowledge. Such a charge will not stick to the bulk of the argument of this book. I have dealt throughout with sundry Marxist propositions, as with any other statements about empirical reality, without paying attention to the putative psychology of the proposers. Given the messianic pretensions and the aggressive cocksureness of most Marxists, such ascetic restraint is not an easy thing. It requires an ongoing suppression of one's sense of humor, among other heroic acts of the mind. At this point of the argument, however, it becomes necessary to at least raise the question,

as a question of social science, as to why the socialist vision persists despite the empirical realities of socialism. If this be then called an argument ad hominem, so be it. Theories, after all, are made by *homines,* and the passions and interests of men are part of what must be explained about a situation in which theories are at work. For the methodological assumptions underlying this view, see Berger and Luckmann, *Social Construction of Reality;* see also, Peter Berger and Hansfried Kellner, *Sociology Reinterpreted* (Garden City, N.Y., 1981), esp. p. 56 ff.

19. Thus throughout his work, but most recently (and most amply—the work has three volumes) in F. A. Hayek, *Law, Legislation and Liberty* (London, 1982).

20. Thus in various works, the best known of which is his *Capitalism and Freedom* (Chicago, 1962). Cf. Irving Kristol, *Two Cheers for Capitalism* (New York, 1978) —the title perfectly expresses the sober, positively *non*mythopoetic character of Kristol's position; one may observe that two cheers for anything are unlikely to inspire or to generate fervent commitment.

21. Two recent efforts along such lines are George Gilder, *Wealth and Poverty* (New York, 1981), and Michael Novak, *The Spirit of Democratic Capitalism* (New York, 1982). Gilder makes the claim that capitalism requires altruism (Adam Smith must turn in his grave); he also extols the near-Promethean virtues of entrepreneurship—as further developed in his more recent work, *The Spirit of Enterprise* (New York, 1984). Novak concludes his book with an outline of "a theology of economics," within which capitalism is defended in Christian terms. Both Gilder and Novak make interesting, in places very original points. It is by no means a denigration of the intellectual verve of these authors to express skepticism about the possibility that their ideas will come to bring about a widely plausible capitalist myth.

22. Max Weber, *Wirtschaft and Gesellschaft* (Tübingen, 1956), p. 142. It is just for this reason that charisma is in tension with the other great historical agent for change that Weber analyzed, that of rationalization—and capitalism was understood by him as a vast rationalizing force. Cf. Guenther Roth and Wolfgang Schluchter, *Max Weber's Vision of History* (Berkeley, 1979), and Wolfgang Schluchter, *Die Entwicklung des okzidentalen Rationalismus* (Tübingen, 1979).

23. See Bob Goudzwaard, *Capitalism and Progress* (Toronto, 1979).

24. See Joseph Schumpeter, *Capitalism, Socialism and Democracy* (New York, 1950).

25. Cf. Juergen Habermas, *Legitimationsprobleme im Spaetkapitalismus* (Frankfurt, 1973), and Daniel Bell, *The Cultural Contradictions of Capitalism* (New York, 1976). One may observe with regard to Habermas that when Marxist or neo-Marxist authors employ the phrase "late capitalism," this is not only an analytic category, but *sotto voce* an expression of pious hope.

26. Frank Parkin, "Social Inequality and Legitimacy in Capitalist Society" (paper for Seminar on Modern Capitalism, 1984).

# INDEX

# Index

*Homo aequalis,* 50
*Homo hierarchicus,* 50
Hong Kong, 24, 128, 129, 141, 147–48, 154, 158; democracy in, 161; income inequality in, 152; individualism in, 169
Horney, Karen, 104
Human rights: capitalism and, 86; democracy and, 85–86; protection of, as value, 219–20
Hungary, 21, 84, 174, 181; New Economic Mechanism in, 186–87; stratification in, 182
Hyper-individualism: of American culture, 106; capitalism and, 111–12; contractual arrangements and, 111

Immiseration, 38, 120–21
Imperialism: capitalism and, 121–22; theory of, 120–21
Imperial Rescript on Education (1890), Japan, 145
Income data: for elite, in Soviet model of socialism, 183
Income distribution: modernization and, 219; in South Korea, 150
Income inequality: in Britain, 44; in Hong Kong, 152; in Japan, 149; labor unions and, 46; in Philippines, 149; in Singapore, 152; in Soviet Union, 44; in Sweden, 44, 149; in United Kingdom, 149; in United States, 44, 149
India, 28, 117, 125, 132, 135, 138, 159, 190; Green Revolution in, 135–36
Indonesia, 125, 128, 135, 138, 141
Individual, collective identification and, 91–92
Individual autonomy: balancing institutions and, 112–13; capitalism and, 93, 95, 96–97, 213; capitalist entrepreneur and, 101; Hellenic experience of, 95–96; as idea, 92; institutions in society and, 92; modernization and, 167–70; Protestanism and, 103; psychic reality of, 92; as value, 220
Individualism: in Hong Kong, 169; in

Japan, 168–69; in Meiji Japan, 168; personal liberation and, 90–91; socialist collectivism and, 190–91; in Taiwan, 169; *see also* Bourgeois individualism; English individualism
Industrial capitalism: bureaucracy and, 56–57; class system and, 52–57; class system in, compared to that in industrial socialism, 70; corporation and, 56–57; democracy and, 64–65; East Asian model of, 142; material equality and, 47–48; middle strata and, 55–56; service sector and, 57; social mobility in, compared to industrial socialism, 64; stratification system and, 62–63
Industrialism, capitalism and, 19–20
Industrialization, social mobility and, 58–60
Industrial Revolution, 17, 19, 34, 35, 57–58, 94–95, 117; capitalism and, 35, 37; inequality and, 44; infant mortality and, 34–35; and material misery, in England, 39–41; working class and, 58
Industrial socialism, 172–93, 215; class system in, 185; class system in, compared to that in industrial capitalism, 70; social mobility and, 63–64; social mobility compared to industrial capitalism, 64; Soviet model of, 175
Inequality: Industrial Revolution and, 44; as term, 50
Infant mortality, Industrial Revolution and, 34–35
Intrinsic linkage, 26
Iranian Revolution, 201, 220
Israel, ancient, 28, 95, 96
Israelite individuation, Hebrew Bible and, 95
Ivory Coast, 155
Iwakura, Tomomi, 144

Jamaica, 135, 154, 156
Japan, 43, 108, 126, 128–29, 140, 142–46, 150, 154, 157–58, 159–60, 162, 164–66, 168–69; condition of the poor and

*257*